Accession no.
01097053

i 25/03/04

LIBRARY

Tel: 01244 375444   Ext: 3301

UNIVERSITY COLLEGE
CHESTER
EST. 1839

This book is to be returned on or before the
last date stamped below. Overdue charges
will be incurred by the late return of books.

2 6 OCT 2004

CANCELLED

D1428884

Contemporary History in Context Series

General Editor: **Peter Catterall**, Lecturer, Department of History, Queen Mary and Westfield College, University of London

What do they know of the contemporary, who only the contemporary know? How, without some historical context, can you tell whether what you are observing is genuinely novel, and how can you understand how it has developed? It was, not least, to guard against the unconscious and ahistorical Whiggery of much contemporary comment that this series was conceived. The series takes important events or historical debates from the post-war years and, by bringing new archival evidence and historical insights to bear, seeks to re-examine and reinterpret these matters. Most of the books will have a significant international dimension, dealing with diplomatic, economic or cultural relations across borders. in the process the object will be to challenge orthodoxies and to cast new light upon major aspects of post-war history.

Titles include:

Oliver Bange
THE EEC CRISIS OF 1963
Kennedy, Macmillan, de Gaulle and Adenauer in Conflict

Christopher Brady
UNITED STATES FOREIGN POLICY TOWARDS CAMBODIA, 1977–92

Peter Catterall and Sean McDougall (*editors*)
THE NORTHERN IRELAND QUESTION IN BRITISH POLITICS

Peter Catterall, Colin Seymour-Ure and Adrian Smith (*editors*)
NORTHCLIFFE'S LEGACY
Aspects of the British Popular Press, 1896–1996

James Ellison
THREATENING EUROPE
Britain and the Creation of the European Community, 1955-58

Helen Fawcett and Rodney Lowe (*editors*)
WELFARE POLICY IN BRITAIN
The Road from 1945

Jonathan Hollowell (*editor*)
TWENTIETH-CENTURY ANGLO-AMERICAN RELATIONS

Simon James and Virginia Preston (*editors*)
BRITISH POLITICS SINCE 1945
The Dynamics of Historical Change

Harriet Jones and Michael Kandiah (*editors*)
THE MYTH OF CONSENSUS
New Views on British History, 1945–64

Wolfram Kaiser
USING EUROPE, ABUSING THE EUROPEANS
Britain and European Integration, 1945–63

Keith Kyle
THE POLITICS OF THE INDEPENDENCE OF KENYA

Spencer Mawby
CONTAINING GERMANY
Britain and the Arming of the Federal Republic

Jeffrey Pickering
BRITAIN'S WITHDRAWAL FROM EAST OF SUEZ
The Politics of Retrenchment

Peter Rose
HOW THE TROUBLES CAME TO NORTHERN IRELAND

L. V. Scott
MACMILLAN, KENNEDY AND THE CUBAN MISSILE CRISIS
Political, Military and Intelligence Aspects

Paul Sharp
THATCHER'S DIPLOMACY
The Revival of British Foreign Policy

Contemporary History in Context
Series Standing Order ISBN 0–333–71470–9
(*outside North America only*)

You can receive future titles in this series as they are published by placing a standing order. Please contact your bookseller or, in case of difficulty, write to us at the address below with your name and address, the title of the series and the ISBN quoted above.

Customer Services Department, Macmillan Distribution Ltd, Houndmills, Basingstoke, Hampshire RG21 6XS, England

Twentieth-Century Anglo-American Relations

Jonathan Hollowell
St Peter's College
Oxford

Foreword by Kathleen Burk

·157226x·

LIBRARY

ACC. No.	DEPT.
01097053	
CLASS No.	

UNIVERSITY
COLLEGE CHESTER

Selection, editorial matter and Introduction © Jonathan Hollowell 2001
Foreword © Kathleen Burk 2001
Chapters 1–10 © Palgrave Publishers Ltd 2001

All rights reserved. No reproduction, copy or transmission of
this publication may be made without written permission.

No paragraph of this publication may be reproduced, copied or
transmitted save with written permission or in accordance with
the provisions of the Copyright, Designs and Patents Act 1988,
or under the terms of any licence permitting limited copying
issued by the Copyright Licensing Agency, 90 Tottenham Court
Road, London W1P 0LP.

Any person who does any unauthorised act in relation to this
publication may be liable to criminal prosecution and civil
claims for damages.

The author has asserted his right to be identified
as the author of this work in accordance with the
Copyright, Designs and Patents Act 1988.

First published 2001 by
PALGRAVE
Houndmills, Basingstoke, Hampshire RG21 6XS and
175 Fifth Avenue, New York, N. Y. 10010
Companies and representatives throughout the world

PALGRAVE is the new global academic imprint of
St. Martin's Press LLC Scholarly and Reference Division and
Palgrave Publishers Ltd (formerly Macmillan Press Ltd).

ISBN 0–333–80404–X

This book is printed on paper suitable for recycling and
made from fully managed and sustained forest sources.

A catalogue record for this book is available
from the British Library.

Library of Congress Cataloging-in-Publication Data
Twentieth-century Anglo-American relations / [edited by]
Jonathan Hollowell.
      p. cm. — (Contemporary history in context)
   Includes bibliographical references and index.
   ISBN 0–333–80404–X
   1. United States—Foreign relations—Great Britain. 2. Great
Britain—Foreign relations—United States. 3. United States–
–Foreign relations—20th century. I. Hollowell, Jonathan, 1964–
II. Contemporary history in context series.
   E183.8.G7 A682 2000
   327.41073—dc21
                                                        00–066561

10   9   8   7   6   5   4   3   2   1
10   09   08   07   06   05   04   03   02   01

Printed and bound in Great Britain by
Antony Rowe Ltd, Chippenham, Wiltshire

Contents

General Editor's Preface

Early in 1962 a Foreign Office paper on 'Britain through American Eyes' warned that

> it is probably true to say that a large proportion of the population is ill-informed about Britain and has no more than a hazy idea of our geography or history, overlaid with certain traditional beliefs about socialism, colonialism and the Royal Family.

Even at the policymaking level, relations could be bedevilled by ignorance or misperceptions, not least in the furore over Skybolt which ensued later that year. The problem, according to the Foreign Office author, was that 'While most foreigners are judged by what they do, we are judged by what Americans think we are.'

Neither this, nor the ignorance of which he complained, necessarily meant that Anglo-American relations had ceased to be important. Indeed, the diplomat's aphorism could simply reflect the extensiveness of the contacts between the two countries. Despite the increasing power disparity between them, with Britain only spending about a tenth of what the US did on defence by the early 1960s, their interests continued to overlap everywhere around the world. In these circumstances it was perhaps easier to operate on normative views of each other, of what each other was likely to do in a particular instance, and of what Ambassador Bruce described in 1961 as 'the essential solidarity of informed self-interest between the English-speaking peoples', even if these views and expectations were to be disappointed, sometimes painfully, on occasion. Indeed, the growing power disparity of the postwar years may have encouraged this tendency. While American policymakers during the cold war tried to structure the international behaviour of Britain to conform to their perceived needs within a Manichaean view of the world shared only to a limited extent by their allies, the British, in turn, repeatedly concluded that they needed to retain what influence they could in Washington. Otherwise, as Harold Macmillan put it, they 'could not count on American support in all circumstances and would be less able to stand up to Soviet threats against the UK or British interests overseas'.

Much of the work on Anglo-American relations in recent years has been concerned with this cold war period. This is unsurprising, reflecting the increasing availability of documents for these years. However, while this book adds to this literature, drawing on recently released archives to cast new light on episodes such as the origins of NATO, McCarthyism, Suez or the Vietnam War, one of its undoubted strengths lies in the historical range that it covers. The essays here span the years from the end of the First World War to the late 1960s, a period in which the relationship between Britain and America was arguably one of the most important dynamics in world affairs. In the process they provide a range of settings in which to examine the nature of Anglo-American relations. Even if such relations may be cemented by Bruce's 'informed self-interest' they can vary over time. They can certainly change according to geographical setting, a variable that could lead to uncharacteristic behaviour – as Macmillan enjoyed noting in 1963,

> We shall not give British Guiana 'independence' only to create a Cuba on the mainland. It is however rather fun making the Americans repeat over and over again their passionate plea to us to stick to 'Colonialism' and 'Imperialism' at all costs.

And, not least, they can change according to the policymaking level being investigated. Anglo-American diplomacy operates at a number of levels: between the respective armed and intelligence services; State Department and Foreign Office; at an informal level involving organisations such as the Council on Foreign Relations; between president and prime minister. The essays collected here touch on all of these dimensions of Anglo-American relations. Authored by leading scholars on both sides of the Atlantic, the result is a book which provides a multifaceted set of analyses of one of the key international relationships of the twentieth century.

PETER CATTERALL
Westminster College
Fulton, Missouri
and
Institute of Contemporary British History
London

Foreword

There is a central theme to Anglo-American relations in the twentieth century: the decline of Great Britain and the rise of the United States. This was not a smooth trajectory: rather, there were episodic rises and falls, but the primary direction was clear. This is not even a case of hindsight. It was clear at the time, perhaps even more clear to Great Britain than it was to the United States. The single most important reason for this was need. The fact that Great Britain was convinced that without the support of the United States she could not maintain her foreign policies – nor even, at one juncture, her independence – betrays this dependence. The United States, conversely, believed that she could afford to ignore the outside world, at least until she was attacked. But she did not fear attack beforehand, as did Great Britain.

It is well to point out that the fundamental basis of this dependence was economic. For much of the period, certainly until 1943, the military forces of Great Britain outstripped those of the United States. The crucial point, however, is that there was – and in theory, is – no limit to the amount which the United States could – and can – spend in order to achieve and maintain military dominance. In the early years of the century, Great Britain had the economic resources to contemplate spending what was in those days an impressive sum. This is no longer the case. If she cannot finance her foreign policies to the extent that she would like, she has to find another country to help. The only country outside the Commonwealth to which she could turn, and can turn, is the United States. The passing across of crude specie is no longer the issue; now it is shared foreign policy goals, and the willingness of the United States to contribute the greater share of the finance needed for joint technology: intelligence and nuclear weapons. The contributions of Great Britain are diplomatic and military prowess, and a willingness and ability to discuss, discreetly, foreign policy problems in the English language.

It is noticeable that the predominant amount of work now being done on Anglo-American relations concentrates on the post-1945 period. There may be several reasons for this. First of all, much work has already been done on the earlier period, and thus it is more difficult to find a truly fresh topic. Secondly, and connected, post-1945 is fresher territory, with the excitement of the frequent opening up of new sources. But thirdly, there is the morbid fascination with decline, and with the occasional and associated pummelling of Great Britain by the United States. Suez comes to mind. This is, of course, leavened with the occasional reversal of fortunes. But it is more often a story of British attempts to co-opt American power, or to prevent the United States from ignoring British policy preferences.

Yet, maintaining a strong Anglo-American relationship was ultimately in the interests of both countries. It was and is a preoccupation of private citizens as well as of politicians, and there were and are many instances of cultural diplomacy on the private as well as the semi-public level. Indeed, while the feeling of political and cultural links is probably a declining commodity, given the demographic changes in the United States, nevertheless these links still remain strong. They are important in policy terms because they enable both countries to recover more easily from bruising encounters, such as Suez.

The essays in this book demonstrate many of these points. They are predominantly on the post-1945 period. In most cases they treat of British dependence. And they include among their number a consideration of the private as well as the public sphere of Anglo-American relations. While this group of essays is not comprehensive in itself, it can be seen as representative of the wide range of Anglo-American relationships and of the work being done on them. It would be interesting to know if, a century hence, it will be thought worthwhile to produce another such collection.

KATHLEEN BURK
University College, London

Introduction

Jonathan Hollowell

The chapters in this text were among those delivered at the 1998 ICBH summer conference on Anglo-American Relations in the Twentieth Century, attended by academics, diplomats, independent scholars, and observers from several countries on three continents. The essays, written by a number of the leading British and American historians, illuminate themes from this pivotal century in our history. The discussions offer new research dealing with some of the prominent aspects – by no means exhaustive – of Anglo-American affairs since the First World War, from the Versailles Peace Conference during the presidency of Woodrow Wilson, to the presidency of Lyndon Johnson and premiership of Harold Wilson; and consider not only the relations of cordiality between the two countries but also areas of considerable friction and mutual exasperation.

Beginning with the post-First World War period, Margaret MacMillan examines an under-explored area of the relationship between the US and the British Empire, in the increasing colonial independence. The dominions, treated by the US as part of a monolithic British empire, were emerging as distinct and sovereign states claiming the right to their own foreign policies and increasingly coming into conflict with their former imperial power. This tension between British policy and the increasingly separate roles of the dominions on occasion gave rise to British-American conflict, as when the colonies pressurised the British government to insist on creating League of Nations mandates for former German territories that would then be placed under dominion control. Thus the extent to which the increasingly independent-minded dominions caused tension between Britain and America presents a new patch of terrain which MacMillan examines with particular regard to the Paris Peace Conference.

The immediate post-First World War period brought some surprises to Anglo-American relations in the American refusal to participate in the League of Nations. Though the enlightened President Wilson led valiant efforts to secure ratification so that the US could participate in the League, the US Senate refused, acting partly out of belief that the League would be an organisation subject to control by a British imperial order, viewing Australia, Canada, New Zealand, the Union of South Africa, and other areas possessing responsible government within the Empire as really constituting British proxies and not really independent countries in their own right. In this regard, the Senators had a point. Though these dominions had achieved internal self-government, their external affairs nevertheless continued to be exercised from London. But this perspective fell somewhat short of viewing the dominions as emerging sovereign entities becoming increasingly vociferous for the exercise of foreign relations in their own right – even if at times their foreign policy would be at variance with that of Britain.

Partly emerging from contacts made during the Anglo-American discussions at Paris, the Council on Foreign Relations was established (1921) during the interwar period and emerged as America's premier international policy organisation, analogous to Britain's Royal Institute of International Affairs. The role of the foreign policy elite in the USA encapsulated by the influential Council has at times been that of an *éminence grise* on the US side of the 'special relationship', and Priscilla Roberts explores its links with the RIIA, the Council's interwar activities, and the impact of its trans-Atlantic contacts upon Anglo-American relations leading up to the US entry to the Second World War.

In the wider social sphere, the activities of an individual who, in some ways, embodied the Anglo-American relationship at a crucial juncture, Eric Knight, is considered by Fred Leventhal. Knight, Yorkshire-born novelist, journalist and screenwriter, and American by adoption, was taken up by Frank Capra to form part of the team producing US wartime films. His reflections of his native Britain at the time of the outbreak of the Second World War and Dunkirk ran the gamut of emotions which mirrored the deliberations of Britain's war cabinet itself, from defeatism to defiance. Leventhal's reviving of this overlooked figure offers a portrayal of a man whose involvement in shaping American sentiment in the battle for the hearts and minds of America during the war reveals Knight's own personal identity crisis – whether British or American, to what extent each – a journey of self-discovery, and its relation to the profoundly different societal institutions masked behind the facade of similarities between both countries.

During the period from 1946 to 1948, witnessing to the widening rift between East and West, direct or indirect discussions about the Byrnes treaty kept alive the concept and the practice of close cooperation between Washington and western European allies with the most dynamic role played by London, from which a primary concern to Foreign Secretary Ernest Bevin was the urgency of maintaining US involvement – and US troops – in Europe. Danilo Ardia reviews the discussions leading up to the Byrnes treaty, examining their significant impact on relations among the Western allies, viz., that the main concept of this US initiative was the direct American responsibility in Europe for the duration of the cold war, and which foreshadowed the role assumed by Washington in the process leading to the Atlantic Alliance in NATO in 1949.

Few topics in postwar US history have aroused such soul-searching into the nature of American democracy than McCarthyism. Yet while books abound about Senator Joe McCarthy's rise and fall in 1950–54, historians, political scientists and contemporaries have only in passing addressed the impact of McCarthyism abroad. In the 1950s, Britons never experienced a domestic upheaval analogous to McCarthyism, and neither did they suffer from a crisis of confidence in civil servants in the Foreign Office and Ministry of Defence. The air of smug pride in operating a parliamentary democracy without manipulation, cynicism and hysteria allowed for an unleashing of criticism directed across the Atlantic. Examining the British public debate over McCarthy during the years in which revelations of Burgess, Maclean, Philby, and other Soviet moles operating within the British government were made, Jussi Hanhimaki's contribution attempts to fill this gap, focusing on British reactions (as evidenced in the popular press and government documents) to McCarthyism and exploring the impact that this almost uniformly negative reaction had on Anglo-American relations in the early 1950s.

In the early to mid-1950s, the role of the British embassy in Washington was instrumental in efforts to prevent a breakdown in Anglo-American relations. Sir Roger Makins' tenure as ambassador has tended to be overshadowed by that of his predecessor, Sir Oliver Franks. But Saul Kelly's research aims to throw light on Makins' very considerable and largely unsung success in establishing relations of confidence with the US Secretary of State, John Foster Dulles, which helped Makins prevent a breakdown during the series of crises in the Far East, the Middle East and in Europe, which occurred during the period of the first Eisenhower administration. Kelly demonstrates the influence and stature Makins had accumulated by, for example, pointing out that after Makins' return to London in 1956, with the 'alliance' breaking down over the Anglo-French intervention in Suez, Makins played an important behind-the-scenes role in restoring the relationship between the US and Britain.

By the 1980s contempt for the culture and politics of the USA was shared by most of the Labour Party's left. One of the defining characteristics among the right was their Atlanticism; indeed, it was one commonly held penchant among those Labour MPs who defected from Labour to establish the SDP in 1981. During the 1940s, however, positive views of America were shared right across the Labour Party, many believing President Truman to be on the same welfare path as Attlee. McCarthyism and the cold war helped undermine this widespread pro-American feeling, yet Labour revisionists continued to view the US in positive terms. By the late 1950s, in the eyes of Anthony Crosland and others, the US had become the paradigm of progress which Labour had to emulate. Steven Fielding focuses on the revisionists and places their vision of the US into a context which embraces both Labour and the period from 1945 to 1960, exploring the reasons for the changing conceptions of the US and indicating the extent to which these views say as much about the reality of America as they do about the assumptions of those holding them.

During the Korean War there was a broad allied consensus about the nature and extent of the strategic embargo that the West conducted against communist states. As the war wound down and with the death of Stalin, controversy rekindled within the Western camp, especially between Britain and the USA concerning both the scope and purpose of export controls. Alan Dobson discusses how this controversy developed, showing how British and American thinking changed and in so doing brought about tension within the alliance. Dobson demonstrates that by the 1960s the USA had moved away from trying to restrict weapons technology and economic growth in communist states and had adopted new goals of a highly symbolic, psychological and normative kind; whereas Britain was more pragmatic and, while retaining the original idea of denying weapons technology, now also emphasised the relative importance of East–West trade to Britain and the possibility of seducing the communists with Western consumer goods. These differences of nuance caused serious controversies which affected the Western alliance; they tell us something about the quality of Anglo-American relations; and they indicate the limits to hardshell American power well before she is normally thought to have been afflicted with hegemonic decline.

Concerning the Suez crisis itself, Peter Boyle argues that President Eisenhower in his correspondence with Prime Minister Eden was clear and consistent in warning that the US would not support but would openly condemn British military action in Egypt. Based on the personal correspondence between Eisenhower and Eden, Boyle analyses Eden's disastrous performance over Suez compared with his very successful earlier diplomatic successes, and assesses the light which the correspondence gives to the crisis.

In the final paper, Sylvia Ellis explores the personal and working relationship between President Lyndon Johnson and Prime Minister Harold Wilson, questioning not only whether this relationship made a fundamental difference to the conduct of Anglo-American relations during 1964–68, but also questioning the validity of the argument that the 'special relationship' is heavily based on the personal affinity between leaders. Using recently declassified documents from the US, oral interviews and numerous British sources, Ellis provides a more sophisticated analysis of a personal relationship long thought to have been poor, tracing LBJ's feelings towards Wilson and showing how his view of the British PM changed over time and circumstances – moving from respect to disdain, and back again – while also tracing Wilson's more constant views of the President. An examination of the major issues affecting British–American relations from 1964 to 1968 serves to illustrate why the relationship between Wilson and LBJ proved to be volatile; Vietnam, the ongoing sterling crisis, and the British decision to withdraw from East of Suez are all assessed in this context, with Ellis offering the proposition that the question of whether the personal relationship between Johnson and Wilson was really only of peripheral importance is not as important as was the ever-increasing power imbalance between the USA and UK and the growing importance of other European nations in the eyes of the USA, which together imply an overshadowing of the bilateral relationship between US and British leaders.

These essays, therefore, present selected highlights of Anglo-American relations, and this volume offers no pretence, therefore, that what follows is a comprehensive overview of the full range of Anglo-American relations in the twentieth century, or a definitive enunciation on the areas alighted upon by the essays included. Rather, the text's purpose is to whet the appetite for further research into these and other areas of Anglo-American relations, towards which end the following chapters offer a modest contribution. The text's chapters are written in large measure from the 'functional' perspective, charting the ups and downs in British–American relations, their increasingly asymmetrical nature, and emphasising the mutual self-interest in a continued relationship; though some may espy the occasional 'evangelical' interpretation as well. Yet lest I presume to interlope upon the ground of the historians whose research is presented in the following pages, it is at this point that an editor – especially one constrained by the imposed limitation to a mere few thousand words of introduction – must allow his contributors to speak for themselves.

JONATHAN HOLLOWELL
St Peter's College,
Oxford

Notes on the Contributors

Danilo Ardia, Department of International Studies at the University of Padua, lectures on the United States' involvement in European integration, postwar American and European diplomatic history, and is author of *Alle Origini dell'Alleanza Occidentale* (1983) and *Il Partito Socialista e il Patto Atlantico* (1976).

Peter G. Boyle, Department of American and Canadian Studies, University of Nottingham, is researching post-1945 America, with a concentration on American foreign policy *vis-à-vis* the Soviet Union and Great Britain. He is the author of *American–Soviet Relations: from the Russian Revolution to the Fall of Communism* (1993), and editor of *The Churchill–Eisenhower Correspondence, 1953–55* (1990).

Kathleen Burke, F.R.Hist.S., Professor of History at University College London, is a specialist on twentieth-century British and American foreign policy, and co-editor of the journal *Contemporary European History*. Among Professor Burke's publications are *The United States and the European Alliance since 1945* (1999), *Deutsche Bank in London, 1873–1998* (1998), and *Goodbye Great Britain: the 1976 IMF Crisis* (1992).

Peter Catterall, F.R.Hist.S., has been Director of the Institute of Contemporary British History, London, since 1989, and during 1999–2000 was Fulbright-Robertson Visiting Professor of British History at Westminster College, Fulton, Missouri. Among his publications are *The Making of Channel Four* (1999), *The Northern Ireland Question in British Politics* (1996), and *Understanding Postwar British Society* (1994).

Alan P. Dobson, Department of Politics, University of Wales, Swansea, a member of the British International Relations Association and a founder member of its International History Group, teaches American politics and foreign policy. His publications include *Anglo-American Relations in the Twentieth Century* (1995), *Flying in the Face of Competition* (1995), and *Peaceful Air Warfare: the United States, Britain and the Politics of International Aviation* (1991).

Sylvia A. Ellis, Department of History, University of Sunderland, teaches modern American history and American studies. Her research interests lie in the Vietnam War and twentieth-century international relations. She has published several articles on recent American foreign policy and is currently working on a book on international reactions to the Vietnam War.

Steven Fielding, Department of Politics and Contemporary History, Salford University, teaches contemporary history, the social and political impact of the Second World War in Britain, and Labour Party history and politics. His publications include *Class and Ethnicity: Irish Catholics in England, 1880–1939* (1993) and *Labour: Decline and Renewal* (1995).

Jussi Hanhimaki, International History Department, London School of Economics and Political Science, lectures on American history and politics, American–European relations from 1945, and cold war history. His publications include *Scandinavia and the United States: an Insecure Friendship* (1997) and *Containing Coexistence: America, Russia, and the 'Finnish Solution', 1945–1956* (1997).

Jonathan Hollowell, Tutor for Politics at St Peter's College, Oxford University since 1999, has degrees from Oxford University, Cambridge University, the London School of Economics and Political Science, and the University of Rochester (USA). He is co-editor of the journal *European Review of History/Revue européenne d'Histoire*, former Research Fellow at the Institute of Contemporary British History (London), and among his publications are *Britain since 1945* (2000) and a forthcoming text on twentieth-century Europe.

Saul Kelly, History Faculty, University of Westminster, is an international historian specialising in Anglo-American relations in the twentieth century. His publications include *Whitehall and the Suez Crisis* (1999) and *Britain, the United States, and the Italian Colonies, 1945–52* (forthcoming). He is currently completing a text concerning the Washington embassy of Sir Roger Makins.

F. M. Leventhal, F.R.Hist.S., Professor of History, Boston University, is a former President of the North American Conference on British Studies, and co-editor of the journal *Twentieth-Century British History*. Among his publications are *Anglo-American Attitudes* (2000), *Singular Continuities:*

Tradition, Nostalgia and Identity in Modern British Culture (2000), and *Twentieth-Century Britain: an Encyclopedia* (1995).

Margaret MacMillan, Professor of History at Ryerson Polytechnic University, Toronto, Canada, is editor of *International Journal* and teaches twentieth-century international relations. Her publications include called *Parties Long Estranged: Canada and Australia* (forthcoming), *Canada and Nato: Uneasy Past, Uncertain Future* (1990), and *Women of the Raj* (1988).

Priscilla Roberts, Director of the Centre of American Studies at the University of Hong Kong, teaches international and United States history. Among her publications are *The Cold War* (2000), *Encyclopedia of the Korean War: a Political, Social, and Military History* (2000), and *Sino-American Relations since 1900* (1991).

1

Isosceles Triangle: Britain, the Dominions and the United States at the Paris Peace Conference of 1919

Margaret MacMillan

On 12 January 1919 the Supreme Council met in Paris. One of the first issues it had to discuss was representation at the Peace Conference. The British Prime Minister, Lloyd George, said that he would have to press the question of separate representation for the self-governing British Dominions and India. President Woodrow Wilson was unenthusiastic; 'the impression amongst those who did not know the full facts would be that they were merely additional British Representatives'. After some discussion, it was decided that the Dominions and India might have one delegate each (the same as Siam and Portugal). Lloyd George hesitated; he had better, he thought, consult with his colleagues in the British Empire Delegation. The following day, he reported that the Dominion leaders had been disappointed and indeed rather annoyed. The Supreme Council thereupon decided that Canada, Australia, South Africa and India would have two delegates each and New Zealand one.[1]

The discussion was revealing. To begin with, Wilson was right in assuming that many contemporaries saw the components of the British Empire as superior sorts of puppets, their strings pulled in Whitehall. But both he and Lloyd George knew that the picture, if it had ever been accurate, was so no longer. Lloyd George had learned to his cost that the Dominion leaders took their own dignity and that of their countries seriously. He was obliged to listen to them. There had been a significant shift of power within the British Empire. That in turn was going to affect one of the key relationships of the first part of this century, that between the two great English-speaking powers of Britain and the United States. Canada, Australia and South Africa, in particular, obliged Britain to take positions which ran counter to the latter's interests; in addition, the

1

Dominions on occasion sided with the United States against Britain. The Paris Peace Conference and the subsequent international conferences of the early 1920s show clearly how what had been a largely bilateral relationship was becoming something rather more complicated.

The main reason for that was that the British Empire was changing. What makes the period at the end of the Great War particularly confusing, both for contemporaries and historians, is that the Dominions were not yet fully independent; nor were they, as was sometimes assumed, merely the loyal foot soldiers of the Empire. Between 1900 and 1926 they were in a state of transition. There were several possible outcomes; even as late as 1926 it was not at all clear that the end-result was going to be a much diminished British Empire and the emergence of completely independent states.

The enthusiasts from the Round Table Movement, and they included by no means the stupid or naive, thought that the Empire was moving towards greater unity. Sir Maurice Hankey, secretary first to the War Cabinet, then British Empire Delegation, and finally to the Peace Conference as a whole, was convinced of it. Never a modest man, he boasted in 1919 to Lord Milner, the new Colonial Secretary and an old friend, that he had already established a British Empire Delegation secretariat, a step 'of tremendous importance to the development of the British Empire'. This group of British, Canadians, Australians, and South Africans was, in Hankey's view, the imperial secretariat which he and others had tried to develop before the war. On the horizon was 'a real Imperial Cabinet Office'[2] and then that great organic empire for which the Round Table had so long laboured.

Colonel Edward House, Wilson's right-hand man, took quite another view. He thought that there might be something to be gained for the United States in separate representation for parts of the British Empire. In the long term, House argued, encouraging a separate dominion role would speed the end of the Empire. What did it matter if the Dominions and India had separate votes at the League of Nations? They would merely come quicker to the realisation that they did not need Britain; the League, which was going to solve many problems, would provide them with security. It means, he confided cheerfully to his diary, 'the eventual disintegration of the British Empire'. Britain would end up back where it started, with only its own islands.[3]

Somewhere in the middle and perhaps not entirely aware of the ambiguity in their position were men like Sir Robert Borden, the Prime Minister of Canada and one of its delegates to the Paris Peace Conference. He maintained that he was a British subject and proud of it but also insisted on Canada's being treated as an autonomous nation. It was Borden, along with Prime Minister Billy Hughes of Australia, who led the demands for separate representation at the Peace Conference.

The easiest way to understand both the speed of the change within the Empire and the resulting uncertainty over what it all meant is to compare the situations in 1900 and 1926. At the start of this century only a few parts of the British Empire – Canada, New Zealand, the Cape Colony, Natal, the Australian colonies – had any degree of self-government, and the notion that these would conduct their own foreign policies was remote indeed. By 1926, Australia and South Africa had become countries, and together with Canada and New Zealand, had established their rights to be represented at major international gatherings, notably the Paris Peace Conference, to join the new League of Nations and International Labour Organisation, and to sign international agreements on their own behalf. (India was usually included at meetings but this was more a matter of courtesy than a recognition of an independent status.) This dramatic change, whatever it meant, was acknowledged in the report in 1926 of the Committee on Inter-Imperial Relations (the Balfour committee after its chairman, Arthur Balfour) which described the dominions as 'autonomous Communities within the British Empire, equal in status, in no way subordinate one to another in any aspect of their domestic or external affairs...'.[4] The formulation was designed to skirt over very real differences of opinion about the future of the British Empire; its ambiguity must have appealed to those masters of ambiguous formulas, Balfour himself and Mackenzie King, the Canadian Prime Minister.

What was this new creature, the British Commonwealth of Nations? And who ran its foreign policy? Many, especially in the United States, thought they knew. The last of Senator Lodge's objections to the Treaty of Versailles assumed that in the League and ILO, the Dominions and India would always vote as Britain told them. The British, however, had learned over the previous decades that they could not take this for granted. In reality, the Dominions supported Britain on general policies while insisting on the right to be consulted and, maddeningly, reserving the right to dissent on particular issues, as for example over the Chanak crisis in the autumn of 1922. It made making imperial foreign policy difficult; as Austen Chamberlain complained, 'I could not go, as representative of His Majesty's government, to meeting after meeting of the League of Nations, to conference after conference with the representatives of foreign countries, and say, "Great Britain is without a policy. We have not yet been able to meet all the governments of the Empire, and we can do nothing." '[5]

The changes within the British Empire between 1900 and 1926 were the result of growing nationalism, of increased confidence on the part of the Dominions, and, above all, of the Great War. Before 1914, complete independence was a rather terrifying prospect for the Dominions. There were advantages, from the financial to the political, in allowing Britain to set foreign and defence policy. As Lionel Curtis concluded ruefully when he visited Canada, South Africa, New Zealand and Australia in 1910 and 1911, 'the majority of people in the Dominions are thoroughly contented with their present situation. After all, they would be more than ordinary human beings if they were not, for the system is one which gives them all the material advantages of independent nations, while relieving them of the insurance which forms the first charge on the public revenue of such nations.'[6] Emotional ties still ran strong. A majority of English-speakers in the Dominions, after all, had emigrated from Britain in the last generation or two. Many took great pride in their British nationality and in their membership in the Empire. It was exhilarating and comforting to be part of a great power; in Canada's case, it also provided a counter-balance to the United States.[7]

There were practical obstacles, too, in the way of greater Dominion independence. The Dominions had small populations and correspondingly small pools of talent and experience. Australia had trouble, for example, finding translators to put documents into French, still the language of diplomacy. In Canada, according to the governor-general, Earl Grey, there were 'only three men in the Government service who have any knowledge of details connected with Canada's foreign relations – one drinks at times – the other has a difficulty in expressing his thoughts, and conversation with him is as difficult as it is to extract an extra tight cork, and the third is the Under Secretary of State, Pope – a really first class official'.[8] Before 1914, all the Dominions had problems finding competent High Commissioners to represent them in London. Only Australia and Canada even had Departments of External Affairs. By 1919, Australia's had vanished; in 1916 the new Prime Minister, Hughes, decided to run foreign affairs out of his own office. Canada's Department, established in 1909 with a staff of five, had only 26 permanent employees in 1919.[9]

Nevertheless, even before the Great War, there were indications that the Dominions were starting to define their own interests and that these were not always the same as those of Britain or indeed as each other's.

Geography clearly played an important part. Australia and New Zealand needed the protection afforded by the British navy against Germany, in the years before 1914; they had no alternative. Canada, by contrast, knew that, if it were threatened by an outside power – which in this case could only mean the United States – Britain would not move to its defence. From the Treaty of Washington in 1871 and the withdrawal of the last British garrisons from Canada, Canadian governments had realised that Canada's best defence lay in friendship between its neighbour to the south and the British Empire. As Canada's first prime minister, Sir John A. Macdonald saw the alternative: 'Canada would be, as a matter of course, the battleground of the two nations. We should be the sufferers, our country would be devastated, our people slaughtered, our prosperity destroyed.'[10] For Canadian governments, of whatever political persuasion, maintaining friendly relations between the United States and Britain was of paramount importance. After 1902, the Anglo-Japanese naval alliance worried Canada, where the government in its gloomiest moments saw itself fighting a war beside Japan against the United States.[11]

In addition, for all the waving of Union Jacks and talk of British citizenship, the Dominions were developing their own nationhoods. Paradoxically, coming to the defence of Britain in the Boer War marked a step towards a national consciousness for Australia, Canada and New Zealand. Joseph Chamberlain may have seen the Boer War as evidence that the bonds of empire were drawing tighter but, in fact, it can seen another way, as the occasion on which the colonials became aware of their own strengths and their own importance to Britain. As Richard Jebb noticed on a visit to Australia, 'Some of the most wholehearted supporters of the sending of contingents were nationalists who knew that the undertaking of responsibility would develop national self-respect, and the respect of the authorities in London for Australian nationhood.'[12] Newspaper reports, patriotic rallies, and, after the war ended, lectures, memoirs and war memorials, all helped to build up the self-confidence of Canadians, Australians and New Zealanders. The heroic sons of Britain had rallied to its defence: 'A nation is never a nation/Worthy of pride or place', boasted an Australian poet, 'Till the mothers have sent their firstborn/To look death in the field in the face.'[13] They had also, at least to their own satisfaction, shown that the transplanted stock flourished in its new soil. Canadian troops were 'grim, solid men as straight as poplars', stronger in fact than their British counterparts. Indeed it became apparent that the British also had problems in running a war; commentaries in the colonies tended to stress British bungling and incompetence, a mild foretaste of what was to be said in the Great War.[14]

Increasingly too, Dominion statesmen and newspapers were ready to criticise the British government when they felt it had failed to do its duty in furthering imperial interests. Canadians complained, with reason, that the British government had been more concerned to improve relations with the United States than to further Canadian interests in the long-drawn-out dispute over the boundaries between Alaska and Canada.[15] Australia, which feared both Japanese power and Japanese immigration, worried that Britain was too inclined to see the Japanese point of view.[16] As Sir Frederic Eggleston, a prominent Melbourne lawyer and a leading member of the Australian Round Table Movement, complained, 'England is notoriously out of sympathy, and does not understand, our exclusion policy.'[17]

The 1914–18 war marked a huge step forward in the self-consciousness of the Dominions and in their relationship to Britain on a number of levels from the financial to the constitutional and the psychological. Whatever deference there had been to the Mother Country and to the wisdom of its leaders melted in the face of what the colonials saw as the Asquith government's incompetence in running the war. The Canadian prime minister, Borden, complained bitterly that the British treated Canadians as 'toy automata' and demanded that Canada share in decisions about the conduct of the war and the shape of the peace to come.[18] Hughes of Australia was, typically, less restrained:

> In the days before the red flood of war, the Dominion representatives had approached the portals of the Imperial Conference in the subdued and reverential spirit of worshippers entering a Buddhist temple, and they had listened to the representatives of Britain – urbane and graciously tolerant – in a mood little removed from that of devotees prostrate before its shrine. But since those far-off days there had been great changes. They, who had been children, were now grown up and had put off childish things. They were no longer impressed by lectures or flattered by being permitted to participate in ceremonious and arid debates.[19]

Dominion leaders were increasingly aware, too, of how much Britain needed their help. By the time the accounts were done at the end of the war, it was clear that the Dominions and India had subsidised the British war effort.[20] They had also made it possible for the Allies to continue fighting until the Americans entered the war. India produced 1.25

million soldiers, the Dominions 1 million out of a total population of only 15 million. Sixty thousand Canadians died, 59 000 Australians, 16 000 New Zealanders, 8000 South Africans, 49 000 Indians. By comparison, the United States lost 48 000 soldiers. Vimy Ridge, Gallipoli, Delville Wood – those were to become part of the fabric of nationhood. 'We were content to be Colonials', according to one of the Canadians who fought at Vimy Ridge, but afterwards 'National spirit was born . . . ; we were Canadians.'[21]

The Asquith government, in its lackadaisical way, made little attempt to accommodate Dominion demands for a greater say. By the time the Lloyd George government took office in December 1916, the Dominions were out of patience. They had earned a voice and they knew it. As Smuts wrote to his wife in May 1917: 'I have told the Government that we no longer want to remain subordinate parts of the British Empire, but wish to be regarded as equal nations on a level with the English nation.'[22]

Lloyd George was an imperialist but in 1916 his first thoughts were to win the war. He was also a brilliant improviser who cared little for the careful procedures of government ministries. He needed manpower above all; if that meant giving more power to the Dominion governments, then he would do it over all the objections of the Colonial Office and the gloomy murmuring of his Colonial Secretary, Walter Long. Lloyd George called into existence the Imperial War Cabinet, which met in 1917 and 1918, and then became the British Empire Delegation to the Paris Peace Conference.

When peace arrived unexpectedly in the autumn of 1918, the Empire representatives made it clear that they were to be part of the decision-making. Hughes and Borden were deeply annoyed that the armistice agreements were negotiated without their consent, and Hughes also objected strongly to Wilson's Fourteen Points being accepted as the basis for negotiations.[23] Shortly after his arrival in England, Borden visited Hankey, 'full of grievances and rather formidable', complaining among other things about the decision that had been taken to try the Kaiser.[24]

The Dominions' sense of what was due to them and their feeling that the British were not taking them seriously enough in the preparations for the peace, came to a head over the issue of representation at the Paris Peace Conference. When it became clear at the meetings of the Imperial War Cabinet in late December 1918 that the British had not considered separate Dominion and Indian representation, there was a heated debate. Lloyd George's suggestion that one Dominion prime minister could stand in for all the rest foundered in the face of Dominion *amour propre*. As Hankey said, 'the Dominions are as jealous of each other as cats'.[25]

In any case, as Borden wrote to his wife the real problem was that the Dominions' position had never been properly sorted out. Canada was 'a nation that is not a nation. It is about time to alter it.' And he noted, with a certain tone of pity, 'The British Ministers are doing their best, but their best is not good enough.'[26] To Hankey, he was threatening; if Canada did not have full representation at the Peace Conference there was nothing for it but for him 'to pack his trunks, return to Canada, summon Parliament, and put the whole thing before them.'[27] Lloyd George, who hoped to avoid quarrels with the United States, was forced to confront Wilson over the issue.

When Lloyd George went to Paris in 1919, he went as leader not of the United Kingdom but of a British Empire Delegation, in which the five British delegates were a minority. The Dominions of Canada, Australia, New Zealand and South Africa were represented by their prime ministers, as well as a former prime minister in the case of Australia, and a statesman of international reputation in the case of Jan Smuts of South Africa. This was not a group to be cowed into line, even by such figures as Arthur Balfour, the British Foreign Secretary, or Lord Milner, the Colonial Secretary. The Dominions and India, included in the Delegation although it was not yet a self-governing dominion, had their own perspectives, policies and goals which did not always mesh with those of Britain. In the course of the 35 meetings of the British Empire Delegation between 13 January and 10 June 1919, all the major subjects from how to deal with Russia to the Covenant of the League of Nations to the peace terms for Germany came up for what was often quite intense and even acrimonious discussion.[28] Hankey recalled some years later, 'Every question was, so far as was humanly possible, discussed at these meetings before it came before the Supreme Council. . . .'[29] Lloyd George or Balfour, one of whom usually took the chair, spoke quite frankly of the difficulties they were encountering in the negotiations and others gave their views with equal frankness.

The shift in the balance of power within the British Empire forced Britain to take positions on certain issues, most notably on the disposition of the German colonies, in opposition to the United States. This created a real dilemma for the British: on the one hand, they wanted to build on the Anglo-American friendship to enhance their own position in Europe and the Pacific; on the other, they had to maintain the unity of the British Empire. The British claim to great-power status rested on the Empire but Britain could no longer manage without partners. It owed the Americans both a moral and financial debt, but so it owed the same to its Empire. The representation issue turned out to be a red herring, but the Empire was going to create substantial difficulties for the British in their dealings with the United States. The United States, conversely, was going to learn that, on occasion, it could use the Dominions against the British.

If the internal dynamics of the British Empire had changed, so too had those between Britain and the United States. In the late 1990s, it is difficult to remember how new Anglo-American cooperation was in 1919. Before the First World War, the United States had not been an obvious friend for Britain. The Americans did not feel a need for any alliances at all and the British moved towards alliances only when they were forced to. Memories of past conflicts, slights and rivalries ran deep and, in the United States, there were significant ethnic groups such as the Irish who had no reason to love the British. And as the United States grew in power, rivalry for trade and influence, especially in Latin America, exacerbated tensions to the point that there was talk of war in 1895 over Venezuela.

While the First World War had brought the United States into a closer relationship with Britain, it was not without strain. American public opinion, after all, was initially divided in its sympathies and on the issue of neutrality. In Britain there was resentment over what was seen as the late entry by the United States. Even an admirer of Woodrow Wilson such as the young British diplomat Harold Nicolson could note at a victory parade in Paris in July 1919 that 'the American flags had flattened, unweighted by history or past achievements'.[30] That feeling was equally strong in the Dominions, which had been at war since 1914. Even Borden, who was disposed to be friendly with the United States, was moved to say on the issue of representation at Paris, that 'Canada should not have less delegates than the United States, whose sacrifices in this war were certainly proportionately much less.'[31]

Among some of the British, too, there was an assumption that the old world, with its experience and sophistication, knew better than the brash Americans. As the bumptious Leo Amery wrote to Smuts about the League, the Americans were also like children in their unpredictability: 'In this case, in order to pacify and please the unconscionable Professor Wilson, you and Bob Cecil put your acute minds together to devise as nice-looking a Constitution as possible, and lo and behold, the whole of the United States takes the thing seriously, imagines it is really going to be carried out and enforced against them or anybody else, and proceeds to work itself up into a passionate frenzy.'[32] For their part, the Americans felt, in the words of Wilson, that the new world was coming in to redress the balance of the old. Gordon Auchincloss, son-in-law and confidant of Colonel House, confided to his diary on 5 November 1919, 'Before we get through with these fellows over here we will teach them how to do things and how to do them quickly.'[33]

British financial dependence on American sources also caused difficulties. While Britain financed the war efforts of its European allies, it in turn borrowed from the United States. In the financial crisis of the fall of 1916, when it became clear that Britain could not continue without increased American funding, John Maynard Keynes sent a memorandum to his superiors in the Treasury: 'the policy of this country towards the U.S.A. should be so directed as not only to avoid any form of reprisal or active irritation but also to conciliate and please'. According to his biographer, Robert Skidelsky, 'These words fix the moment when financial hegemony passed irrevocably across the Atlantic.'[34] Where the Americans saw their lending as a lever, certain of the British and their colleagues from the Dominions saw it as no more than was owed them for having stood off the German menace.

At the end of 1918, as the Paris Peace Conference was about to open, Wilson gave his first impressions of the British leaders to his confidant, Colonel Edward House. He had got on well with Lloyd George, less so with his foreign secretary Arthur Balfour. House, who could not bear Lloyd George and liked Balfour, behaved with his customary discretion but took the opportunity to tell the President, 'in my opinion we would have to work with England rather than France if we hoped to get the things for which we were striving through'.[35] In general this was to be true. Although Britain and the United States could not entirely trust each other, given their common history, and although there was still the distinct possibility of a naval race between the two, there was a willingness on both sides to work together on such issues as the League of Nations, the treatment of Germany, or the drawing of new borders in Europe. The fact that neither had any territorial ambitions in Europe enabled them to take the high moral ground against countries such as France and Italy. If there was some scepticism about the more idealistic aspects of Wilson's programme among senior British officials, it enjoyed considerable support among the younger generation.[36] Among the Dominions, Canada supported the League while Australia opposed it, mainly because Hughes could not bear Wilson or his 'toy', as he rudely put it.[37] On the question of the treatment of the losers, especially Germany, the Americans and the British agreed that a harsh peace

would be foolish. They also agreed that the French were being impossible, the Italians absurd.

On a practical level, British, Dominion and American experts generally worked well together on the special committees and commissions
which were set up during the Paris Peace Conference to grapple with
such issues as reparations and borders.[38] When their own interests
were not at stake, Dominion delegates were willing to work under the
direction of the British. Borden, for example, was asked to lead the
British delegation to the proposed meeting with Bolshevik and other
Russian delegates on Prinkipo island off Istanbul. Smuts went on his
famous mission to Hungary. Men from the Empire staffed the British
secretariat at the Peace Conference and were representatives on the
numerous committees and commissions set up to consider specific
questions. Harold Nicolson liked the colonials because they generally
did what they were told: Borden was 'easy and intelligent and will make
a good representative'. Sir Joseph Cook on the Czecho-Slovak Committee was 'a nice sensible man and an angel of obedience'.[39]

Dominion representatives worked as part of the British team, but
they also represented themselves. In Paris, the Empire delegates grew
accustomed to behaving as independent agents, going directly to representatives of other nations. Hughes met frequently with Clemenceau;
the two old radicals amused each other. Borden and Botha renewed their
friendship. Lesser figures chatted and dined with their counterparts.
Where it was necessary Dominion leaders met to hammer out a common position in opposition to the British. On 5 February, for example,
Borden called a meeting of the Dominion prime ministers on the issue
of their signing the peace treaty with Germany; the meeting agreed that
each Dominion should give its own assent to the treaty.[40]

On what was the single most difficult issue between the United States
and Britain, the naval one, it appeared that the Dominions had definite
views of their own. The British had, admittedly rather grudgingly,
accepted Wilson's Fourteen Points as a basis for peace settlements.
'Freedom of the seas', though, had worried them. At the time of
the armistice with Germany, the British tried to modify the principle
because it clashed with the traditional reliance of Britain on a naval
blockade against its enemies.[41] When the issue was discussed
in the Imperial War Cabinet at the end of 1918, Prime Minister Hughes
was all for sticking to the right to blockade in time of war even at
the cost of a rift with the United States.[42] Canada, on the other
hand, urged acceptance of the American position on freedom of the
seas.[43]

What was more troubling was a potential for serious naval rivalry between the two great powers. While Britain had expanded its navy to deal with Germany before the war, the United States had built its Pacific fleet to counter Japan, Britain's ally. The British were irritated by the competition from the United States; the Americans were equally irritated at British suggestions that they limit the size of their navy. The friction surfaced repeatedly during the Peace Conference. The chief American naval representative and chief of naval operations, Admiral William Benson, complained to Colonel House that the British wanted an agreement that the United States would never build a navy as large as theirs: 'This is perfectly preposterous. The British are just as crazy on the question of ships as the French are on other questions. We will undoubtedly have trouble with them about this before long.'[44] The fear was not entirely an unreasonable one; indeed naval planners in both the United States and Britain felt obliged to consider the prospect of a war between their two countries.[45]

That raised the issue of Britain's naval alliance with Japan, the potential enemy of the United States. Australia and New Zealand, and to a lesser extent South Africa, were torn. They feared Japan, its navy, its expanding economy and its growing population.[46] They most definitely did not want Japanese competition or Japanese immigrants (on that at least they had common ground with both Canada and the United States). On the other hand, both Australia and New Zealand continued to support the Anglo-Japanese Naval Alliance until it was finally abrogated at the Washington Naval Conference as the best means of ensuring peace and stability in the Pacific. Canada, which had little to fear from Japanese naval power, was more concerned about relations with the United States.[47] In the years after 1919, the Canadian government under Borden's successor, Arthur Meighen, played a key role in pushing both for an end to the alliance and for the general naval disarmament agreements of the Washington Conference at the end of 1921.[48]

The Americans, or some of them, gradually became aware that the British Empire was not the monolith they had feared. In Paris, in 1919, Wilson eventually decided that he had no objection to separate representation for the Dominions, 'providing they acted independent of the British Government and were not simply at the beck and call of the British authorities'.[49] This, he knew, was a safe bet, because Sir William Wiseman, the liaison for the British with the Americans, had passed on to House the minutes of the acrimonious discussions in the Imperial War Cabinet over representation and the peace terms.[50]

Moreover, as the Americans in Paris came to realise, the divisions within the British Empire could be useful. House, confided Sir William Wiseman to his diary, was 'very anxious that BORDEN and SMUTS should "play in" with the President's policy.'[51] Wilson made a point of having a private interview with Borden near the start of the Peace Conference to encourage his cooperation.[52] Both Borden and Smuts were going to help in the complex negotiations between the British and the Americans which shaped the League Covenant.[53] The racial equality clause, in particular, was a tricky one for the Americans. The Japanese wanted such a clause in the Covenant largely as a symbol of their new status as a power. They also deeply resented restrictions on Japanese immigration into the United States (and into Australia and Canada). Wilson saw the merits of the Japanese case; on the other hand, he did not want trouble from the West coast of the United States where feeling against Japanese immigration ran strong.[54]

The subsequent negotiations show how the Dominions were starting to pursue their own interests in international relations. House tried to come up with an anodyne formula which would not affect the domestic policies of members of the League; even that was probably too much for American domestic opinion. The British, by contrast, had no objection to a request from what was after all an ally; they had to deal, though, with the Australians and New Zealanders who vehemently opposed any mention of racial equality. Hughes in particular refused to support it. When the League of Nations Commission discussed the issue on 13 February 1919 the British accordingly voted against the racial equality clause; as House confided to his diary, 'It has taken considerable finesse to lift the load from our shoulders and place it upon the British, but happily, it has been done.'[55] The Japanese, for their part, held the British Dominions, rather than Britain, responsible.[56]

Of all the members of the British Empire Delegation, apart of course from the British themselves, the Americans found that they could work best with the Canadians. This was partly a matter of personal ties and shared values, partly because the Canadians saw themselves as a bridge between Britain and the United States. Indeed as Borden wrote to Lloyd George in 1918, if the larger League of Nations did not work out, there might be one between 'the two great English speaking commonwealths who share common ancestry, language and literature, who are inspired by like democratic ideals, who enjoy similar political institutions and whose united force is sufficient to ensure the peace of the world'.[57] No mention, it should be noted, was made of the British Empire. The Canadians stressed, in their customary high-minded way, that they did not want anything for themselves and, in general, disapproved of territorial annexations. (In fact that did not stop a lot of delightful chat with the Americans and the British about the possibility of letting Canada have the panhandle in exchange for, say, British Guiana.)

The most contentious issue at the Paris Peace Conference, and the one which showed clearly the three-sided and shifting nature of the relationship between Britain, its empire and the United States, was that of the disposition of Germany's former colonies. No one suggested they should become independent; rather the question was whether they should go as spoils of war to the victors as annexations to existing British colonies (which is what the South Africans, New Zealanders and Australians wanted), or, as the Americans insisted, as mandates under the new League of Nations.

The fate of the Pacific islands, in particular, also touched relations between Japan on the one hand and the British Empire and the United States on the other. The British, mindful of their need for Japanese assistance in the Far East, had promised German possessions north of the equator to the Japanese in a secret agreement during the war. Australia, though, arguing on grounds of security against Japan and other vaguely defined Asiatic threats, tried to make a case for getting all the islands, north and south of the equator. On that at least the British stood firm; Australia had to content itself with the southern islands only. The United States was torn; it disapproved of secret agreements and opposed annexations, whatever the power. It also had not decided which was the greater threat in the Pacific: Britain or Japan. On the one hand, it was alarmed about the growth of Japanese naval power, which would only increase if Japan got more island bases; perhaps, suggested a memorandum of 2 December 1918 from the Naval Planning Committee, Japan might be given a free hand on the continent of Asia to turn its attention away from the Pacific.[58] Given the potential for naval rivalry with Britain, it would be foolish to alienate the third naval power in the Pacific. On the other hand, did the United States want Britain to acquire more strategic positions in the Pacific?[59]

The question also caused considerable heat within the British Empire Delegation. Britain itself, the enthusiasts in the Colonial Office apart, did not want any of the German colonies. Its main concern was with grabbing large parts of the Ottoman Empire and there it had already arranged matters to its own convenience before the war ended. Neither Britain nor Canada wanted to antagonise the Americans on the matter. Before the Peace Conference opened, the British tried to reassure Wilson; on 28 December 1918 the President told Auchincloss that the

British were 'strongly opposed' to the Australians having the islands; 'he didn't think they would press it'.[60]

On the other hand, the British Empire had to be kept together and several of its members wanted territory. Even India (although this probably reflected the imperialist designs of its officials more than anything else) put in its claims. In a document drawn up before the Peace Conference started, the India Office hinted that India might be a suitable power to run Mesopotamia and asked outright for German East Africa. Indians, it argued, were prevented from emigrating to the white Dominions, and this caused political difficulties within India. Why not open up East Africa for, say, demobilised Indian soldiers? They would be loyal to the crown, hardworking, and probably much nicer to the local inhabitants than the white planters.[61] Australia wanted German New Guinea and several archipelagos, New Zealand German Samoa. Although South Africa, notably Smuts, supported the League (indeed Smuts claimed he had invented it) on this issue, specifically its claim to German South West Africa, it stood with Australia and New Zealand. Given recent history, Britain wanted to keep South Africa happy. What caused particular trouble with the Americans is that the British Dominions and India talked in terms of outright annexation, not some irritating mandate which might encourage the native inhabitants to make trouble.

Even Smuts, who had developed the idea of mandates, did not intend them to apply to Africa.[62] As he reported to a friend in January 1919, a long discussion with Wilson about the League went well until the issue came up: 'He is entirely opposed to our annexing a little German colony here or there, which pains me deeply and will move Billy Hughes to great explosions of righteous wrath.'[63] Smuts was prepared to do some horse-trading to gain his ends. Wilson, he reported in a letter of 20 January 1919 to Lloyd George, was sound except on one point. Lloyd George should speak strongly to him about his opposition to the annexation of German colonies: 'I need not point out the trouble you are going to have with these Dominions in this matter. You are helping Wilson in getting the League established, but he must be made to realise your difficulty and assist you to overcome them.'[64]

The difficulty was going to be to persuade Wilson that annexation was desirable. Wilson agreed that Germany should lose its colonies but insisted that the League take over responsibility. On 22 January, Borden confided to his diary that Wilson had insisted to him that there be no annexations: 'Is opposed to claims of Australia and New Zealand. Says world would abhor annexations and in interest of B.Emp. Hopes they will not insist and agreed with me that good relations between B.E. and U.S. best asset either c'd have.'[65] Colonel House's cynical assessment was that the debate over annexation versus mandates was academic because the mandatory power in charge would in short order persuade the colony for which it had been given responsibility to request annexation itself, but his view was unlikely to satisfy either side.[66]

The Pacific islands came up for discussion on 24 January in the Council of Ten. Clémenceau, in the chair, invited Lloyd George to bring in his cannibals – Hughes and William Massey of New Zealand.[67] (This was to be a running joke at the conference.) Hughes reassured Wilson when he asked about freedom for missionaries to work in New Guinea: 'there are many days when the poor devils do not get half enough missionaries to eat'. Hughes' claim for outright annexation of the islands was based on defence – they were 'as necessary to Australia as water to a city'; on Australia's payment in the war – the 90 000 casualties, the 60 000 killed, the war debt of 300 million pounds sterling. 'Australia did not wish to be left to stagger under this load and not to feel safe.' (The Australians had also considered using the argument that the locals were welcoming them with open arms after the horrors of German rule; but when the Australian government carried out some inquiries in New Guinea it found that the inhabitants had liked the German officials who generally respected their customs.)[68] Massey followed Hughes with his demand for Samoa.

The French, who were as cynical as Hughes about the League, were sympathetic to the claims. Before the war ended, in July 1918, Hughes had held friendly discussions with Leo Amery and two French officials concerned with colonies, at which he had outlined his claims on the islands and stressed that he wanted France to stay in the Pacific.[69] Some observers in Paris believed that the French were egging Hughes on as a way to get at Wilson.[70]

Wilson, for his part, dug in and threatened to take the whole issue to the public.[71] The meeting on 24 January was followed by a series of meetings behind the scenes, involving, as Hankey put it, 'an infinity of delicate negotiations'[72] as the British tried to bring their reluctant Dominions to heel and keep the Americans happy. Hankey blamed Hughes and Massey for insisting on annexation but he also found Wilson unnecessarily stubborn in insisting on the affiliation of the former German colonies to the League.[73] On both sides, the British Empire and the American, there was alarm at the possibility of a rift, especially at a time when other important issues, notably the League of Nations Covenant, were under consideration.[74]

On 29 January, House and Smuts met to consider a compromise which had been drafted by Lloyd George and 'some of them' on the British Empire Delegation. (It had not however been shown to either Massey or Hughes.)[75] The proposal was to have three sorts of mandates: A for nations nearly ready to run their own affairs, B where the mandatory power would run them and C (which was really annexation under another name) where the mandatory would administer the territory as part of its own, subject only to certain restrictions on the sale of alcohol and firearms. Not surprisingly, the C mandates were to apply in Africa and the Pacific. John Latham, from the Australian delegation, with or without the knowledge of Hughes, helped Smuts to work out the details.[76]

The pressure on Hughes increased. On 29 January, there was a meeting of the British Empire Delegation, which, Borden told his diary primly, produced a 'pretty warm scene'.[77] Lloyd George produced the deal which had been agreed upon with House; and Hughes, fighting 'like a weasel',[78] quibbled over every point until Lloyd George finally lost his temper and told him that he had been arguing his case with the United States for three days but that he did not intend to quarrel with the Americans over the Solomon Islands.[79] (That remark does not appear in the official record.)

Hughes also used the press. The next day an article in the continental *Daily Mail* accused Lloyd George and Balfour of kowtowing to Wilson and of disappointing the Dominions. There was a danger, it continued, that the Empire would break up.[80] The author had lunched with Hughes and had also spoken to Ward of New Zealand.[81] The whole interview was very unfortunate, Philip Kerr, Lloyd George's secretary, wrote to Milner:

> It is difficult to see what its effects will be because the suggestion has been put out that the Prime Minister has been sacrificing the vital interests of the Dominions for the sake of the *beaux yeux* of America, whereas the fact is that he has fought their battles from start to finish subject only to putting pressure on them to go as far as they can in accordance with the Imperial Cabinet resolution to accept the mandatory principle and not break up the Peace Conference altogether.[82]

Wilson, who was always sensitive about press attacks, was in an angry mood when the Council of Ten met on 30 January. There was, House commented, 'a first-class row'. According to Lloyd George, Wilson

delivered a rambling and muddled criticism of proposed British compromise, and was noticeably rude to Hughes. 'Mr Hughes was the last
man I should have chosen to handle in that way.'[83] Borden, for all his
dislike of Hughes, was also dismayed.[84] Even House felt his President
was unwise: 'The British have come a long way, and if I had been Wilson
I should have congratulated them over their willingness to meet us
more than half way.'[85] Wilson ended by demanding of Hughes, 'am I
to understand that if the whole civilised world asks Australia to agree to
a mandate in respect of these islands, Australia is prepared still to defy
the appeal of the whole civilised world?' 'That's about the size of it,
President Wilson.'[86] There was a grunt of agreement from Massey.
Things calmed down when Botha made an eloquent appeal, condemn-
ing the article in papers that morning (he had thrown it away, he said, in
contempt) and asking for compromise. Think, he told his audience, of
the peace of the world. Give way on small things. Lloyd George later
wrote, 'It is difficult to convey the power of General Botha's deliverance
by a mere summary of the words. Behind it was the attractive and
compelling personality of this remarkable man.' Wilson told Lloyd
George immediately afterwards that Botha had made 'the most impressive speech to which he had ever listened.'[87] The deal ultimately went
through. Borden later went round to House and apologised for
Hughes.[88] The crisis over the German colonies was not as serious as
that over Italy's claims in the Adriatic but it does reveal the balancing
act Britain now had to do.

After 1919, the Dominions continued to complicate Britain's foreign
relations. As Hankey said wearily to Balfour in 1926, 'There is always
some Dominion that gives trouble at an Imperial Conference, but it is
hardly ever the same one twice running.' Before the war, in Hankey's
view, Australia had caused problems but it was 'now one of the most
loyal'.[89] Hughes, for all his threats and bluster, did not lay the founda-
tions for a more independent foreign policy. Both Australia and New
Zealand, partly through inclination, partly for security reasons, chose to
remain good team players; both opposed ending the Anglo-Japanese
naval alliance and, at the three Imperial Conferences between 1921
and 1926, argued for a united Empire with a common foreign and
defence policy.

South Africa moved in the opposite direction, partly as a result of
pressure from its Afrikaans minority. When Lord Milner, then Colonial
Secretary, announced in 1920 that an imperial conference would be
held the following year to look into the whole issue of imperial
government, the South African Opposition saw it as a threat to national

independence. As one politician put it, 'The Conference to be held next year had only one aim, that of making the whole of the Empire speak with one voice, and against that the whole of Dutch-speaking South Africa protested, as it did not wish to be tied forever to the British Empire.'[90] Under the prime ministership of General Hertzog in particular, South Africa moved further down the road to independence.

Canada went furthest. Like South Africa, it also had a strong minority which had no reason to love the British tie. Most important, though, was its proximity to the rising power of the United States. The liberal government under Mackenzie King, which took office at the end of 1921, was openly committed to Canadian management of its international affairs but the difference with their Conservative predecessors was more apparent than real. Borden had talked of an imperial foreign policy but it was he who had insisted on separate Dominion representation at the Paris Peace Conference and in the League of Nations. His government had appointed the first Canadian representative in Washington.

Mackenzie King, of whom it was said by a Canadian wit that he never did anything by halves which could be done by quarters, was an unlikely standard-bearer of Canadian autonomy. Fussy, anxious, preoccupied by domestic affairs in his first term in office, he nevertheless took opportunities as they arose to mark out a position for Canada. When the British government precipitously summoned its Dominions to its aid in September 1922 during the Chanak crisis, King argued that the Canadian Parliament would have to decide on Canada's role; typically, he had no intention of calling parliament back.[91] When the British finally managed to make peace with Turkey at Lausanne in 1923, Canada went along with Curzon's assertion that his signature bound the Empire as a whole; King, however, issued a typical proviso to the effect that Canada was bound by the treaty in so far as it ended a war but was not accepting any obligations as to the future.[92]

At imperial conferences, notably in 1923, King infuriated the British and the more imperial-minded Dominion representatives by his passive resistance to anything that smacked of imperial centralisation. Like Laurier before him, he quibbled, delayed, split hairs to whittle every statement down into a bland non-committal formula. 'The timidity of even speaking about the Empire as a single unit is getting too ridiculous', complained Leo Amery.[93] In March 1923, Canada signed the Halibut Treaty with the United States on its own behalf; the British Embassy in Washington sulked but again Britain found it politic to acquiesce. It was yet another reminder of the changed relations both within the Empire and between Britain, the Empire and the United States.

It is tempting, but dangerous, to see in this the inevitable disintegration of the British Empire and the rise of an American hegemony. Without the Second World War, it is possible that the Empire or rather Commonwealth would have lingered on as a significant political force. Indeed the transformation of world communications, with the jet engine, long-range aircraft, satellites and the Internet would have gone a long way to overcoming the disadvantages of a widely dispersed collection of territories. Leo Amery saw at least some of the possibilities as early as 1917 when he sketched out a greatly expanded Empire from Cape Town to Cairo and from Egypt through the Middle East to India and on to Singapore and the Antipodes. 'They will have the Indian Ocean free for their shipping; as aviation develops they will have a continuous chain of aerodromes, etc.; and to a very large extent it will be possible to secure railway communication as well.'[94]

The Second World War closed the door on that possibility forever. By 1945 Britain was worn down financially and militarily. More important, perhaps, its people were no longer prepared to pay the price of Empire. Nor of course was the Labour Government which took office in the summer of 1945. In India, the Middle East, the Far East, then in Africa, the growth of nationalist movements had significantly raised the costs of keeping large parts of the globe pink. Furthermore, the United States was not prepared to hand over money or military equipment if it went to keeping the British (or any other European) empire going; and help from the United States was essential. The sterling crisis of 1947 showed that, if any demonstration were still needed.

There were of course still those, and not just in Britain, who hoped to salvage the core of the old Empire, the Dominions perhaps without India, and build an economic bloc based on sterling and internal trade. That did not happen, for two reasons: the Cold War and Britain's decision to move into the European Economic Community. These factors forced each of the self-governing parts of the Empire to reconsider its relations with both the United States and Britain. As the leader of the coalition against the Soviet Union and as the possessor of the deterrent, the United States now occupied the position that Britain had once held in imperial defence; it no longer made sense to deal with the Americans through London. In 1951 Australia and New Zealand signed the Pacific Security Agreement with the United States, the first treaty either had signed with a foreign power. Canada, which had dealt directly with the United States for years, tried through NATO, as it had done through the

Empire, to find counterweights to its neighbour to the south; but in reality the ties, military, political and economic, between the two North American nations grew even closer. South Africa withdrew itself from the Commonwealth in the face of criticism of apartheid but maintained close, if troubled, relations with both Britain and the United States.

Britain for its part talked of a 'special relationship', not with its Commonwealth but with the United States. In 1971, when Edward Heath asked for House of Commons approval of the government's decision to apply to join the EEC, he said: 'The Commonwealth . . . is a unique association which we value. But the idea that it would become an effective economic or political, let alone military bloc has never materialised.' Today the great imperial buildings still line Whitehall but the world that built them seems a long way off. So does a common imperial foreign policy with its complicated balancing act between internal and external relations. Perhaps the United States has gained greater sympathy for coping with these difficulties.

Notes

1 *Papers Relating to the Foreign Relations of the United States 1919: the Paris Peace Conference, 1919* (Washington, 1942–47), I, pp. 482–6, 531–3.
2 Stephen Roskill, *Hankey: Man of Secrets, Volume II. 1919–1931* (London, 1972), p. 44.
3 See, for example, diary entries for 28 October 1918; 6 February 1919. Yale University Library. Edward M. House Diary, Series II c, Binder 14.
4 Nicholas Mansergh, *The Commonwealth Experience, Volume 2: From British to Multiracial Commonwealth* (Toronto and Buffalo, 1983), pp. 27–8.
5 Quoted in Nicholas Mansergh, *The Commonwealth Experience, Volume 2: From British to Multiracial Commonwealth* (Toronto and Buffalo, 1983), pp. 19–20
6 John Kendle, *The Colonial and Imperial Conferences, 1887–1911* (London, 1967), pp. 93–4.
7 See Norman Hillmer and J.L. Granatstein, *From Empire to Umpire: Canada and the World to the 1990s* (Toronto, 1994), chapter 1 *passim* for a discussion of this point.
8 Kendle, p. 226.
9 See John Hilliker, *Canada's Department of External Affairs, Volume 1: The Early Years, 1909–1946* (Montreal and Kingston, 1990), pp. 42–5, 79.
10 Quoted in Hillmer and Granatstein, p. 5.
11 National Archives of Canada [NAC]. Borden Papers, Volume 12069, f65926.
12 Quoted in Charles Grimshaw, 'Australian Nationalism and the Imperial Connection 1900–1914', *The Australian Journal of Politics and History*, Vols 3 and 4 (November 1957–November 1958), p. 164.

13   Quoted in Barbara R. Penny, 'Australia's Reactions to the Boer War – a Study in Colonial Imperialism', *Journal of British Studies*, Vol. VII, 1–2 (November 1967), p. 101.

14   Carman Miller, *Painting the Map Red: Canada and the South African War, 1899–1902* (Montreal and Kingston, 1993), pp. 437–8.

15   See, for example, Hillmer and Granatstein, pp. 24–5 and Pope, Maurice, ed., *Public Servant: the Memoirs of Sir Joseph Pope* (Toronto, 1960), pp. 86–8.

16   See, for example, Ian Nish, *Alliance in Decline: a Study in Anglo-Japanese Relations 1908–23* (London, 1972), pp. 45–6.

17   Quoted in Leonie Foster, *High Hopes: the Men and Motives of the Australian Round Table* (Melbourne, 1986), p. 75.

18   Borden, Robert Laird, *Robert Laird Borden: His Memoirs, edited and with a preface by Henry Borden* (New York, 1938), Vol. 2, pp. 622–3.

19   Hughes, William Morris, *The Splendid Adventure; a Review of Empire Relations within and without the Commonwealth of Britannic Nations* (Toronto: Doubleday, 1928), p. 118.

20   See, for example, Robert Bothwell, Ian Drummond, John English, *Canada, 1900–1945* (Toronto: University of Toronto Press, 1987), p. 179.

21   Quoted in Hillmer and Granatstein, p. 63.

22   Smuts, Jan Christiaan, *Selections from the Smuts Papers*. Edited by W.K. Hancock and Jean van der Poel (Cambridge, 1966), 3, 498.

23   L.F. Fitzhardinge, *The Little Digger 1914–1952. William Morris Hughes. A Political Biography*, Vol. 2 (London and Sydney, 1979), p. 354.

24   Roskill, p. 29.

25   Ibid., p. 30.

26   R. Craig Brown, *Robert Laird Borden: a Biography*, vol. 2 (Toronto, 1980), p. 152.

27   Roskill, pp. 29–30.

28   Public Record Office, London (PRO). The Minutes of the British Empire Delegation. CAB 29/28.

29   House of Lords Records Office, Lloyd George Papers, G/8/18/39.

30   Nigel Nicolson, ed., *Vita and Harold: the Letters of Vita Sackville-West and Harold Nicolson* (London, 1993), p. 96.

31   PRO. Minutes of the British Empire Delegation, 13 January 1919 (CAB29/28).

32   *Selections from the Smuts Papers*, 4, 78.

33   Yale University Library. Gordon Auchincloss Papers: Diary. Series I, Box 2.

34   Skidelsky, Robert. *John Maynard Keynes. Volume 1: Hopes Betrayed 1883–1920* (London, 1983), p. 335.

35   Entry for 31 December 1918. Yale University Library. Edward M. House Diary, Series II c, Binder 14.

36   See, for example, Harold Nicolson, *Peacemaking 1919* (London, 1964), pp. 30–3, 36–8.

37   David Lloyd George, *The Truth about the Peace Treaties* (London, 1938), 1, 196.

38   See, for example, Charles Seymour, *Letters from the Paris Peace Conference*. Edited, Harold B. Whiteman, Jr (New Haven and London, 1965), p. 152.

39   Harold Nicolson, pp. 259, 272–3.

40   See memorandum of 7 February 1919 in *Documents on Canadian External Relations. Volume 2: The Paris Peace Conference of 1919* (Ottawa, 1969), p. 200.

41   See Roger Dingman, *Power in the Pacific: the Origins of Naval Arms Limitation, 1914–1922* (Chicago and London, 1976), pp. 70–2.

42 David Lloyd George, *The Truth about the Peace Treaties* (London, 1938), 1, p. 196.

43 See Dingman, p. 74.

44 Entry for 3 April 1919. Yale University Library. Gordon Auchincloss Papers: Diary, Series I, Box 2; see also Seth P. Tillman, *Anglo-American Relations at the Paris Peace Conference of 1919* (Princeton, New Jersey, 1961), pp. 287–94.

45 See, for example, Dingman, pp. 97, 108.

46 See, for example, Hughes to Lloyd George, 4 November 1918. House of Lords Records Office. Lloyd George Papers F/28/2/7.

47 See, for example, NAC. Borden Papers. Vol. 12069, folio 65926.

48 C.P. Stacey, *Canada and the Age of Conflict. Volume 1: 1867–1921* (Toronto, 1984), pp. 341–5.

49 Entry for 13 January 1919. Yale University Library. Gordon Auchincloss Papers: Diary. Series I, Box 2.

50 Entry for 12 January 1919. Yale University Library. Sir William Wiseman Papers. Peace Conference Diary of Sir William Wiseman. Series I, Box 7.

51 Entry for 17 January 1919. Yale University Library. Sir William Wiseman Papers. Peace Conference Diary of Sir William Wiseman. Series I, Box 7.

52 Entry for 21 January 1919. Yale University Library. Sir William Wiseman Papers. Peace Conference Diary of Sir William Wiseman. Series I, Box 7.

53 See, for example, entry for 5 February 1919. Yale University Library. Edward M. House Diary, Series II c, Binder 14.

54 See Roy Watson Curry, *Woodrow Wilson and Far Eastern Policy, 1913–1921* (New York, 1968), pp. 254–7.

55 Entry for 13 February 1919. Yale University Library. Edward M. House Diary, Series II c, Binder 14.

56 Nish, pp. 270–1.

57 Borden to Lloyd George, 23 November 1918. House of Lords Records Office. Lloyd George Papers. F/5/2/28.

58 Curry, p. 258.

59 See Dingman, pp. 79–80.

60 Entry for 28 December 1918. Yale University Library. Gordon Auchincloss Papers: Diary. Series I, Box 2.

61 PRO. The Minutes of the British Empire Delegation. Indian Desiderata for Peace Settlement (CAB 29/2, p. 42).

62 See W.K. Hancock, *Smuts, Volume 1: The Sanguine Years, 1870–1919* (Cambridge, 1962), p. 507.

63 *Selections from the Smuts Papers*, 4, 50.

64 House of Lords Records Office. Lloyd George Papers. F/45/9/30.

65 Entry for 22 January 1919. NAC. Borden Diary.

66 Edward Mandell House, *The Intimate Papers of Colonel House Arranged as a Narrative by Charles Seymour*. Vol. 4 (Boston and New York, 1928), p. 296.

67 Arthur Walworth, *Wilson and his Peacemakers: American Diplomacy at the Paris Peace Conference* (New York, 1986), p. 71.

68 Hudson, W. J., *Billy Hughes in Paris: the Birth of Australian Diplomacy* (West Melbourne, Victoria, 1978), pp. 78, 93–4, 17.

69 John Barnes and David Nicholson, eds, *The Leo Amery Diaries, Volume 1: 1896–1929* (London, 1980), p. 225.

70 Eggleston diary, quoted in Hudson, pp. 116–17.

71   *The Intimate Papers of Colonel House*, 4, p. 296.
72   Roskill, p. 53.
73   Ibid., p. 54.
74   See, for example, Sir William Wiseman's diary for 27 January 1919, Yale University Library, Sir William Wiseman Papers, Series I, Box 7 Peace Conference.
75   *The Intimate Papers of Colonel House*, 4, p. 298.
76   Roskill, p. 54.
77   Borden, Robert Laird, *Memoirs*, p. 908.
78   Alan Sharp, *The Versailles Settlement: Peacemaking in Paris, 1919* (London, 1991), p. 162.
79   Borden, *Memoirs*, p. 906.
80   Walworth, p. 79.
81   Lord Riddell, *Lord Riddell's Intimate Diary of the Peace Conference and After, 1918–1923* (London, 1933), p. 16.
82   Kerr to Milner, 31 January 1919. Bodleian Library. Ms. Eng. Hist, c. 700 Additional Milner Papers.
83   Lloyd George, *The Truth about the Peace Treaties*, 1, 542.
84   Entry for 30 January 1919. NAC. Borden diary.
85   *The Intimate Papers of Colonel House*, 4, 299.
86   Roskill, p. 55, footnote 3.
87   Lloyd George, *The Truth about the Peace Treaties* 1, 546.
88   Entry for 1 February 1919. Yale University Library. Edward M. House Diary, Series II c, Binder 14.
89   Roskill, p. 429.
90   Hancock, p. 38.
91   See Hillmer and Granatstein, pp. 87–8.
92   See H. Blair Neatby, *William Lyon Mackenzie King. Volume 2, 1924–1932. The Lonely Heights* (Toronto, 1963), pp. 33–5.
93   *The Leo Amery Diaries*, 1, 354.
94   Ibid., 1, 173.

2
Underpinning the Anglo-American Alliance: the Council on Foreign Relations and Britain between the Wars

Priscilla Roberts[1]

The Council on Foreign Relations has given rise to its own mythology, attracting attacks from both Right and Left in American politics as an example of the ability of anti-democratic, elitist groups to set governmental policy.[2] Robert D. Schulzinger, Michael Wala, and Inderjeet Parmar have also studied the Council's role and influence upon American foreign affairs.[3] Their works largely concentrate upon the period from approximately 1940 onwards, when the United States began to take an increasingly important part in world affairs, and upon the Council's contribution to its country's international transformation. This essay focuses on the Council's earlier interwar activities, in the fifteen or twenty years after its foundation, and in particular upon its impact upon Anglo-American relations. In recent years historians have drawn attention to the development between the wars among certain sections of the foreign-policy elite in both Britain and the United States of sentiments in favour of closer Anglo-American relations.[4] This essay suggests that the roots of the transformation in American international policies, most notably the dedication and commitment with which the United States government supported the Allies, especially Britain, during the Second World War, owed something to the Council's previous efforts to improve Anglo-American relations.

The Council on Foreign Relations originated in a joint Anglo-American initiative at the Paris Peace Conference of 1919. The British and American experts assembled to advise their country's diplomats and statesmen as to the peace already felt among themselves, and some of their European colleagues, a sense of confraternity and collegiality. They initially contemplated creating a bi-national Anglo-American Institute of International Affairs, with branches in both countries. The British quickly established the Royal Institute of International Affairs, but in the pervading malaise afflicting the United States after the Senate rejected membership in the League of Nations, its American counterpart lagged behind. In early 1921, it merged with another near-moribund organisation, the Council on Foreign Relations, 'a group organized in 1918 by leading lawyers, bankers and other men of affairs in New York to discuss wartime problems and entertain foreign visitors', which by mid-1920 found itself 'languishing' and 'old and waning'.[5] Under the energetic direction of the youthful Hamilton Fish Armstrong, appointed executive director in 1922, the Council rapidly became a formidable intellectual presence in American foreign affairs. Like the RIIA, the Council deliberately eschewed adopting any institutional position on any question. Yet in practice the organisation attracted and represented primarily those elite Americans who had supported American intervention in the First World War and firmly believed that the United States should have been more involved than it was in post-1920 world affairs. While CFR members might differ over the exact parameters of such involvement, the great majority shared this broad consensus.

From the beginning the Council emphasised the influential rather than simple mass appeal: early speakers included Georges Clémenceau, the French President, Édouard Herriot, the French Premier, J. Ramsay MacDonald, the British Prime Minister, his compatriot Lord Robert Cecil, and similar luminaries. Its journal, *Foreign Affairs*, likewise deliberately solicited articles not only from political and academic commentators but from leading statesmen, financiers and economists: just a few examples of the early contributors include V. I. Lenin, Hjalmar Schacht, Heinrich Brüning, Raymond Poincaré, Leon Trotsky, and Thomas W. Lamont, all writing on highly topical issues which they themselves were in a position to affect. It quickly became a tradition that before each presidential election representatives of the major political parties should publish pieces on their party's foreign policy achievements and outlook, and that Secretaries of State should deliver at least one address before the Council. The generosity of its business sponsors, among them the leading bankers Thomas W. Lamont of J. P. Morgan & Company, Otto H. Kahn of Kuhn, Loeb & Company, the latter's quondam partner, Paul M. Warburg, and former Secretary of State Elihu Root, facilitated the Council's early efforts. It sponsored study groups which considered such topical issues as Anglo-American relations, disarmament policy, Latin American affairs, Far Eastern affairs, economics, and raw materials policy, groups which generally included some participants from the

State Department. The organisation's emphases and activities in turn won it further memberships and financial backing from the powerful internationalist New York business community, always the Council's economic mainstay, and from the Carnegie Corporation and the Rockefeller Foundation.[6]

Although political considerations and fears of being perceived as a British front finally persuaded the Council's officers to establish an independent organisation which did not even share the RIIA's name, in practice the two institutions remained rather close. This sprang not solely from their common origins, but also from the outlook on international affairs which many of both bodies' most prominent and active officers shared. In particular, many believed that closer Anglo-American relations and even the creation of an Anglo-American alliance were essential to the maintenance of international stability, a viewpoint which they hoped the two institutions would promote, possibly in partnership. While some of the Council's most active officials, notably Armstrong and John Foster Dulles, were far less Anglophile and throughout their lives tended to define their foreign policy views according to Wilsonian principles of universalism and the rejection of the Rooseveltian balance-of-power worldview, many shared a decidedly Anglophile propensity.[7]

Such Anglophilia was a pronounced feature of the internationalist views of such officers as Root, the Council's first and only honorary president; John W. Davis and George W. Wickersham, its first two presidents; Paul D. Cravath, its first vice-president; and several of its founding directors, including Cravath, Kahn, Whitney H. Shepardson, and Wickersham, together with one of its greatest benefactors, Lamont of the Morgan firm, whose views generally represented those of his partners. These men were active and prominent not just in the Council itself but in other transnational organisations to promote Anglo-American solidarity, including the Pilgrims Society and the newly-established English Speaking Union, of which Davis was the American president and Wickersham the chairman.[8] Most of these individuals had strongly supported American intervention in the First World War, identifying themselves almost completely with the Allied cause. The Morgan firm not only acted as the Allies' war purchasing agent in the United States but also helped the British and French governments to raise the American credits and loans they desperately needed to finance their war effort.[9] After the war, such men were lukewarm towards Woodrow Wilson's vision of a universalist League of Nations based upon the equality of nations, disarmament and anti-colonial principles.

From well before the Armistice, such men as Cravath, Davis, Kahn, the Morgan partners, Root and Wickersham reiterated their continuing belief that Anglo-American political and economic cooperation must be the postwar settlement's central and most essential principle, the mainstay on which a satisfactory resolution of all other international problems would depend. In 1919 and 1920, during the negotiation of the Treaty of Versailles and the League fight, such men continued to hope that a *de facto* continuation of the wartime alliance between Britain, France and the United States, and these nations' mutual collaboration to enforce world peace and order and promote Europe's economic recovery, would characterise the postwar settlement.[10]

Since the late nineteenth or early twentieth century, important elites in both the United States and Britain had shared such views. In Great Britain, belief in the need to strengthen the Empire's defences through a *de facto* alliance with the United States was fundamental to the thinking of various leading British statesmen, notably Lord Grey, Arthur Balfour, Lord Bryce, and Lord Robert Cecil, the British press magnate Lord Northcliffe, proprietor of *The Times*, St John Loe Strachey, editor of *The Spectator*, and some members of the consciously imperialist group associated with the periodical *The Round Table*.[11] These last, in particular, would prove central to the RIIA's foundation and subsequent operations. Prominent among them were the academic and philosopher Lionel Curtis; Philip Kerr, later Lord Lothian, Lloyd George's wartime private secretary; the American-born Lord Astor and his wife Nancy; her brother-in-law, the banker Robert H. Brand; the novelist John Buchan; and Geoffrey Dawson (Robinson), later editor of *The Times*. Several had served under the imperialist Lord Milner in South Africa; they were pillars of the Rhodes Trust and thought it essential both to reinforce links between the constituent parts of the British Empire and to bolster Britain's international position by encouraging closer ties with the United States.[12] The RIIA quickly became the home of those who shared this outlook: Astor, Lothian, Curtis, and Cecil were among its most active presidents and directors. It is perhaps significant that both Lamont and the Carnegie Corporation generously funded its programmes in international studies.[13]

While the Anglophile viewpoint was perhaps slightly less dominant within the Council, undoubtedly many of its leading directors believed that the United States should enhance its international activities in close collaboration with the British Empire. The Council on Foreign Relations contributed substantially to this objective's attainment and to better Anglo-American relations. No other country benefited to anything like the same degree, not only from a special relationship with the Council itself, but also from its officers' dedicated attempts to improve Anglo-American relations and to present Britain's case on assorted issues. Council officers' efforts encompassed a coordinated range of activities, including hosting British speakers and authors and mounting a long-running series of Council study groups and conferences consciously designed to enhance Anglo-American relations, an endeavour intensified first by the naval difficulties of the later 1920s and then by the Great Depression's economic impact upon such divisive and contentious issues as war debts, reparations and international trade.

The Council provided a forum in which eminent Englishmen could explain their country's policies to a knowledgeable United States audience in a relatively frank and confidential atmosphere. Over the years the Council's speakers programme featured many individual Britons, more than any other nationality. Every year Council members could listen to one or more British guests, among them Cecil, H.A.L. Fisher, Robert Seton-Watson, John Maynard Keynes, Brand, Curtis, Sir Arthur Salter, the British Ambassadors Sir Ronald Lindsay, Lord Lothian and Lord Halifax, and numerous others. The most favoured, such as Salter, a top League of Nations official, might even be invited to make an office in the Council's New York headquarters their base. They covered a wide variety of topics, usually setting forth the British viewpoint on such often-vexatious issues as war debts, trade, financial and monetary policy, India, the League of Nations, the Far East, and naval policy.[14] Some speakers attracted large audiences, while others appeared before a small but carefully chosen group of invited guests. Such occasions provided useful opportunities to initiate new contacts and strengthen existing relationships. *Foreign Affairs* also published numerous articles by leading Britons, for example Cecil, the former British Foreign Secretary Viscount Grey of Fallodon, Sir Austen Chamberlain, Sir Basil Blackett and Salter, on such subjects as the League of Nations and collective security, the freedom of the seas, principles of British foreign policy, finance and India.[15]

In addition, the Council sometimes asked Americans to discuss Anglo-American relations, either on some specific issue or generally. In March 1922 a minor furore arose in the Senate when the press obtained the stenographic record of a Council address of Cravath in February. He had allegedly stated that the most important feature of the recently concluded Washington Conference treaties was the 'understanding' reached between Britain and the United States on the Far East.[16]

Cravath's fellow officers Davis, Kahn and Wickersham shared his stance; arguing for the Washington Treaties, the latter stated: 'The essential vital interests of Great Britain and the United States are and must always be the same.'[17] As the decade ended, such Council stalwarts as Davis and the influential political commentator Walter Lippmann likewise argued in *Foreign Affairs* that the most significant result of the 1929–30 London Naval Conference was its contribution to Anglo-American harmony in resolving a festering naval dispute, a viewpoint shared by the Secretary of State, Henry L. Stimson.[18]

The first Council study group on Anglo-American relations held its opening meeting in November 1928 and submitted a report in June 1929, a document intended to influence policymakers at the London Naval Conference. This was in every sense a transatlantic venture; the Council's endeavours had their counterpart in the RIIA in Britain, which provided a friendly forum where American visitors such as Allen W. Dulles could speak on Anglo-American naval relations. In 1928–29 the RIIA likewise established a 'Special Group on Anglo-American Relations', chaired by Philip Kerr, which contended that close cooperation between the two powers was in the best interests of both.[19] The American group was chaired by Charles P. Howland, a Boston lawyer, and its membership of 17 included Davis, Allen W. Dulles, Wilson's former adviser Colonel Edward M. House, Arthur Bullard of the League of Nations, Philip C. Jessup, Shepardson and Lippmann, together with various academics, New York lawyers and representatives of other organisations interested in international affairs.[20] Its purposes were to hammer out a possible American position in the then impending naval disarmament conference; and to devise means of strengthening the recently concluded Kellogg–Briand Pact to outlaw war by considering methods of exerting sanctions, military or otherwise, in collaboration with either or both Britain and the League of Nations, against nations which resorted to war.[21] The final report stated that the study's objective 'was of course to see how the attitudes of the two countries could be harmonised so as to avoid competitive navy building, recriminatory language and ill-will where there should be community of interest'.[22] The hope was that the Council's deliberations and conclusions would reach the president through what Howland described as Allen Dulles' 'private channel to Hoover's ear'.[23] The group made every effort to accommodate the British position. In January 1929 Salter addressed it over dinner, while in mid-February Dulles and Howland spoke respectively on 'technical aspects of the naval situation' and 'broader political questions'. Three English visitors, Salter, George Young and Professor

C.K. Webster, were invited to sit at the speakers' table and comment on the addresses for five minutes each 'from the British point of view'.[24] Even after the group presented its report in mid-1929, its members still reassembled in January 1930 to hear Kerr discuss Anglo-American relations in view of the London Naval Conference.[25] *Foreign Affairs* also published related articles by Howland and Kerr, in which each suggested that Anglo-American naval cooperation was the best means of achieving a harmonious conference settlement.[26]

The group's June 1929 report drew substantially upon recent writings of Kerr in the RIIA's journal, *International Affairs*.[27] It argued that war between the United States and Britain should be unthinkable and that, while economic concerns might cause dissension, the only reason such a conflict might arise was potential British interference with United States shipping in a war in which America remained neutral. Conceding that 'public opinion in the United States is determined to have a substantial navy and has a firm intention that it shall be equal to the British', it suggested that the two countries should accept parity of 400 000 tons apiece in cruisers, the major point of contention between the two sides. It also suggested that, since one could not assume that the Kellogg–Briand Pact alone would prevent future wars, Britain and the United States should coordinate their policies toward subsequent controversies between other nations. Fearing that the Senate would not ratify such a treaty, the group recommended that, following the precedent of the hallowed Monroe Doctrine, it should be implemented by executive action.[28] In effect, such a strategy would have realised the Anglo-American condominium which many leading Council figures had long envisaged.

In 1930, as international economic difficulties began to threaten continued harmonious relations between Britain and the United States, the Council decided to establish a second Anglo-American group to study 'possible points of economic friction between the two countries', including disputes over the control of such raw materials as oil and rubber and rivalries in overseas commerce and merchant shipping. Unlike its predecessor, this group did not contemplate suggesting solutions to these problems.[29] Conspicuously missing from its agenda were war debts and international economic policy, issues which would subsequently precipitate serious Anglo-American dissensions. Although the group's membership overlapped with that of its predecessor, it also included several economists, businessmen, and former Treasury officials. Interestingly, Allen W. Dulles was not included, though his brother John Foster Dulles, who since the First World War had been far more involved in economic questions, was.[30] Over the following months the group held several dinner meetings, at which these questions were discussed, but produced neither report nor recommendations. Its deliberations were effectively overtaken by negotiations over the moratorium on the payment of European war debts and reparations, Britain's abandonment of the gold standard, and the increasing international economic competition, including the raising of tariff barriers, which simultaneously engulfed the world.[31]

Throughout the 1930s the Council ensured that the British view on contentious issues dividing the two countries received at least a fair hearing within its portals. In the early 1930s the Council hosted at least 16 British speakers, including Ivison MacAdam, secretary of the RIIA, and Stephen King-Hall, its director of research, Lindsay, Sir Frederick Whyte and Sir George Paish of the British Treasury, Keynes, the former Prime Minister, Ramsay MacDonald, Lord Reading, a former viceroy of India, Salter, Brand, H.G. Wells, Sir Josiah Stamp of the Bank of England, and Kerr, who addressed the Council at least four times. Speakers concentrated particularly on economic issues, but also included policy toward India and, as the thirties progressed, the broader international situation and American neutrality policy.[32] *Foreign Affairs* likewise published articles by leading British figures on Far Eastern policy and the world economic situation.[33] As another London Naval Disarmament Conference approached in 1935, leading British and American experts, including Norman H. Davis, the Council's president-elect and a perennial American naval negotiator, again used the journal's pages to publicise the desirability of closer Anglo-American collaboration, particularly given the increasingly menacing European and Asian situations.[34]

Such interchanges culminated in 1936 in a more substantial undertaking, a joint dinner conference on Anglo-American relations held in New York which the Council and RIIA co-organised. This in turn was the prelude to probably the Council's most ambitious project on Anglo-American affairs, a two-year study group, in collaboration with Chatham House, on various aspects of Anglo-American relations. Ivison MacAdam of the RIIA first mooted the idea of the conference in 1934.[35] As Edwin F. Gay, a Harvard academic and long-time Council director, commented, it was decidedly a British initiative.[36] After much deliberation, it was arranged that a delegation of RIIA members who were in the United States to attend a meeting of the Institute of Pacific Relations, another joint Anglo-American enterprise, should also participate in a lengthy evening session with CFR members. This occurred on 8

September 1936. Only 17 people were present in all: for the British A.V. Alexander, former First Lord of the Admiralty; C.I.C. Bosanquet of Chatham House's Council; Sir Frederick Hayward, Chairman of the British Cooperative Movement; Hamilton W. Kerr, Financial Under-Secretary to the Treasury; Lord Snell, former Under-Secretary of State for India; and Rear-Admiral A.H. Taylor. The Americans included Norman H. Davis; Armstrong, Mallory, and Shepardson of the Council; Allen Dulles and Lamont; Herbert Feis, Economic Adviser to the Department of State; John M. Franklin of the International Mercantile Marine; Philo W. Parker of Standard Vacuum Oil; retired Admiral William V. Pratt; and Allan Sproul of the New York Federal Reserve Bank.

Opening the meeting, Norman Davis declared 'that there is nothing more important for the welfare of the world than for Great Britain and the United States to go step in step', stating that if the two countries could collaborate, they would also promote world peace. Speakers expressed the hope that the Americans would send a small reciprocal delegation to a similar gathering in London. Frequent reference was made to the possibility of a broad European conflict, with Americans, including Dulles and Lamont, expressing their belief that should this occur the United States, even if formally neutral, would nonetheless favour the Western democracies. Lamont brought up the desirability of improving Anglo-American relations by resolving the continuing impasse on the war debts which the British owed the United States, and by implementing international currency stabilisation. Feis suggested that mutual tariff reduction would also facilitate this objective. Shepardson recalled the longstanding ties between the two organisations, despite their formal independence of each other, tracing the Council's roots to a memorandum written by Curtis in 1919 and reminding the British that one of their first large donations came from Lamont.[37]

The September conference's fruits included the Council's most ambitious project to date, a two-year joint study group on Anglo-American relations, mandated to consider those questions of war debts, currency stabilisation, and reciprocal tariff reduction which Lamont and Feis had pinpointed as particular sources of friction. In early 1937 the Council and the RIIA each established sub-groups on War Debts and Trade Practices, who exchanged highly confidential memoranda and other documents across the Atlantic and commented on their proposals and analyses. The United States and Britain had by this time opened negotiations aimed at tariff reduction, which the sub-group's deliberations were consciously designed to affect, and both Council and RIIA study groups included some government officials. Feis even gave the sub-group access to government materials and a colleague's comments on its draft report.[38] Differences between the Americans and their British counterparts revolved around the vexed questions of British Empire preference and America's most-favoured-nation policy.[39] Percy Bidwell, the University of Buffalo economist heading the American commercial group, used *Foreign Affairs* to publicise the 'Prospects of a Trade Agreement with England'.[40] Dinner talks featuring various British speakers, including Sir Otto Niemeyer of the British Treasury, Sir George Schuster of the Westminster Bank, and Graham Hutton of *The Economist*, supplemented the discussions.[41] Even though Chatham House stalled in responding to the American group's memoranda on free trade, in November 1938 the United States and Britain concluded a reciprocal trade agreement which also included Canada.[42]

The question of war debts, whose payment the British had suspended in 1933, was more controversial. Chatham House submitted a memorandum written by a British group including Alexander, Lord Astor, Bosanquet, Brand, Geoffrey Crowther and H.D. Henderson. This emphasised that British public opinion regarded the debts as an American contribution to their joint wartime effort, and would not support payment in full; and, while recognising that the United States government might find this politically impossible, expressed the hope that the debts might be written down to a level acceptable to the British public.[43] In response, the Council established a small group, consisting of George P. Auld, a New York accountant who had served on the Reparation Commission; Shepard Morgan of the Chase National Bank; Professor Winfield Riefler of Princeton's Institute of Advanced Study; Raymond Gram Swing; and Garrard B. Winston, a former Under Secretary of the Treasury. Auld's report suggested that most Americans no longer expected to realise any substantial sums on the war debts, but that 'the continued existence of this un-liquidated controversy provides an element of strength to isolationist sentiment in this country'. Stating that a merely 'nominal' payment would be insufficient to remove this irritant in Anglo-American relations, the Council group proposed the British offer to pay the principal, without interest, over relatively few years.[44] While welcoming any definite figure, the British group, after budgetary calculations, suggested that the amount proposed was still too high and should be substantially reduced, perhaps by as much as two-thirds.[45] At this impasse the matter was left to rest: the Americans believed the British counter-offer far too low to be politically acceptable, but recognised the force of their opposite numbers' arguments that the British public would find the figure they proposed equally unpalatable.[46] At Shepardson's suggestion, the British response was forwarded to Feis at the State Department, on the grounds that 'People like Brand (on the British Committee) don't suggest figures unless they have a pretty good idea of the government's view.'[47] Although *Foreign Affairs* published an article by Auld on the topic, when the Second World War began the war debt issue remained unresolved.[48]

Perhaps more important than the specific impact of these assorted talks, study groups and conferences on Anglo-American relations was their overall influence upon the broader climate of elite opinion between the two countries. From 1933 onwards the Council was dominated by those who believed the United States should be far more proactive in Europe, who opposed the decade's neutrality legislation, who tended to deplore the international behaviour of Germany, Italy and Japan, and believed that both the United States and the West European powers, separately or preferably in collaboration, should oppose these states far more firmly than they did.[49] During the 1930s Armstrong, whom an interview with Hitler in 1933 left convinced the German leader was highly dangerous and could not be ignored, opened the pages of *Foreign Affairs* to those Americans and Europeans, such as Dorothy Thompson, Arnold Toynbee, Allen W. Dulles and various refugee intellectuals, who demanded that European nations and the United States cease tolerating the Fascist powers' disrespect for the League of Nations and international law.[50] The Council's continuing support for cooperation between Britain and the United States, with the common objective of blocking further advances by Hitler, Mussolini, and Japan, was apparent in the prominence which it gave to endeavours designed to promote these aims.

In the late 1930s, as always, the Council provided a friendly venue in which prominent Englishmen could share their views with a broadly elite American audience and on occasion discuss future plans. Increasingly, such gatherings focused upon the European situation, Britain's potential role therein, and what support Britain could expect from the United States in efforts to restrain Germany and Italy. In 1937 and 1938 the Council heard the journalist H. Wickham Steed and the Labour Party figures Herbert Morrison and Harold Laski, while in December 1938 Anthony Eden, after resigning as British Foreign Secretary, gave a Council banquet 'his views on the world situation'.[51] In January 1939 Hutton spoke on Munich, telling his audience that Chamberlain had erred by permitting Britain to find itself in a situation in which such a crisis could occur.[52] A few days later the RIIA's Curtis and MacAdam discussed future international machinery to maintain peace.[53] *Foreign Affairs*, meanwhile, published a sympathetic assessment of Eden.[54]

During this period prominent Council members exhibited divisions resembling those simultaneously characterising the British elite. Some of the directors, such as Lamont, his fellow Morgan partner, Russell C. Leffingwell, and the lawyer Frederic R. Coudert, shared the pro-appeasement outlook of such leading Institute figures as Lords Lothian and Astor, supporting the Munich agreement, not because they liked or admired Hitler, but in the belief that a European war would be disastrous for the British Empire's survival.[55] Others, such as Armstrong, Allen W. Dulles, and Stimson, contended that Britain and, indeed, the United States, should oppose the Fascist powers much more resolutely.[56] With few exceptions, however, the most notable anomaly being John Foster Dulles, Council members generally united in support for American re-armament, opposition to the neutrality legislation of the later 1930s, and a deep conviction that, should war eventuate, the United States should range itself decisively with the Allies and take every possible measure to facilitate an Allied victory over the Fascist powers.[57]

In the late 1930s this viewpoint clearly informed the Council's delib-erations. Following upon the Munich crisis, for example, a 'European Policy Group' led by Allen W. Dulles and featuring the strongly anti-Nazi American diplomat George W. Messersmith suggested that German economic penetration endangered the Western Hemisphere and that the United States must strengthen its air force and Atlantic fleet. Its members also discussed the potential revision of American neutrality legislation to allow United States neutrality 'policy to be in harmony with British policy'.[58] In March 1939, in a two-day conference on 'Amer-ican Foreign Policy' towards Europe, Asia and Latin America, leading Council members joined American government officials to discuss and reassess United States economic, defence and neutrality policies overall. As Raymond Gram Swing noted, not one speaker recommended that the United States 'reconstruct our economy, and live a life of complete and highly defended isolation like a sealed fort in a welter of anarchy'; rather, they contemplated countering 'lawlessness in Europe and Asia' through formal government protests, economic sanctions and, if neces-sary, actual combat. The discussants suggested that in Latin America, Asia and Europe the policies of the dictators threatened United States interests, and that existing neutrality legislation must be modified to permit the United States government to assist those powers which it favoured in any conflict.[59]

Once war began, the supposedly apolitical Council arrayed itself firmly behind the Allies. Several of its leading officials, including Armstrong and Shepardson, helped to establish the Century Group, interventionists who often met at the Century Club and who eventually formed the ultra-pro-Allied organisation Fight for Freedom; the Century Group's most energetic organiser, Francis Pickens Miller, was also a Council employee on temporary sabbatical. The Century Group advocated that their country join Great Britain outright in the war against Hitler. They publicly urged President Franklin D. Roosevelt to repeal the neutrality legislation, introduce conscription, strengthen American defences, and give all assistance possible to Britain, whatever the risk of war with Germany, arguing that American national security and Britain's fate could not be separated. In particular, in autumn 1940 they spearheaded a public campaign urging the President to conclude the 'Destroyers-for-Bases' deal with Britain; in 1941 they pressed the United States Navy to escort convoys of merchantmen bound for Britain, notwithstanding the risk of war, and also advocated that the United States should include Greenland in its defensive perimeter, a policy the Roosevelt administration adopted.[60]

In the two years of American neutrality the Council also provided a forum in which prominent British officials could present their country's case and provide helpful advice as to how best to persuade both the Roosevelt administration and Americans in general of its validity. In the pages of *Foreign Affairs* Sir Arthur Willert, head of British censorship, justified 'British News Controls', while Lord Cranborne idealistically depicted Britain's war aims and Lionel Robbins described British war financing.[61] British officials also paid numerous personal visits to New York. In April 1940 the Labour parliamentarian Sir Stafford Cripps discussed the Far Eastern situation, fielding questions from the influential Lamont as to how the United States might assist China.[62] The following October, shortly before the American presidential election, Sir Walter Layton of the British Purchasing Commission discussed his country's economic war effort, stressing Britain's determination to persevere but warning that 'the length of the war will largely depend on how much aid this country can send Britain in 1941'.[63] In March 1941 Wendell Willkie, the defeated pro-Allied Republican presidential candidate of 1940, whom several of the Council's more prominent members, particularly the Morgan partners, had endorsed, described his recent trip to Britain, praising Winston Churchill, characterising British morale as 'unbelievably high', and stating that, since Britain most needed ships, he had 'proposed [to President Roosevelt] that we make available to Britain 5 to 10 destroyers a month'.[64] Three months later the Council's long-time associate Lord Brand addressed 'The Future of Anglo-American Relations', assuring his listeners that Hitler 'seeks world domination', and that the only choice before the United States was whether it should 'face Hitler later but alone, or... face him now with Britain as an ally'. Brand requested more food aid, shipping and long-range bombers, and that the American navy escort the merchant convoys carrying supplies to Britain. He also expressed 'hope that after the war, there will be extensive peace-time cooperation between the United States and Britain', preferably through relatively informal collaboration as opposed to the League of Nations or 'any formal machinery'.[65]

Brand's address to the Council not only described those policies which, as his country's representative, he hoped the United States would choose, but encapsulated the plans for a *de facto* Anglo-American alliance which many members of British and American elites had advocated since the early twentieth century. Like the RIIA, the Council on Foreign Relations provided a focus and meeting-point for those who shared this vision, which its activities and publications helped to propagate. The ultimate significance of the Council's endeavours to promote Anglo-American concord and cooperation manifested itself in the later 1930s. As a general European war approached and the Asian situation became increasingly menacing, the Council effectively swung its substantial weight behind those forces in the United States, within and outside the Roosevelt administration, which wished their country to abandon neutrality, move firmly to Britain's side and, if necessary, assist the British and their Allies in any potential armed international conflict. While its tangible impact is difficult to quantify, after September 1939 the Council's past endeavours to minimise tensions in the Anglo-American relationship and help the British to present their own case to an influential public undoubtedly facilitated the Roosevelt administration's efforts to pursue and win public support for pro-Allied policies which might and ultimately did draw the United States into the Second World War.

Notes

1   Thanks are due to the University of Hong Kong's Committee on Research and Conference Grants and the Research Grants Council of Hong Kong for generous financial support of the research on which this article is based.

2 Examples of criticism from Right and Left are, respectively, Dan Smoot, *The Invisible Government* (New York: Americanist Library, 1962); Laurence H. Shoup and William Minter, *Imperial Brain Trust: the Council on Foreign Relations & United States Foreign Policy* (New York: Monthly Review Press, 1977).

3 Robert D. Schulzinger, *The Wise Men of Foreign Affairs: the History of the Council on Foreign Relations* (New York: Columbia University Press, 1994); Michael Wala, *The Council on Foreign Relations and American Foreign Policy in the Early Cold War* (Providence, RI: Berghahn Books, 1994); Inderjeet Parmar, 'The Issue of State Power: the Council on Foreign Relations as a Case Study', *Journal of American Studies* 29:1 (April 1995), pp. 73–96. See also the Council's own historical publications, esp. William P. Bundy, *The Council on Foreign Relations: Notes for a History* (New York: Council on Foreign Relations, 1994); Peter Grose, *Continuing the Inquiry: the Council on Foreign Relations from 1921 to 1996* (New York: Council on Foreign Relations, 1996).

4 See e.g. Nicholas Cull, 'Selling Peace: the Origins, Promotion and Fate of the Anglo-American New Order during the Second World War', *Diplomacy and Statecraft*, Vol. 7, No. 1 (1996), pp. 1–14; Inderjeet Parmar, 'Chatham House and the Anglo-American Alliance', ibid., Vol. 3, No. 1 (1992), pp. 23–47; idem, *Special Interests, the State and the Anglo-American Alliance 1939–1945* (London: Frank Cass, 1995), esp. chapters 2–3; Priscilla Roberts, 'The Anglo-American Theme: American Visions of an Atlantic Alliance, 1914–1933', *Diplomatic History*, Vol. 21, No. 3 (1997), pp. 333–64.

5 Quotation from Hamilton Fish Armstrong, *Peace and Counterpeace from Wilson to Hitler: the Memoirs of H.F. Armstrong* (New York: Harper and Row, 1971), pp. 4–6, 181–5; see also Otto H. Kahn Papers, Princeton University Library [henceforward MS Kahn], boxes 132, 149, 172, files Council on Foreign Relations 1920, 1921, 1922; Thomas W. Lamont Papers, Baker Library, Harvard Business School [henceforward MS Lamont], files 21–6 to 21–7, 22–1 to 22–8; Schulzinger, *Wise Men*, 3–10; Wala, *Council on Foreign Relations*, pp. 1–9; Grose, *Continuing the Inquiry*, pp. 1–9.

6 Schulzinger, *Wise Men*, pp. 10–57; Wala, *Council on Foreign Relations*, pp. 15–29; Grose, *Continuing the Inquiry*, pp. 9–20; Shoup and Minter, *Imperial Brain Trust*, esp. chapter 3.

7 On Armstrong, see my conference paper delivered at the annual conference of the British Association of American Studies, April 1998, ' "The Council Has Been Your Creation": Hamilton Fish Armstrong, Paradigm of the United States Foreign Policy Establishment?'; on Dulles, see esp. Ronald Pruessen, *John Foster Dulles: the Road to Power* (New York: Free Press, 1982).

8 *New York Times*, 4 May 1919; Robert T. Swaine, *The Cravath Firm and Its Predecessors, 1819–1948*, 3 vols (New York: Ad Press, 1946–48) Vol. 2, p. 256; William H. Harbaugh, *Lawyer's Lawyer: the Life of John W. Davis* (New York: Oxford University Press, 1973), p. 424; MS Lamont, files 27–5 and 27–6.

9 On the Morgan firm's wartime financial activities, see MS Lamont, file 213–7, 'Memorandum Relative to Financing by J. P. Morgan & Co. during the World War', no date; Kathleen Burke, *Britain, America and the Sinews of War, 1914–1918* (Boston, 1985), chapters. 1–5; idem, *Morgan Grenfell 1838–1988: the Biography of a Merchant Bank* (Oxford, 1989), pp. 103–34; Ron Chernow, *The House of Morgan: an American Banking Dynasty and the Rise of Modern Finance* (New York, 1990), chapter 10.

10   A lengthier discussion of this outlook, giving more detailed references, is Roberts, 'Anglo-American Theme'.

11   George W. Egerton, *Great Britain and the Creation of the League of Nations: Strategy, Politics, and International Organization, 1914–1919* (Chapel Hill: University of North Carolina Press, 1978), pp. 63–109; Michael G. Fry, *Illusions of Security: North Atlantic Diplomacy, 1918–22* (Toronto: University of Toronto Press, 1972), pp. 5–67; D. C. Watt, *Succeeding John Bull: America in Britain's Place, 1900–1975* (Cambridge: Cambridge University Press, 1984), pp. 24–163.

12   Prominent among the voluminous literature on this topic are those works by Egerton, Fry, and Watt cited above; Watt, *Personalities and Policies: Studies in the Formulation of British Foreign Policy in the Twentieth Century* (London: Longmans, 1965); John E. Kendle, *The Round Table Movement and Imperial Union* (Toronto and Buffalo: University of Toronto Press, 1975); DeWitt Clinton Ellinwood, Jr, 'Lord Milner's "Kindergarten": the British Round Table Group and the Movement for Imperial Reform, 1910–1918' (PhD diss., Washington, University, 1962); A. M. Gollin, *Proconsul in Politics: a Study of Lord Milner in Opposition and in Power* (New York: Macmillan, 1964), esp. pp. 160–7, 323–46; John Marlowe, *Milner: Apostle of Empire* (London: Hamilton, 1976), esp. pp. 209–16; John Evelyn Wrench, *Alfred Lord Milner: the Man of No Illusions 1854–1925* (London: Eyre and Spottiswoode, 1958), esp. pp. 292–4; idem, *Geoffrey Dawson and Our Times* (London: Hutchinson, 1965), esp. pp. 72–6; David Astor, *Tribal Feeling* (London: J. Murray, 1963), esp. pp. 47–9, 65–79; Christopher Sykes, *Nancy: the Life of Lady Astor* (London: Collins, 1972), esp. pp. 117–31; John Grigg, *Nancy Astor: a Lady Unashamed* (Boston: Little Brown, 1980), esp. pp. 108–12, 137–53; J.R.M. Butler, *Lord Lothian (Philip Kerr) 1882–1940* (New York: St. Martin's Press, 1960), esp. pp. 42–8, 68–70; John Turner, *Lloyd George's Secretariat* (Cambridge: Cambridge University Press, 1980), pp. 123–38.

13   Parmar, *Special Interests*, p. 131.

14   See Council on Foreign Relations Papers (microfilm ed.), Council on Foreign Relations, New York [henceforward MS Council], records of meetings.

15   For example, Viscount Cecil, 'American Responsibilities for Peace', *Foreign Affairs*, Vol. 6, No. 3 (1928), pp. 357–67; Viscount Grey of Fallodon, 'Freedom of the Seas', ibid., Vol. 8, No. 3 (1930), pp. 325–35; Chamberlain, 'The Permanent Bases of British Foreign Policy', ibid., Vol. 9, No. 4 (1931), pp. 535–46; Blackett, 'The Economics of Indian Unrest', ibid., Vol. 8, No. 1 (1929), pp. 41–51; Salter, 'England's Dilemma: Free Trade or Protectionism?', ibid., Vol. 10, No. 2 (1932), pp. 188–200.

16   MS Council, records of meeting, 17 Feb. 1922; see also *New York Times*, 21, 22 March 1922; Thomas H. Buckley, *The United States and the Washington Conference, 1921–1922* (Knoxville; University of Tennessee Press, 1970), p. 181; H.C. Allen, *Great Britain and the United States: a History of Anglo-American Relations (1783–1952)* (New York: St. Martin's Press, 1955), pp. 741–2. The stenographer's transcript makes it clear that the scepticism which greeted Cravath's subsequent disavowal that he had ever made such remarks was entirely justified.

17   Wickersham, quoted in *New York Times*, 13 Nov. 1921; John W. Davis Papers, Sterling Memorial Library, Yale University, Davis, diary, 23 Dec. 1920, 15

March 1921, Davis to Arthur Murray, 24 January 1922; MS Kahn, box 169, Kahn to Arthur Balfour, 9 Jan. 1922, box 179, Kahn to Sir Reginald Wingate, 3 May 1922; Kahn, *Of Many Things* (New York: Boni and Liveright, 1926), pp. 343–4.

18 Davis, 'Anglo-American Relations and Sea Power', *Foreign Affairs*, Vol. 7, No. 3 (1929), pp. 345–55; Lippmann, 'The London Naval Conference', ibid., Vol. 8, No. 4 (1930), pp. 509–10; Stimson, 'Bases of American Foreign Policy', ibid., Vol. 11, No. 3 (1933), pp. 366–8.

19 Peter Grose, *Gentleman Spy: the Life of Allen Dulles* (Boston: Houghton Mifflin, 1994), pp. 97, 124; Parmar, *Special Interests*, pp. 69–70.

20 The other members were Hamilton Fish Armstrong; Isaiah Bowman; Raymond L. Buell; Charles C. Burlingham; Joseph P. Chamberlain; Walter H. Mallory; Raymond B. Fosdick; James G. McDonald; and James T. Shotwell.

21 MS Council, records of groups, records of Anglo-American Group 1928–30, Memorandum by Professor Jessup, 16 Nov. 1928.

22 Ibid., 'Report of Study Group of Members of the Council on Foreign Relations on the Anglo-American Naval Question', 1 June 1929.

23 Ibid., Howland to Mallory, 18 Feb. 1929.

24 MS Council, meetings file, Walter H. Mallory to John W. Davis, 13 Feb. 1929, Mallory, to Frank L. Polk, 15 Feb. 1929.

25 Ibid., list of those attending dinner for Philip Kerr, 23 Jan. 1930.

26 Kerr, 'Navies and Peace: a British View', *Foreign Affairs*, Vol. 8, No. 1 (1929), pp. 20–9; Howland, 'Navies and Peace: an American View', ibid., pp. 30–40.

27 MS Council, records of groups, Howland, 'Outline for the Report of the Anglo-American Group', 17 Jan. 1929.

28 Ibid., Report of Study Group of Members of the Council on Foreign Relations on the Anglo-American Naval Question, 1 June 1929.

29 Ibid., Records of Anglo-American Group 1930–31, Howland, circular letter, 17 Oct. 1930.

30 The group's full membership was: Prof. James W. Angell, Hamilton Fish Armstrong, Isaiah Bowman, Joseph P. Chamberlain, John W. Davis, Henry S. Dennison, John Foster Dulles, Herbert Feis, Edwin F. Gay, Charles P. Howland, Philip C. Jessup, Oswald W. Knauth, Sam A. Lewisohn, Walter Lippmann, Walter H. Mallory, George O. May, Prof. Parker T. Moon, William Phillips, Albert Rathbone, Leland Rex Robinson, Franz Schneider, Jr, James T. Shotwell, Charles A. Stone, Frank W. Taussig, Arthur C. Veatch, Garrard B. Winston and David A. Wainhouse.

31 MS Council, records of groups, Files of Anglo-American Group, 1930–31.

32 Ibid., records of meetings.

33 For example, Whyte, 'The East: a Survey of the Post-War Years', *Foreign Affairs*, Vol. 11, No. 1 (1932), pp. 148–60; T.E. Gregory, 'Britain and the Gold Standard', ibid., Vol. 11, No. 2 (1933), pp. 268–78; Sir Walter Layton, 'After the World Economic Conference', ibid., Vol. 12, No. 1 (1933), pp. 20–9; Stamp, 'The Economic Consequences of the Peace', Vol. 13, No. 1 (1934), pp. 104–12.

34 Admiral Sir Herbert W. Richmond, 'Immediate Problems of Naval Reduction', ibid., Vol. 9, No. 3 (1931), pp. 371–88; Admiral William V. Pratt, 'The Setting for the 1935 Naval Conference', ibid., Vol. 12, No. 4 (1934), pp. 541–52; Richmond, 'Naval Problems of 1935: a British View', ibid., Vol. 13, No. 1

(1934), pp. 46–58; Lippmann, 'Britain and America: the Prospect of Political Cooperation in the Light of Their Paramount Interests', ibid., Vol. 13, No. 3 (1935), pp. 363–72; Pratt, 'Pending Naval Questions', ibid., pp. 409–19; Sir Willmott Lewis, 'The Paramount Interests of Britain and America', ibid., Vol. 13, No. 4 (1935), pp. 549–62; Davis, 'The New Naval Agreement', ibid., Vol. 14, No. 4 (1936), pp. 578–83.

35 MS Council, records of conferences, file Conference on Anglo-American Relations 1936, Mallory to MacAdam, 8 Sept. 1934.

36 Ibid., Edwin F. Gay to A. Lawrence Lowell, 23 March 1935.

37 Ibid., transcript of 'Conference on Anglo-American Relations', 8 Sept. 1936.

38 MS Council, records of groups, file Anglo-American Relations Group 1937–38, Mallory to Percy W. Bidwell, 16 March 1937, Feis to Mallory, 27 April 1937.

39 Ibid., memoranda submitted by each side to the other, and the American comments thereon.

40 *Foreign Affairs*, Vol. 16, No. 1 (1937), pp. 103–14.

41 MS Council, records of meetings.

42 Schulzinger, *Wise Men*, pp. 35–8; David Reynolds, *The Creation of the Anglo-American Alliance 1937–41: a Study in Competitive Co-operation* (Chapel Hill: University of North Carolina Press, 1982), pp. 17–18; Richard N. Kottman, *Reciprocity and the North Atlantic Triangle, 1932–1938* (Ithaca: Cornell University Press, 1968), chapter 7.

43 Ibid., records of groups, File Anglo-American Relations Group 1937–38, 'The War Debts: a British View', Sept. 1937.

44 Ibid., 'The British War Debts: an American View', April 1938.

45 Ibid., 'The War Debts: a Further Contribution to the Discussion of the Problem', Sept. 1938.

46 Ibid., Winston to Auld, 19 Sept. 1938.

47 Ibid., Shepardson to Mallory, 16 Sept. 1938, Mallory to Shepardson, 1 Oct. 1938.

48 Auld, 'The British War Debt: Retrospect and Prospect', *Foreign Affairs*, Vol. 16, No. 4 (1938), pp. 640–50.

49 Schulzinger, *Wise Men*, chapter 2; Grose, *Continuing the Inquiry*, pp. 19–21.

50 Roberts, ' "The Council Has Been Your Creation" ', pp. 11–12.

51 MS Council, records of meetings.

52 Ibid., Digest of meeting, 'British Public Opinion since Munich', 3 Jan. 1939.

53 Ibid., Digest of meeting, 9 Jan. 1939.

54 Victor Gordon Lennox, 'Anthony Eden', *Foreign Affairs*, Vol. 16, No. 4 (1938), pp. 691–703.

55 Priscilla Roberts, 'The American "Eastern Establishment" and the First World War: the Emergence of a Foreign Policy Tradition' (PhD dissertation, Cambridge University, 1981), p. 577; MS Council, records of meetings, comments by Coudert in digest of talk by Sir Graham Hutton, 3 Jan. 1939; Edward M. Lamont, *The Ambassador from Wall Street: the Story of Thomas W. Lamont, J. P. Morgan's Chief Executive* (Lanham, MD: Madison Books, 1994), pp. 427, 436–8.

56 Roberts, ' "The Council Has Been Your Creation" ', pp. 10–16; Grose, *Gentleman Spy*, chapter 6; Godfrey Hodgson, *The Colonel: the Life and Wars of Henry Stimson, 1867–1950* (New York: Knopf, 1990), pp. 216–20; Henry L. Stimson

with McGeorge Bundy, *On Active Service in Peace and War* (New York: Harper, 1947), pp. 313–20.

57   Roberts, 'American "Eastern Establishment"', pp. 576–81; Pruessen, *John Foster Dulles*, pp. 179–90; Lamont, *Ambassador from Wall Street*, pp. 444–77; Schulzinger, *Wise Men of Foreign Affairs*, chapter 3; Grose, *Continuing the Inquiry*, pp. 18–22.

58   MS Council, records of groups, Records of European Group, 1938–39.

59   Ibid., records of conferences, Records of Conference on American Foreign Policy, 21–2 March 1939.

60   See Hamilton Fish Armstrong Papers, Mudd Manuscripts Library, Princeton University, box 44, Francis P. Miller files; The Fight For Freedom Committee Papers, Mudd Manuscripts Library, Princeton University; also Francis Pickens Miller, *Man from the Valley: Memoirs of a 20th-Century Virginian* (Chapel Hill: University of North Carolina Press, 1971), pp. 89–104; Mark Lincoln Chadwin, *The Warhawks: American Interventionists before Pearl Harbor* (New York: Norton, 1970).

61   Willert, 'British News Controls', *Foreign Affairs*, Vol. 17, No. 4 (1939), pp. 712–22; Cranborne, 'Why Britain Fights', ibid., Vol. 18, No. 2 (1940), pp. 220–8; Robbins, 'How Britain Will Finance the War', Vol. 18, No. 3 (1940), pp. 525–34.

62   MS Council, records of meetings, digest of dinner discussion, 8 April 1940.

63   Ibid., digest of dinner discussion, 21 Oct. 1940.

64   Ibid., digest of dinner discussion, 5 March 1941.

65   Ibid., digest of dinner discussion, 3 June 1941.

3
Eric Knight's War: the Campaign for Anglo-American Understanding

F. M. Leventhal

Eric Knight's name is now virtually forgotten, although during his short life he attained a considerable measure of notoriety and literary success. His last book, *This Above All*, hailed by *The Times Literary Supplement* as 'one of the outstanding novels of the war'[1] and by the *Yale Review* as 'the finest novel of the war',[2] was the best-selling work of fiction in America for several months during 1941.[3] Even without the Book-of-the-Month imprimatur, the American edition sold roughly 200 000 copies, and the book was speedily adapted into a major commercial film. During the less than two years that remained of his life after *This Above All* was published in the spring of 1941, Knight abandoned fiction for propaganda work in England and the United States, especially through the medium of film, in order to win over public opinion to the British cause and persuade Americans to take the war seriously.

Knight's early background was itself the stuff of fiction, and he was to exploit it fully in his novels. Born in Menston, in the West Riding of Yorkshire, in 1897, the third son of a prosperous, but profligate Quaker jeweller and diamond merchant, Eric Mowbray Knight experienced childhood poverty. Before he was 3, his father (whose life seems to have been shrouded in mystery) was killed in South Africa, probably in the Boer War, although there was some suspicion that he had simply absconded to Australia. With the family immediately reduced to penury, his mother Hilda, 24 at the time she was widowed, dispersed her sons among Yorkshire relations and accepted a position in St Petersburg as a governess in a noble household.

Until the age of 12 Eric was a pupil at the Bewerley Street School in Leeds, his sole continuous period of formal education, later recalled as 'the only nice thing in a miserable and grubby childhood'.[4] He was then reduced to attending school as a 'half-timer', working as well as a bobbin-setter in a worsted mill. The next year he was apprenticed in an engineering works in Leeds, but a protracted strike led him to find employment successively in a sawmill, a bottle-blowing factory and in a Halifax spinning-mill until his mother, by now remarried and settled in Philadelphia, sent for him and his brothers.

The reconciliation when he was 15 proved traumatic: Eric's Yorkshire dialect and proletarian habits offended his mother's sense of propriety. Finding it difficult to adjust, he left home to work in a lumber yard and then a carpet mill before finding his way to Cambridge, Massachusetts, where for a time he attended Cambridge Latin (High) School and the Boston Museum of Fine Arts School. Married at 20, he subsequently enlisted in the Princess Patricia's Canadian Light Infantry and saw action in Flanders. Disenchanted with army life, he survived physically unscathed but emotionally battered. As he later described it to his friend, the filmmaker Paul Rotha:

> Certainly I was far too young and impressionable to have gone to war, certainly I couldn't have stayed out because I believe too fiercely in what I believed. The utter coarseness and monotony of training in the South of England, the vileness of the army system, nearly killed me outright. I wasn't emotionally stable enough to get through it.[5]

His two brothers were both killed on the same day, and family ties were impossible to rekindle after the war, Eric having become 'always a reminder of the other two who didn't come back' to his mother.[6]

During the next decade he struggled fitfully to make a living as a newspaperman, but – neither Englishman nor American – could not find his bearings. When he decided to join the US Army Reserve as an artillery specialist at Fort Sill, Oklahoma in 1925, his wife refused to accompany him and the marriage soon dissolved. He drifted around Europe and South America before settling in Philadelphia as a reporter and film critic and remarrying, this time more happily. A six-month stint in Hollywood as a screenwriter whose scripts were ignored left him with a distaste for the crass materialism of the studio bosses. On the basis of a handful of published stories and an unsuccessful first novel, *Invitation to Life* (1934), Knight resolved to devote himself to writing full time.

It was only when, after several attempts to emulate the contemporary American style of Dashiell Hammett and Raymond Chandler, including a hard-boiled California thriller,[7] Knight returned to his roots that his

LIBRARY, UNIVERSITY COLLEGE CHESTER

literary talent began to develop. Modest success followed with a series of short stories about Yorkshire village life, most notably a novella about a character named Sam Small, who discovers his distinctive ability to fly.[8] Most of these, published in popular American magazines like *Esquire*, *Colliers*, and the *Saturday Evening Post*, employed dialect for humorous effect, offering vignettes of ordinary village people, laconic, shrewd, warm-hearted.

If nostalgia inspired the more sentimental stories, his serious work combined passionate loyalty to the land of his birth with outrage over the complacency of businessmen, all too indifferent to the ramifications of the closing of mines and factories. *Song on Your Bugles*, published in Britain in 1936 and in America the next year, told the story of an artistically gifted, young Yorkshire mill-worker, torn between class solidarity and creative self-fulfilment, impeded by an unsympathetic wife and by concern for fellow workers, and ultimately crushed by mob violence.

Although the book smacked of authenticity, it was set, as one critic noted, in 'the vague present, unrealistically isolated from the shadows of such things as national politics or European battles'.[9] The human misery that Knight chronicled might as easily have been drawn from recollections of prewar Yorkshire as from the late 1930s. After observing photographs of Welsh miners in Dowlais, Knight decided to travel to Britain to investigate conditions in the distressed areas and persuaded the *Saturday Evening Post* to finance his trip in early 1938.[10]

'Britain's Black Ghosts', as his May 1938 article was titled, described once-prosperous industrial valleys where 'unsmoking chimneys stand like stumps of blackened teeth', where workers now waited for times to change while, 'unwanted, useless, they exist on the dole'. As one unemployed worker told him, 'For the decency of England and ourselves, the most respectable thing we could do is to go right home now and die. But we don't die. And we won't die.'

Knight denounced the dole system for encouraging unemployed workers to stay put rather than migrate to jobs elsewhere. It was an 'economic opiate' that 'not only paralyses the initiative of labour but also deadens the senses of the poorer type of employer', discharging union employees only to replace them with lower-paid workers supplied by the Labour Exchange.[11] As he described the visit,

> I just got back from Yorkshire, and it's the end of an era, with rotten decay of a system evident, and the damned good people left there by

the thousands, living in the houses that were built for them, looking at the factories that they helped to build, and everything is just as it was except that the system has collapsed, they don't know why, and the mills don't open again, and they exist on the dole.... If you are homesick, you must go home and cure it. You will come back so gladly, wanting the things of this continent. I was ill for the sight of home for twenty years. One visit removed it.[12]

Although these sentiments made for compelling journalism, Knight was dissatisfied. He felt that he had tried to cram too much into a single article, but 'still it says something which the *Post* has never quite dared to say before'.[13]

The experience galvanised Knight into denunciations of Britain's business and political leaders, exempting only his new acquaintance, Stafford Cripps, whose views he endorsed.[14] Shortly after his return, he wrote one American friend,

I cannot tell you of all the sensations and impressions I have had suddenly in that trip, nor of my deep feelings about England – how now I hate it and find myself truly an American in thought, in wish....[15]

It is not clear whether the *Saturday Evening Post* declined to publish a further instalment, but Knight was sufficiently moved by what he had observed to want to turn his experience into a book. Committed to documenting the lives of people he had encountered or known in childhood, Yorkshire colliers whose pride and independence was eroded by unemployment, Knight hoped that his message 'rips the pants off the smug Tories'.[16] What emerged was the story of the collapse of a family whose loss of earnings forces them on to the dole, despite the heroic efforts of the daughter Thora, who has held the family together, to remain self-sufficient. Knight saw the story of the Clough family as emblematic of an entire region:

As whole sections of England have lost their pride, their manhood, their dignity of being, through industrial paralysis, the narcotic of the dole, the meaningless slavery of the labor camps, the dunder-headed stubbornness of the middle class, the inertia of the leaders, so does this family disintegrate and, despite the girl's ambition and stubbornness, break down bit by bit until it is worthless, defeated, disrupted as a valuable unit of society.[17]

And yet, his characters also revealed a tenacious patriotism, taking pride in their Britishness, seeing the ability to endure hardship as a testimonial to national character.

By the spring of 1939 he was ready to submit a draft to Harpers, but extensive revisions were required before its publication the next year as *The Happy Land* in the United States and *Now Pray We for Our Country* in Britain. Reviews were unstinting in praise for its 'thorough grasp of what happens to common, ordinary, everyday people',[18] and its honesty in writing about unemployment.[19] By the time it appeared, however, interest in the subject had been displaced by the war.

More successful was his juvenile novel also published in 1940, which Knight claimed, 'seems fair to bring me more than all the others put together'.[20] Originating as a *Saturday Evening Post* story in December 1938, it was, in his opinion, 'a neat job of bread-and-butter workman-ship'.[21] Like *The Happy Land*'s, its locale was Yorkshire and dealt, more obliquely, with family poverty, but in this case the book's hero was modelled on his own pet collie. The book, retaining its magazine title, *Lassie Come-Home*, was destined to become an instantaneous classic. Written just as the war was breaking out, it may be regarded as Knight's first venture in pro-British propaganda targeted at an American audience. Even though he returned from his 1938 visit affirming his American identity, the onset of war resuscitated a patriotic longing to contribute to the war effort.

While recognising that it might be unfair for Americans, invulnerable to attack by German bombers, to castigate the British for betraying Czechoslovakia, Munich prompted a diatribe against Britain's rulers:

> It seems incredible to me that [Chamberlain] can stay in power, or that the British nation can be so short-sighted as not to see his deter-mined, edging, incessant drift to Fascism – working always without courage but with no letup toward conscription, and mass regimenta-tion of unemployed labor.... England needs the most sweeping housecleaning it ever had in its history. Out with the bloodsuckers – a reorganization from the bottom to the top, bringing in a true Eng-land, an England worth those thousands of damned good, starving men I saw and talked to in Durham, Wales, Yorkshire, and Lanark.

What he characterised as 'the utter collapse of Britain as a bulwark against Fascism'[22] did at least prod Americans to recognise that the European crisis was their concern as well. Initially he sought merely to awaken American sympathies, but increasingly the need to enlist the

United States more directly in support of Britain came to dominate his thinking and writing. To preserve and promote American friendship 'is the job of fellows like myself. . . . The men of England, and the heritage of England, are something any good salesman can sell to America. And we shall sell it.'[23]

After the fall of France, doubtful that Britain could defeat Germany by itself, he pondered whether a negotiated peace might not be preferable, allowing time for a massive internal reform which would 're-house, re-feed, re-employ, start great work projects for the sake of national employment and unity'. He recommended the introduction of a British equivalent of Roosevelt's Civilian Conservation Corps in order to 'make a country that English youth would serve as fervently as German youth serves now-victorious Germany'. To be sure, such subversive speculation was confined to personal correspondence. When Knight spoke and wrote publicly, he delivered a different message: 'I speak only of democracy, the evils of Nazism, the need for help to England. If England fights, naturally I want her to win, even if I'd rather see her get away with an honorable peace now.'[24]

He was convinced that Americans would not enter the war unless they could anticipate what would happen after the fighting ended:

> What we say is that we are not willing to fight for the preservation of British imperialism. . . . But we are willing to fight for the great march forward into a new world. . . . We know what will happen if Britain loses, and we don't like that picture. But if the same thing is to happen if she wins, then let us not go to war.[25]

In the aftermath of Dunkirk, Knight began writing what was to be his last and most successful novel, *This Above All*. Even more than *The Happy Land*, it reflected both profound misgivings about the condition of England and his conviction about the ultimate validity of its cause. The plot revolves around a budding romance between the seemingly mismatched Clive Briggs, embittered, orphaned, self-educated product of Yorkshire slums, and Prudence Cathaway, an idealistic, privileged daughter of a prominent surgeon and granddaughter of a general. What begins as impulsive sexual encounter in a haystack between a lonely soldier and a WAAF volunteer ripens into a love affair during a shared leave in a seaside hotel against a background of nightly German attacks. Although they ultimately agree to marry, fate intervenes: Clive sustains a serious head injury rescuing a woman and child during a bombing raid, fails to recover from brain surgery (due primarily to the after-effects of childhood tuberculosis and pneumonia contracted at Dunkirk), and dies in a London hospital in the course of another air raid, leaving Prue, determined to fight for a better England for their unborn child.

To characterise *This Above All* as a war romance is to describe only its most marketable feature. Clive, its hero, stigmatised for being illegitimate, unemployed, and lacking educational qualifications, had joined the army at the beginning of the war and survived the retreat from Douai and the Dunkirk evacuation, courageously subordinating his own welfare to the needs of fellow soldiers. But if Clive has proved his manhood in heroic fashion, he has also returned disenchanted, no longer believing that England was worthy of his loyalty and courage. Even before he meets Prue, he has decided to desert, whatever the consequences. As he explains,

> When we went to France, we went, believing something. Well – but when we, or at least I, came out of Dunkirk, we knew *that* something wasn't true. We knew that we weren't in a place where we were being asked to die because of justice or equality or anything else. We were being asked to die because other people had been blind and incapable and blundering and smug. And I know those things are not the things I'll die to preserve.

Clive feels betrayed by those who automatically assumed British superiority despite deficient weaponry. 'Who sent us out', he asks, 'to pit our bodies against steel? Who employed us with arms and techniques as out of date as those of the Boer War's red uniforms?'[26] He questions whether it makes sense for soldiers to go on being massacred because of the incompetence of leaders who understand neither the war, nor the aspirations of those being sacrificed.

When Prue, admitting past errors, denies British responsibility for the collapse of France and Belgium, Clive responds that those in charge should have anticipated what was coming. Blinded by their fear of communism, they preferred to leave the nation vulnerable rather than concede economic benefits to the working class:

> It goes back to the entire government of Britain ever since the last war – a series of governments so rotten that they should be shot.... Sitting contentedly on an internal industrial and social scheme that has stunk of its own stagnation and the poverty of a quarter of the nation it couldn't employ and daren't let quite die of hunger![27]

Without an ally, England could not defeat Hitler: the prospect was for stalemate, each side trying to starve the populace of the other.

At first neither his friend Monty's injunctions about the obligation of obedience (or of 'sticking it') – and the penalties for desertion – nor Prue's invocation of patriotism weaken his resolve. Indeed she realises that her plea to 'fight for England', which in her mind evokes Shakespeare, thatched roofs and Magna Carta, sounds hollow against his burning indignation. In the end she appeals to those qualities of British manliness that had led him to help weaker men into boats at Dunkirk instead of trying to save himself: 'For whatever you are, blood and bone and mind and heart and spirit, England has made you – every part of you.'[28] Her rosy image of a progressive, enlightened England hardly accords with his own experience of deprivation, his 'mean, grubby, dirty, useless little makeshift life...so much like ten or twenty or thirty million other lives in this land'. It was all very well for the middle class to rally in defence of their privileges, but 'what have we to fight for in England? Why should we preserve the rose we've never been allowed to smell – to be the guardian of the feast whose very garbage we have not been allowed to share?' But the traditional England that Prue recalls fondly, was, in any event doomed. The common people will demand their due:

> those who paid the bills would share the rewards. And they must. This time, I believe they shall.... Win, lose, or draw, your smug middle-class England is gone.... If there are things in England that can be killed by the loss of war, then they deserve to die. But what is fine and enduring in England cannot be killed by a military defeat. That is why I won't go back. I want my life so that I can go into the bigger fight of the new England that will rise after the war. And I refuse to offer it to be squandered now to preserve the bad things of Britain which I know surely will have to go even if we win.[29]

Despite the undercurrent of defeatism in Clive's disbelief that Britain's ruling class can win the war, the novel sought to instil the notion that a new, classless England would arise upon the ashes of the old. His repudiation of effete leadership was coupled with a paean to the common people of Britain, indomitable and ultimately triumphant. But the novel did not wholly reconcile the contradictions in Knight's argument. He identified revolutionary possibilities in the war, and trusted to popular will to supplant discredited leaders. He idealised ordinary Englishmen, yet they had hitherto been powerless to change a system which exploited them for the benefit of a privileged minority. It was easier for Clive to know what he was fighting against than what he could realistically fight for, and desertion seemed the most appropriate option. But Knight wanted to encourage American participation, not foster isolationism, and he had therefore to suggest the likelihood both of social change and military victory.

Clive never entirely overcomes his disillusionment, but in the end, unable to live as a fugitive or face imprisonment, he resolves to rejoin the army. He tells Prue, somewhat unconvincingly and perhaps unconvinced, that only by returning will he be able to gain a hearing for his views: 'If everyone who believes it's the new world of peace we've got to live for, and not the old world of war we've got to die for – would say it loud enough – I don't know what would happen.'[30] It is a half-hearted recantation, but it is never put to the test, since Clive is fatally injured before he can surrender himself to the authorities. If the logic and drama of the novel make his death obligatory, it is significant that he is not a casualty of battle, but of the bombing of civilians and of his own physical impairment.[31]

In the final scene, after Clive dies, Prue emerges into the London streets during a bombing raid, defiantly oblivious to the danger around her, and speaks to her unborn child:

> Without a father – like your father. But you're going to have a better time of it than he did. You're going to have a better England to live in! Because we were both right. We have to fight now for what I believe in. And after that, we'll have to fight for what he believed in. We'll win this war because – because we can stick it. And then, God help us, we're going to win the peace, too.[32]

If Clive's grievance against the system is, in the author's view, fully justified, it is Prue who is vindicated, recognising past failures, but confident that a victorious Britain will be regenerated. As pro-British propaganda, the novel is all the more effective for not seeking to gloss over defects in leadership and economic injustice, but, having excoriated the British, concludes on a note of resounding optimism.

Published in the United States in April 1941 to critical acclaim, *This Above All* was an immediate success. The *New York Times* did not hesitate to call it 'the most important [novel] about this war'. Disclaiming its propagandistic intention, the reviewer cited it as 'the first novel which shows us in human terms why we should not only give all our help to Britain, but why we should help solve Clive's problem, which is the problem of millions as well as it is our own'.[33] The *Saturday Review of Literature* was more circumspect about what it called a 'hurried piece of work by an admirable writer and a British patriot' keen to take advantage of the current American interest in the war. Even so, its reviewer hailed it as an 'honest and meritorious' novel that 'presents a picture of England's wartime development from dazed bewilderment to stoicism...in a manner which digs deeper than newspaper bulletins or politicians' diaries'.[34]

By the end of May it topped the bestseller list, and discussions were proceeding for stage and film versions.[35] The novel was quickly translated into Dutch, Norwegian, Spanish, Italian, Portuguese and Finnish. It also attracted the attention of Eleanor Roosevelt, who invited Knight to Hyde Park and to the White House to meet the President,[36] and he was deluged with invitations to lecture about Britain and the war.

By July, with considerable trepidation, he had sold rights for the movie version, over which he was to have no control. Fearing, correctly as it happened, that the film would become a star vehicle, he believed that he was best suited to transform the book into a film script. But producer Darryl F. Zanuck had his own ideas and hired English playwright R.C. Sherriff, author of *Journey's End* and scriptwriter for the movie version of *Goodbye Mr Chips*. With Anatole Litvak directing, and Tyrone Power and Joan Fontaine (who had just won an Oscar) in the leading roles, Twentieth Century-Fox released it in May 1942. Like the novel, it was commercially and critically successful, a trade journal labelling it 'one of the truly great pictures to come out of this war'.[37] It was, in fact, hardly that, despite several lesser Academy Award nominations. Zanuck had sanitised the plot, eliminating the haystack sequence and the pregnancy so as to avoid offending the Hays Office and family audiences. As he justified himself to a studio subordinate: 'Prue and Clive fall in love – and nothing else.... Why should we assume that they have consummated an illicit affair? What have they said or done, or what do they later indicate to prove they have gone the whole way?'[38]

War conditions precluded filming on location as originally intended, so the film was shot in Hollywood, with an exaggeratedly quaint English country pub thrown in for atmosphere.[39] In January 1942 *Life* magazine published a ten-page photo essay to supplement advance publicity for the film. A staff photographer in England sought out locations referred to in the book and hired models and actors (who looked like the Hollywood originals) to simulate film scenes and give the article a semblance of verisimilitude that the film lacked.[40]

Almost from the start of the war, Knight sought ways to engage more fully, not made any easier by his age – 42 in 1939 – and the ambiguity of his national identity. In September 1940, while still writing *This Above All*, he found he could not 'get used to the idea of being, for the first time, too old'. He had written to the Militia Bureau in England, offering to rejoin the army, but his suggestion was politely refused, which left him 'just where I am – doing nothing'.[41] He and Rotha had begun to discuss collaborating on a film that would stress the need for more equitable world food distribution in the belief that 'food will win the war' and also volunteered his services to the Ministry of Information. Being an expatriate only intensified his sense of impotence, and he was desperate to make restitution for his long absence.

In October 1941 he persuaded the *Saturday Evening Post* to send him to London to assess the impact of Lend-Lease on British diet and nutrition. By now convinced that Britain could not win the war without American participation, he saw the need to make American opinion 'understand that Britain is fighting now not a mere Imperialist war, but somehow a war that is deciding the way the whole world is going to live'.[42] Flying by clipper to Lisbon and then to London, Knight had to be hospitalised for many weeks for acute food poisoning, which temporarily immobilised him. Yet his debilitated condition could not dampen his spirits, as a letter from England indicates:

> I am very happy to be in London – because it is a good city. The people here have been somehow purified – any twerps and self-seekers left long ago. It is a fine city and one feels very clean here. I have swung around the North – through Yorkshire. There is no failing of heart here ... the ultimate victory never lies in doubt among the common man and woman, and they want no compromise with Fascism.[43]

During the few weeks remaining after he left hospital, Knight began to work on the script of the documentary film *World of Plenty* for the Ministry of Information, lectured and broadcast about America to British audiences, visited his former schoolteacher in Leeds, and inspected the Canadian army for a scheduled broadcast in Canada on his return. He had become convinced, as the article and film script were to show, that Lend-Lease should not terminate with the war, but should instead be linked with a long-term programme through which American agricultural abundance would ensure adequate nutrition for the masses in Britain.[44]

Knight returned by sea in a convoy that took three weeks, arriving in Canada in late February 1942, where he broadcast a blistering indictment of North American complacency. Subsequently published as a pamphlet entitled *They Don't Want Swamps and Jungles*, it contrasted carefree life in Canada and the United States with the privations endured by the British, chastising the North American democracies for failing to realise that 'if we are a united front, when it happens to one of us, it happens to us all'. Exploiting audience fears, he warned that when Nazis talked about *Lebensraum*, their designs were not on crowded Britain, but on rich, sprawling Canada and the United States.[45] Knight's broadcast, repeated four times, evoked the biggest response in the history of the CBC: 300 000 copies of the reprint were requested, and he received 7000 letters and telegrams.[46]

'The British Eat to Win', his article published in the *Saturday Evening Post* in May 1942, attributed improved health in Britain to Lend-Lease and better nutrition. Despite the shortage of fresh fruit and meat, rationing ensured that children and factory workers were adequately nourished. Morale remained high, because, amid the Blitz and overcrowded shelters, working people were better fed than before the war. Without underestimating the importance of American food contributions, he was more concerned to emphasise the courage with which people endured shortages.

Once again at home, he became depressed 'marking time and feeling I'm doing nothing to help', made all the more painful because he found none of the commitment to shared sacrifice that so impressed him in England.[47] As he commented to his *Saturday Evening Post* editor, 'I am, like everyone else, wanting to do something important in the war and not knowing what, but knowing I should know how to apply what abilities I have.'[48] He registered for the draft, volunteering for any corps, only to be classified as medically unfit for service. Within a month, however, he was recruited by Frank Capra, who had been given the task of directing orientation films for the US Army, to become a Special Assistant to the Secretary of War.[49] Capra, a Sicilian-born immigrant who achieved commercial success during the 1930s with a string of populist comedies, knew little about documentary films. Knight was not merely a successful novelist: he had spent time at Fort Sill in 1934, observing how the Army made official training films, was knowledgeable about the British documentary movement as a result of his friendship with Rotha, and had been invited by the Ministry of Information to produce a sketch for a film explaining the American people to the British.

Capra proposed that he write a script about Britain that would become the basis for the film *Know Your Ally – Britain*.[50] In addition Capra turned over for his criticism preliminary versions of the projected *Why We Fight* series. Knight found their tone too negative, inclined to demonstrate the odds against victory and calculated to foster defeatism. As he told Capra, 'You've got to have scripts that will make you ache in the guts as you read them.'[51] Above all, they needed to persuade soldiers that the present war was justified, that Germany was not invincible, and to do so in language simple enough for ordinary soldiers to understand. Knight was willing to lend a hand in transforming the scripts into more effective propaganda. Most of the team Capra assembled were inducted into the army, Knight himself receiving a commission as a Captain in the Special Services Division. He wrote scripts for the first four films in the *Why We Fight* series in Washington, helped to revise others, and then worked at the Disney Studio in Hollywood in July 1942 on animated maps and diagrams. In addition he brought to the enterprise an understanding of propaganda sorely lacking in the Army Morale Branch, the division officially responsible for producing the films.[52]

Shortly after joining, Knight provided an analysis of the uses of propaganda for Col. Lyman Munson, the Chief of the Army Information Branch, to be circulated to top brass. In it he claimed that, because its impact was instantaneous, film was 'the best means of spreading ideas and mental attitudes on the home front'. After tracing the history of documentary film in Britain and on the Continent, especially the work of Rotha and John Grierson, he asserted that American film could contribute to 'national moral unity' by showing our desire for peace, while underscoring 'the full intention of the aggressor nations to solve world problems by brutal, undeclared attack and by ruthless force'. Rather than produce 'defensive films' to uphold American beliefs, it was essential to wage a 'savage and pitiless attack upon the aggressor nations'. He further stressed the value of films that would explain America's allies, suggesting that the most effective propaganda would show people 'in their homes, on the streets of the cities, at the factories and in the training camps and fighting fronts'.[53]

When the *Why We Fight* team began to collaborate, members shared a sense of camaraderie. As Knight described it, 'I'm just a cog – but what a happy one – in the military machine. It's a grand outfit I'm with in the Special Services. I feel very clean inside at last, being in some sort of national effort where I flatter my ego that I count a little.'[54]

But the production process invariably became less harmonious than initially anticipated because of the pressure of time and continuous tampering with every script. Seven films were eventually completed, in addition to *Know Your Ally – Britain* and two *Know Your Enemy* films, with Knight involved, to a greater or lesser extent, in nearly all of them, only two of which were released before his death.[55] Despite his insistence to Capra that personal attribution was irrelevant – the films themselves never identified authorship – he inevitably became proprietary about his own writing. Capra, assuming a supervisory role after the first few films, did little to mitigate friction once the production team moved from Washington to Hollywood. There were additional disagreements about shooting new film as opposed to using newsreel clips, with Knight, a practitioner of the documentary technique, holding out for the latter. He told Rotha:

> My battle is to make the big directors understand that we are never going to get out films if we stage and shoot everything – that we must cut, cut, cut from acres of existing film of actuality, and maybe shoot three maps, and two animated charts, in one finished film.[56]

It was a battle that Knight to a large extent won.

The first film, *Prelude to War*, released in November 1942 with a script mostly written by Knight, was a huge success: reviews were favourable, it was seen by millions of soldiers before being made available for commercial distribution in the United States and abroad, and received an Academy Award as the best documentary film in 1943.[57] In reviewing political events of the prewar years, it contrasted two worlds opposing each other – a free world and a slave world, underscoring its theme with film footage of children and soldiers marching, of dictators gesticulating before cheering throngs, and of allied peoples – and especially children – at work and play. Film historians have recognised the series as a landmark in documentary film, employing extraordinary technical expertise in order to explicate recent history through motion pictures. That its presentation involves oversimplification and occasional distortion in no way diminishes its impact as propaganda.[58]

Of all the films, Knight was most closely identified with *Know Your Ally – Britain*. Originally conceived in March 1942, even before he had became involved, it was his first assignment. 'I wanted to get into it', he said, 'everything that London and Britain meant and felt to me when I was there.'[59] The production, underway by June, was sidetracked by *Why We Fight* films and not released until January 1944. The film introduced the British as team players, who had learned to live together amicably despite 'more congestion than anywhere except the

New York subway or a can of sardines'. This explained their cherished privacy, but also the low incidence of crime. While Nazi propaganda sought to divide the Allies by underlining differences between Britain and America, the film focused on shared traditions of representative government and freedom of speech, religion and the press. Although 'John Britain' – counterpart to the American John Q. Public[60] – lived in an old house, 'cluttered up with ancient traditions', institutions like the monarchy and the House of Lords had evolved democratically. The King, stripped of authority to make laws or impose taxes, was now the 'servant of the people not its ruler', working as hard as any other citizen.

Countering the charge that Britain had entered the war merely to protect its empire, the film stressed that the Dominions were independent nations whose actions Britain could not control, but circumvented the turmoil in India, with a cursory reference to Indian participation in the Viceroy's Council and the conditional promise of postwar self-government. It also refuted the allegation that the British left the burden of fighting to their allies and colonial subjects. Among casualties, seven out of ten had been sustained by British citizens, while the bulk of Allied planes and ships were being manned by British airmen and sailors. Yet, their propensity for understatement meant that it was considered 'bad form' to publicise what they were doing for themselves. Insisting that 'everyone is in the front line', the film went on to explain conscription of men and women, high taxes, food shortages and rationing. Everyone, it asserted, was on short rations, except children, but these were 'the rations of a free people', opting to use their ships to transport troops rather than to import food. The concern for children's welfare was a recurrent theme, the narrator emphasising that children got four times the number of eggs as adults, all the oranges, and most of the extra milk, clearly indicating that the British were thinking beyond the immediate crisis to 'the new world that his children and ours will inherit'. Alluding implicitly to prewar appeasement, the film concludes by saying:

> They are an old people, a stubborn people; and sometimes they have moved slowly. But in three years of blood and sweat and tears John Britain has found his soul. Now he is tough. Now he is determined and now he knows where he is marching...to victory and to a new world. He's a good man to have on our team.[61]

In addition to working for Capra, Knight found time to revise his script for *World of Plenty* and to write a scenario for another Rotha project, a counterpart to *Know Your Ally* to be called *USA: the Land and Its People*. No longer regarding himself primarily as an expatriate, he assured Sidney Bernstein that he was 'extremely honored by the right to wear' an American uniform,[62] and by the end of 1942 had finally become an American citizen.[63]

It was his hybrid character that made him a logical choice to write *A Short Guide to Great Britain*, a manual distributed to American soldiers on the point of embarkation. Like *Know Your Ally*, it was intended to acquaint GIs with the British, their country, and their customs. Its approach emulated the film, underlining the fact that 'in their major ways of life the British and American people are much alike'. Quaint though their traditions might seem, they instilled feelings of security and comfort: 'The important thing to remember is that within this apparently old-fashioned framework the British enjoy a practical, working twentieth century democracy which is in some ways even more flexible and sensitive to the will of the people than our own.'[64]

Most of the pamphlet consisted of a series of admonitions either to explain British behaviour or to ensure that American soldiers conducted themselves inoffensively. The British, depicted as reserved and polite, disliked boasting or seeing money squandered. Soldiers were warned not to criticise the King, steal a Tommy's girl, or fail to acknowledge the adversity that the British army had faced. It was inadvisable to bring up historic grievances or to suggest that the Americans had won the last war. It was important to 'look, listen, and learn before you start telling the British how much better we do things'.[65] Soldiers invited to a family meal should refrain from eating their fill, lest they inadvertently consume the weekly rations. Obvious though such suggestions were, they needed to be spelled out to young recruits ignorant about conditions in Britain and oblivious to the impression their brashness might make.

The *Short Guide* was the last thing he ever wrote. By the end of 1942 his writing for Capra and Rotha was winding down, and he had been promoted to the rank of Major as reward for his contributions. With less to do, Knight began once again to chafe at inactivity. 'I think I'd be much more effective somewhere nearer the front', he wrote, 'and continually agitate perfectly nice people and irritate them with the idea.'[66] Finally in early January he was ordered to proceed abroad for temporary duty – probably to establish a radio station – in Cairo.[67] On 15 January his plane crashed over Surinam, and all 35 passengers aboard were killed.[68] As this was the route President Roosevelt was scheduled to fly the next day to Casablanca, there was some speculation that the

Germans mistook the plane for the one carrying the President, but no evidence of sabotage was uncovered.

Several months before he died at the age of 45, Eric Knight wrote, 'This war we're in is too big to make any one man or his life of the slightest importance.'[69] A statement made in the context of publicity for the movie of *This Above All*, it cannot be taken as a valid indication of its author's sentiments. Knight was justifiably proud of his contributions to the war effort, striving, through his novels, articles, and film scripts to awaken the public in America to consciousness about the war and to promote a just peace in which food and social benefits would be more equitably distributed. Although his only lasting monument is *Lassie Come-Home*, its name immortalised as his never was, Knight deserves a measure of credit for his successful campaign to achieve greater Anglo-American understanding.

Nor was his contribution limited to the war years. In its several incarnations *Lassie* continued to shape the consciousness of young Americans about Britain and to reinforce an image of 'deep England' as a pastoral landscape where history sometimes stood still and where eternal values like loyalty and affection for animals persisted. It was perhaps ironic that Knight's incisive critique of industrial decline and class exploitation in the 1930s, inspired by his own childhood experience, had less appeal for his American audience than his more sentimental and whimsical depictions of British life. His own intentions notwithstanding, Knight's legacy situated him in the world of James Herriot rather than that of George Orwell.

Notes

1   *Times Literary Supplement*, 12 Nov. 1941.
2   *Yale Review*, Summer 1941.
3   *Publishers' Weekly*, 17 Jan. 1942.
4   Eric Knight to Frederick Leathley, 24 May 1940, copy in Knight Papers [hereafter EKP], Box 2 (Uncat ZA MS 146, Beinecke Library, Yale University).
5   Eric Knight to Paul Rotha, 25 Apr. 1933, Paul Rotha Collection [hereafter PRC], University Research Library, UCLA. He recalled that initial enthusiasm that burned in the Canadian volunteers was replaced by 'repulsion as we were lined up before British sergeants at Seaford and treated to the filthiest line of gibberish ever free men listened to'. Eric Knight to Paul Rotha, 16 Aug. 1941, PRC. He also described the experience in *Invitation to Life*, pp. 59–60.
6   *Current Biography 1942*, p. 463.

7 Richard Hallas (pseud.), *You Play the Black and the Red Comes Up*. Written in 1936, the novel was published in Britain and the United States in 1938.
8 'The Flying Yorkshireman', *Story* (July 1937), republished in *The Flying Yorkshireman* (New York, 1938).
9 Earle Birney in *Canadian Forum*, Dec. 1937.
10 Eric Knight to Paul Rotha, 1 Feb. 1940, PRC.
11 'Britain's Black Ghosts', *Saturday Evening Post*, 28 May 1938.
12 Eric Knight to Herbert Heaton, 21 June 1938, EKP, Box 1.
13 Eric Knight to Paul Rotha, 24 May 1938, PRC.
14 Eric Knight to Paul Rotha, 22 June 1938, PRC.
15 Eric Knight to Peter Hurd, 23 Mar. 1938, copy in EKP, Box 2.
16 Eric Knight to Paul Rotha, 24 May 1938, PRC.
17 Eric Knight to Norman Holmes Pearson, 2 Nov. 1938, EKP, Box 2.
18 *Nation*, 30 Mar. 1940.
19 *Saturday Review of Literature*, 9 Mar. 1940.
20 Eric Knight to Norman Holmes Pearson, 28 Dec. 1940, EKP, Box 2. Knight told Rotha that he had 'made enough from the juvenile version of *Lassie* to live another six months'. Eric Knight to Paul Rotha, 28 June 1940, PRC. It was a Junior Literary Guild Selection, guaranteeing substantial sales.
21 Eric Knight to Paul Rotha, 1 Feb. 1940, PRC.
22 Eric Knight to Paul Rotha, 18 Nov. 1938, PRC.
23 Eric Knight to Paul Rotha, 24 Aug. 1939, PRC.
24 Eric Knight to Paul Rotha, 28 June 1940, PRC.
25 Eric Knight to Paul Rotha, 10 June 1941, PRC.
26 *This Above All* (New York, 1941), pp. 290–1.
27 *This Above All*, pp. 293–4.
28 *This Above All*, p. 302.
29 *This Above All*, p. 321.
30 *This Above All*, p. 386.
31 Knight felt that for Clive to die from injuries sustained rescuing somone in an air raid was a cliché. As he noted in a radio forum, 'I wanted the indictment to go along that his death was due not to any action in the war, but to his whole life, or I might say, to the illness that he had contracted in life due to previous illnesses of his youth. Had the conditions been better, Clive would have lived.' *Wilson Library Journal*, Apr. 1943, p. 612.
32 *This Above All*, p. 473.
33 *New York Times Book Review*, 13 Apr. 1941.
34 *Saturday Review of Literature*, 5 Apr. 1941.
35 Knight reported that the book was advancing to the top of the list, but 'even a national best seller doesn't sell above 1200 copies a week'. Eric Knight to Peter Hurd, 22 May, 17 June 1941. By July weekly sales figures reached 4700 copies. Eric Knight to Peter Hurd, 6 July 1941. Copies in EKP, Box 2. Katherine Hepburn wanted to play Prue in the film, but MGM was 'terrifed of a "war picture"'. Eric Knight to Paul Rotha, 14 July 1941, PRC.
36 In her newspaper column 'My Day' Eleanor Roosevelt described the book as 'interesting reading, parts of it are so painful that I could hardly go on, but other parts are very beautifully written...'. 9 May 1941, Eleanor Roosevelt Papers, Box 3081. See Eleanor Roosevelt to Eric Knight, 7 June 1941, Eleanor Roosevelt Papers, Box 1608, Franklin D. Roosevelt Library, Hyde Park, New

York. The Knights visited Hyde Park in September 1941 and the White House in November 1942. Eric Knight to Paul Rotha, 11 Dec. 1942, PRC.

37   *Motion Picture Herald*, May 1942.

38   Rudy Behlmer, ed., *Memo from Darryl F. Zanuck: the Golden Years of Twentieth Century-Fox* (New York, 1993), p. 57.

39   *Monthly Film Bulletin*, 31 July 1942.

40   *Life*, 26 Jan. 1942, pp. 68–77. Knight was originally supposed to oversee the illustrated story, with his wife Jere posing as Prue, but delays in travel and his bout with food poisoning en route to England altered plans. Eric Knight to Paul Rotha, 24 Sept. 1941 PRC; Eric Knight to Peter Hurd, 4 October 1941, copy in EKP, Box 2. Prue was impersonated by Joy Frankau, a young actress, and Clive by an ARP worker. The same feature also appeared in *Illustrated*, 14 Feb. 1942.

41   Eric Knight to Peter Hurd, 20 Sept. 1940, copy in EKP, Box 2.

42   Eric Knight to Paul Rotha, 24 Sept. 1941, PRC.

43   Eric Knight to Witter Byner, 12 Jan. 1942, EKP, Box 2.

44   Eric Knight to Mr Frost, 27 Nov. 1941, EKP, Box 2.

45   *They Don't Want Swamps and Jungles* (Ottawa, 1942). Also see *The Monetary Times*, 14 Mar. 1942.

46   Eric Knight to Paul Rotha, 25 Mar. 1942, PRC; Eric Knight to Frederick Leathley, 26 Aug. 1942, copy in EKP, Box 2.

47   Eric Knight to Peter Hurd, 30 Mar. 1942, copy in EKP, Box 2.

48   *Saturday Evening Post*, 27 Feb. 1943.

49   In his autobiography Capra stated that 'it was love at first sight with Eric Knight. He had all the talents that could be compressed into a single writer: wit, compassion, sensitiveness, an intriguing style, and a great, great love for human beings.' Frank Capra, *The Name Above the Title* (New York, 1971), p. 331.

50   'I do a script for him about Britain – what the people are like, the land, habits – take 'em apart.' Eric Knight to Paul Rotha, 17 Apr. 1942, PRC.

51   Eric Knight to Frank Capra, 15 Apr. 1942, Frank Capra Archive [hereafter FCA], Wesleyan Cinema Archives, Wesleyan University, Middletown, Connecticut.

52   'The basic shape of the *Why We Fight* series was decided between April and August 1942, with a crucial contribution from the British-born writer Eric Knight.' Joseph McBride, *Frank Capra: the Catastrophe of Success* (New York, 1992), p. 467. Also see David Culbert, ' "Why We Fight": Social Engineering for a Democratic Society at War', in K.R.M. Short, ed., *Film and Radio Propaganda in World War II* (London, 1983), pp. 173–91.

53   Memorandum, 25 May 1942, reprinted as Document #25 in David Culbert, ed., *Film and Propaganda in America: a Documentary History*, Vol. III, 2 (New York, 1990), pp. 107–17.

54   *Saturday Evening Post*, 27 Feb. 1943.

55   Knight told Rotha, 'It is a fine and sensible job, and I've got eight scripts done already – five being cut.' Eric Knight to Paul Rotha, 27 June 1942, PRC. These would have been the seven *Why We Fight* plus *Know Your Ally – Britain*.

56   Eric Knight to Paul Rotha, 20 May 1942, PRC.

57   See Charles Wolfe, *Frank Capra: a Guide to References and Resources* (Boston, 1987), pp. 139–49; Richard Griffith, *Frank Capra* (London, 1984), pp. 29–32.

Viewing by soldiers before going overseas was compulsory. The total attendance for the seven films by the end of the war exceeded 45 000 000. See Thomas William Bohn, *An Historical and Descriptive Analysis of the 'Why We Fight' Series* (New York, 1977), p. 108.
58 William Thomas Murphy, 'The Method of *Why We Fight'*, *Journal of Popular Film*, I, 3 (Summer, 1972), pp. 185–96.
59 Eric Knight to Paul Rotha, 20 May 1942, PRC.
60 The film critic James Agee, who found the repeated references to John Q. Public 'embarrassing', believed that they reflected an underestimation of the audience. *Nation*, 12 June 1943, reprinted in James Agee, *Agee on Film* (New York, 1958), p. 41.
61 Script of *Know Your Ally – Britain* in FCA, Box 10; print in Department of Film, Imperial War Museum, London. I am grateful to Toby Haggith for making this available to me. Also see Wolfe, *Frank Capra*, pp. 144–5.
62 Eric Knight to Paul Rotha, 27 June 1942, PRC.
63 Eric Knight to Frank Capra, 21 Nov. 1942, FCA, Box 6A/418.
64 US Army Special Services Division, *A Short Guide to Great Britain* [1943], pp. 2, 10.
65 *Short Guide*, p. 16.
66 Eric Knight to Paul Rotha, 11 Dec. 1942, PRC.
67 Eric Knight to Dradha, 11 Jan. 1943, EKP, Box 2.
68 *New York Times*, 22 Jan. 1943.
69 *New York Times*, 10 May 1942.

4
The Byrnes Treaty and the Origins of the Western Alliance, 1946–48

Danilo Ardia

The drawing together of the Western alliance resulted from the operation of a complex web of a number of gradual processes. Foremost among those processes was the development of the German question.[1] It was in this framework that the so-called 'Byrnes treaty' had a significant impact on the relations among the Western allies. The main concept at the base of that US initiative, i.e. American direct responsibility in Europe, foreshadowed the role assumed by Washington in the first steps of the process leading eventually to the Atlantic Alliance. During the period 1946–48, witnessing the widening rift between East and West, direct or indirect discussions about the Byrnes treaty kept alive the concept and the practice of a close cooperation between Washington and the Western European allies.

The British played the most dynamic and consistent role in this process. They felt they needed help from the United States to maintain their international position and to build some form of western European cooperation against Soviet pressure: 'Anxious about Russia, uncertain about America, inclined to lead in organising western Europe – this was the mood of British policymakers in 1945–46.'[2]

Paris, April–July 1946

Secretary of State James F. Byrnes presented his Draft Treaty on the Disarmament and the Demobilization of Germany to his British, French and Soviet colleagues a few weeks before the opening of the second session of the Council of Foreign Ministers (CFM) in Paris. The text recalled the quadripartite declaration of 5 June 1945 on the Reich's capitulation. Clauses had been added providing for the establishment of a quadripartite inspection commission and for measures to be taken in case of violation by Germany of the terms imposed upon her by the four powers.

What was the purpose of this initiative? During the winter of 1945–46 American foreign policy had reached a turning-point: with a Soviet Union now perceived as aggressive and expansionist, relations could no longer be established on the basis of compromises and of efforts towards cooperation but of a policy of firmness. Soviet policy in Germany was interpreted as an attempt to draw the whole of the country into the Soviet sphere of influence. Byrnes's proposal was meant to test real Soviet intentions. If Soviet policy was dictated solely by security fears in relation to Germany, Moscow should have accepted the guarantee offer; a refusal would have meant proof of expansionist objectives.[3]

For a meeting in which the German problem would have been a pivotal issue, 'Byrnes's strategy...was to proclaim an American commitment for German unity', reaffirming at the same time the joint allied commitment to Germany's total disarmament and demobilisation.[4]

Armand Bérard, Minister Counsellor at the French Embassy in Washington, reported that at the Department of State the opinion was that an initiative originating from Washington rather than Paris or London would appear less interested and would give less room for suspicion from the Soviet side.[5]

In fact Moscow appeared to be the main target of Byrnes's move: the draft treaty, argued the French Embassy in Washington again, had to be a reassurance particularly to the Soviet Union and France. It was to be proof to the Soviets that the Western allies wanted to keep Germany disarmed, and to the French that America did not intend to escape her responsibilities in Europe nor prematurely terminate the obligation she had undertaken with regard to Germany.

Recent scholarship[6] has argued that since Potsdam the Americans were suggesting that a German disarmament and demobilisation treaty would signal to the Soviet Union the end of any threat from the West and would allow Moscow to adopt a more liberal policy in Eastern Europe: 'Also this treaty would "strengthen" US influence in Europe by removing the fear of US troop withdrawal and another retreat to isolationism.'[7]

That those were really relevant issues with the western European partners is witnessed by their reaction to the American proposal. The French Chief of Staff, General Juin, argued that the US draft reflected the American desire to end the total occupation of Germany in order to reduce the American military burden. According to Juin, the Byrnes draft as it had been proposed entailed 'substantial amputations' to

French security, and even the guarantee by the three other great powers could not be seen to balance the dangers embedded in the proposed new security system.[8]

Involving the same themes, but within a completely different perspective, were the comments from the French ambassador in Washington. Reporting widely the mostly favourable comments of the American press and stressing the definition of the Byrnes proposal given by the *New York Times* as a 'fact of basic importance' and a 'revolutionary change' in American foreign policy, Ambassador Bonnet argued: 'That the United States is willing to shoulder such responsibilities even before the terms of the European peace treaties are known, would be the proof that they are decided whatever may happen not to disengage from Europe.' The ambassador also informed the Quai d'Orsay that in the exchanges he had had with Congressmen on Capitol Hill, all of them had stressed how the United States Government had never before proposed to undertake such definite engagements outside the Western hemisphere and that they saw in that step the rejection of isolationism and the Monroe Doctrine.[9] This was a rejection of great significance, one should stress, as the whole American Senate, Democrats and Republicans together, were behind the Secretary of State in supporting his initiative: 'The tragedy of 1920', was the comment from the Embassy, 'will not be repeated. . . .'[10]

The Chargé of the French Embassy in Washington, reporting on the enquiries he had conducted at the State Department upon request from Paris, reported that American officials considered the Byrnes draft as an answer to the fears of an early withdrawal of the American troops from Germany and a reassurance that the United States would not disinterest themselves from that country. The conclusions of Bérard were as compelling as those of Ambassador Bonnet and compounded them: 'The proposed treaty would give us for 25 years that international and notably American guarantee we were looking for after the First World War.'[11]

Yet the official French reaction to the American initiative was late, cautious, and almost elusive and reflected the first of the two sets of opinion; Bidault 'neither favoured the treaty in principle nor endorsed it.'[12] In fact the proposal of a similar treaty had already been broached by President Truman and Byrnes to General de Gaulle in Washington after Potsdam, but it had not received much attention from the French. On the German problem, Bidault and the French foreign office were still pursuing a policy of resistance to any step which could imply an implementation or even could open the way to an implementation of the Potsdam agreement or any part of it, as she considered any such development as undermining the very basis of her own security.[13] In a certain sense the tone and the content of the French reaction justified some American comments that the Byrnes idea, although revolutionary from the American perspective, was 'too little, too late' for the west European partners.[14]

The British response was much more forthcoming both in tone and substance. In presenting to the Cabinet the draft of the treaty, Foreign Secretary Bevin did not conceal that the American proposal was designed to facilitate an early US withdrawal from Germany (a notably similar appreciation to that made in the French capital), but at the same time he argued that it should have been welcomed for the assurance it contained of continued United States participation in European affairs; the Americans would have been bound for 25 years to the principle and practice of inspection in Germany and of the use of force by means of contingents to be agreed in advance. Eventually the Foreign Secretary was granted authority from the Cabinet to inform Washington that the British government welcomed their proposal 'as most useful for discussion'.[15]

Bevin's stance becomes much more significant when considered together with the mention he made to his Cabinet colleagues of the views of the Chiefs of Staff about the strategic aspects of the key issue of West Germany and the Ruhr Basin. In summarising their report, Bevin wrote: 'Our policy towards Germany should be guided by the consideration that Russia is our most likely potential enemy and is a more serious danger than a revived Germany.' What Bevin did not mention in the resumé, but which the Cabinet could read for themselves in the Chiefs' report, was one of the main provisos: i.e. that Great Britain had to be able to carry the United States with them in any proposal they decided to make.[16]

Within the process of developing the 'Western strategy' during the first months of 1946,[17] we may perceive in Bevin's attitude towards the Byrnes proposal a hidden supporting element of that strategy. The Western strategy 'meant the organisation of either the British or the Western zones as a separate unit, a division which was envisaged as being permanent'.[18] Of the two conditions considered as 'crucial' for the success of that policy, the one to be stressed from our point of view is that the British side had 'to be assured of the full and continued financial and military support of the United States'; and that was what Bevin told his officials on 3 April, that 'we must carry the Americans with us' on Germany.

Given that Bevin had told the Cabinet on 7 May that 'the danger of Russia has become certainly as great as, and possibly even greater than, that of a revived Germany', one might be left to wonder which of the two main aspects, the economic or the security, weighed more in the Foreign Secretary's reflections.[19] This could also help to put his support of the American draft treaty in a more proper light.

At the Foreign Office, officials were perceiving that a new US attitude was emerging. The earlier perspective of a short occupation of a couple of years was being substituted by the mounting awareness of 'the need to maintain their forces if they wish to exercise their proper influence in European policy'.[20] The British were also possibly aware in some measure that the American proposal concealed a manoeuvre to revise the Yalta and above all the Potsdam agreements in order to con-ciliate the French.[21] If this was so, it was certainly to be welcomed by the British as a step forward in drawing the French into the Western strategy.

The British decision to support the Byrnes proposal then fitted in perfectly with the 'major shift' in British foreign policy which was emerging in the spring of 1946 and was to develop fully the following summer.[22] The British attitude in fact was to keep open two strategic perspectives: to prod the Americans to make clear their intention to stay in Europe, and to strengthen the western zones of Germany. The British also intended to test Soviet intentions but they were less and less willing to sacrifice their strategic aims to win Soviet compliance with allied (i.e. four-power) cooperation.[23]

A revealing if indirect proof of this double-edged nature of the British attitude towards the Byrnes proposal is how Bevin tackled the discussion of the draft treaty at the Paris CFM. Bevin and the British delegation went to Paris 'without much hope or enthusiasm for quadripartite integration'; yet, even if caught by surprise by Byrnes's decision to publicly discuss the American proposal, the Foreign Secretary expressed his government's full support for the initiative[24] and when the discus-sion on it became too hot he suggested, and Byrnes accepted, that the issue be frozen for the time being,[25] thereby avoiding the danger that the issue would be shelved for good. But the Soviets had failed the test; the British, and Bevin in the first place, had showed their 'enthusiastic' support for the treaty;[26] and now it was time to go ahead with the new strategy.

When the July session of the Paris conference ended with the perspect-ive of the establishment of the Anglo-American bizone, this new devel-opment 'was to help to seal a peacetime Anglo-American relationship, and it gave Bevin the best way forward that could be hoped for to contain the spread of communism without yet openly declaring the breakdown of the four-power unity'.[27] In fact throughout the discussion that had led to the American proposal to set up a joint zonal administration, Bevin had referred to four-power cooperation and had specifically advocated the four-power treaty. Besides, the Americans themselves recognised that only the British were supporting the Byrnes proposal, whereas the French, fearing that the Four Power Treaty might be considered a sort of substitute for other guarantees they believed necessary, paid 'lip service' and the Soviets were 'highly critical'.[28] On the other hand, the Americans did not know, nor did the British inform them, that the main attraction of the Byrnes draft for London was the perspective it involved of 'the retention of American troops in Europe for a prolonged period' and that the military advantage gained 'would be so great that we should not allow other and less important considerations to prejudice the acceptance of the Treaty'.[29]

In the meantime, the French ambassador in London was told at the Foreign Office that the US Senate should not be discouraged from engaging in Germany, that is, in Europe.[30] With the negotiations progressing at the Paris CFM, as Allan Bullock notes, 'the more Bevin thought about the Byrnes proposal, the more he liked it. To anyone who remembered the American withdrawal after the First World War, this seemed an enormous step forward toward a stable peace settlement after the second.'[31] All this is evidence of how thoroughly the British had grasped what the *New York Times* had described as 'a revolutionary change' in American foreign policy and Byrnes himself had indicated to the Counsellor of the French Embassy in Washington as 'revolutionary from the point of view of traditional American policy'.[32]

This is not to argue that the Byrnes treaty was a major element in the evolving British strategy towards the United States and Europe, but that it was a permanent, albeit backstage, feature of that strategy as it represented an essential link with the Americans in the perspective of European security. A link much more important if considered in the light of the acceptance by Bevin of the fusion of the Anglo-American zones in Germany accompanied by the full awareness that it was 'a measure which implied a clear division between Eastern and Western Germany' and that it meant to 'abandon hope of Russian co-operation'. Bevin advised the Cabinet that 'there was the danger that we should thereby increase the tendency for Europe to split into two parts', but he justified the initiative by arguing that 'the action proposed would not make matters worse than they were', and ended his exposition by mentioning the possible 'salutary effect upon the Russians' of the initiative.

Speaking in that way to the Cabinet, Bevin had certainly in mind what his ambassador in Washington had reported to him a few days before: that in the light of the Soviet refusal of the Byrnes treaty and of Moscow's negative attitude towards the administration of Germany as an economic unit, in the United States 'it is generally realise[d] that events are shaping themselves towards a solution which will leave Germany divided into two parts'.[33] Bevin was also consistent in his unrelenting efforts to maintain and strengthen the link with America, as could be seen in January 1947 with the issue of the revision of the Anglo-Soviet treaty of 1942. The British Chiefs of Staff at that time were holding conversations with the Americans about standardisation of military equipment and exchange of information. Bevin had proposed entering negotiations with the Soviets, indicating that in case Moscow desired 'definite military commitments for the containment of Germany, the best way to handle the matter' would have been the Byrnes treaty; on the other hand, the arrangements which were to be made with the Americans were 'essential' to British security and to lose them would have been a 'disaster'.[34]

As soon as Bevin became aware of the American anxiety lest Stalin wanted 'to split the Anglo-American front', he stalled the negotiations with Moscow and assured the State Department of Britain's desire to pursue the closest Anglo-American collaboration.[35] At the beginning of October, in a paper on 'The Strategic Aspect of British Foreign Policy', the Foreign Office had indicated as first in the list of 'principal objects' of British policy: 'to find with the United States Government a basis on which the Soviet world and the Anglo-Saxon world can live together, if not in friendship, at any rate without open conflict', considering that 'present Soviet policy (even on the hypothesis that it is dictated primarily by considerations of security) is directed to undermine British and American influence in all parts of the world and, where possible, to supplant it'.[36]

Moscow, March 1947

It may be debated whether the Four Power Pact has been a 'cornerstone' of Secretary of State Marshall's diplomacy at the Moscow CFM in March 1947,[37] but it goes unquestioned that it was one of the main issues he proposed for discussion at the meeting. As has been recently and convincingly argued, in Moscow Marshall pursued a diplomatic line which, while accepting the general policy of containment, 'wanted to try harder to find some basis for pragmatic cooperation' with the Soviet Union on reparations and demilitarisation in Germany.[38] This pragmatism of Marshall was suspicious to the British and dangerous for their strategy which since the second half of 1946, as we have noted, was 'to press ahead with policies that would make the "Western" option viable' and whose first priority 'was now to secure the British and American zones, not the whole of Germany, for the West', pursuing a new policy for containing the Soviet Union and restoring the Western part of Germany.[39] Support of the Four Power Treaty could weaken the British strategy and give more ground to Marshall's 'pragmatism'. Why then did Bevin choose to throw all his diplomatic weight behind the American proposal?

Sure enough, one explanation that could narrow the gap would be that Bevin 'still toyed with hopes that the Americans could be committed to the defence of Europe without an open breach with the Soviet Union'.[40] More satisfying and maybe fairer to Bevin, is to point out that his diplomatic line would be a further proof that 'he was certainly more reluctant to abandon hope of an agreement with the Russians than either the United States or his own officials.'[41]

But there is a body of evidence shedding new light on another aspect. On 4 March 1947 on their way to Moscow, the British Foreign Secretary and the French Minister of Foreign Affairs, Georges Bidault, signed the Treaty of Dunkirk – an event which requires some consideration in order to discern and appreciate properly the clues explaining the progress of British diplomacy in Moscow. The conclusion of the Anglo-French Pact was the first initiative of the British government in what has been defined an 'eventful period' of British foreign policy between the end of 1946 and March 1948.[42] During the winter of 1946–47, Great Britain had reshaped her undertakings in Germany and in the Eastern Mediterranean, both moves being dictated by the impossibility of maintaining her current level of international burdens.[43] Why, then, right at the moment in which she was dramatically experiencing the limits of her position as a 'great power' and the Cabinet was making 'a series of fateful decisions', did Great Britain decide to undertake a new engagement?[44]

As Lord Strang recalls in his memoirs, Bevin considered that 'there was always a right moment to act and he never would have accelerated the pace', but once he had decided to act 'he would have never acted without a definite purpose'; and Frank Roberts, who was to become Bevin's Private Secretary, added that 'Although pragmatic in his tactics, Bevin had an overall strategic concept which protected him from the all too prevalent diplomatic disease of simply reacting to events as they occur....'[45]

Now at the end of February 1947 the British Foreign Secretary was anxious to sign the new engagement 'as soon as possible', whereas only a few months earlier he had declared, 'I even did not urge for an alliance with France and the other Western Powers because I have always been moved in this matter by the desire of not dividing Europe.'[46] But the alliance with France was one of the long-sought objectives of Bevin's strategy in Europe and when the opportunity arose eventually to realise it, he did not hesitate to get 'the Treaty with France safely in the bag'.[47] The treaty then appeared as 'completing a triangular Anglo-Franco-Soviet system in Europe directed against Germany'.

Yet one cannot forget that there were some officials considering the pact as a sort of a cornerstone of a future anti-Soviet reinsurance system.[48] The Dunkirk treaty in fact went as far as it was possible to go in that direction at that international juncture. The two European powers talked security against Germany, but that was only part of the real issue. The true problem was western European security in perspective and on that account the treaty was functional in the prevailing phase of uncertainty as to the final frame of the European system.[49]

In January 1948, a few days after Bevin's famous speech on Western Union, the British ambassador in Washington, Lord Inverchapel, in informing the State Department of the Anglo-French scheme, and proposing to the Benelux countries bilateral treaties directed primarily against Germany on the model of the Dunkirk treaty, explained: 'Mr. Bevin regards this approach as the only way in which any progress can be made towards closer unity in Western Europe pending the adoption of some wider scheme in which the United States will play its part.'[50]

By spring 1947, the phase of uncertainty was fast receding. On the eve of the Moscow conference, Bevin, although decided for a negotiating line of definite toughness, certainly did not intend to force a break with the Soviets and above all shoulder the responsibility should a breach occur. This is why every care had been taken to give to the pact a clear anti-German flavour.[51] This preoccupation in turn raised a new problem with regard to the American-proposed four-power treaty.

Since the beginning of the negotiations in mid-January, the main British preoccupation was to avoid the insertion within the pact of any principle which could 'risk affecting the adoption of the Byrnes treaty'; at the same time, it was stressed that 'the importance of doing nothing to encourage the Russians to reject the treaty as being superfluous and the importance of the United States being committed to participation in the control of Germany'. On the same point Sir Orme Sargent, Permanent Under-Secretary at the Foreign Office, advised French Ambassador René Massigli that it was of the utmost importance 'that neither the French nor the British do anything to discourage the Americans to proceed with the Byrnes proposal'.[52] (Those utterances seemed to express more a concern for an American disengagement from Europe than for the sort of Byrnes treaty as was witnessed by the opinion circulating in the Foreign Office, and subscribed to by Bevin himself, that the American proposal could be destroyed by Molotov's refusal irrespective of the Anglo-French pact.)[53]

At this stage, then, the Byrnes treaty was more important to the British for its form than for its substance, as it was a visible sign of the Anglo-American link to Europe: as Foreign Office officials explained to their State Department counterparts, 'Anglo-American solidarity against the Soviet Union was the foreign secretary's top priority.' At the same time, Bevin was advising the Cabinet that if the United States withdrew from Europe Britain would have been placed in an impossible position.[54]

In Moscow Bevin was, besides Marshall, the staunchest supporter of the Byrnes treaty, declaring significantly that 'had such a treaty existed after World War I, the recent war might have been prevented' and urging Molotov to accept the American proposal. In fact consultations on strategy between London and Washington prior to the Moscow conference had resulted in quite close negotiating positions: 'the British goal at Moscow was like that of the US State department: to set prohibitive conditions for Soviet cooperation, and, when these were rejected, to proceed vigorously with the development of the bizone'.[55] That meant that neither London nor Washington was inclined to compromise with Moscow except on the basis of Soviet access to the bizone – that is, unless there was a reversal of the current Soviet position.

Thus British support of the American draft had seemingly a double purpose: to try as far as possible to keep at least the semblance of quadripartite political cooperation in Germany, this cooperation being perceived as a possibility, and a rather dim one; and second, to try and secure American participation in European affairs, this being perceived as an absolute necessity. And much more a necessity, as the situation was seen as moving fast, 'getting perilously near a position in which a lineup is taking place', as Bevin told the Prime Minister.[56]

Bevin's evaluation of the state of the quadripartite relations was strikingly similar to that entertained by the American delegation as expressed by Robert Murphy, that 'It had been the Moscow conference of 1947 to draw the iron curtain', and confirmed by the declaration of Marshall 'that it was at Moscow that he finally came to the conclusion that it was impossible to reach a settlement with the Russians'.[57] Even the French foreign minister, Bidault, was found entirely changed in his views about the Soviet Union and decided to work wholeheartedly with his Western partners.[58]

Back from Moscow and reporting to Cabinet on the discussions about the Byrnes treaty and how the Soviets had tried to delay them, Bevin had commented on the decision by Marshall to propose once again at the next CFM the American draft treaty as meaning the confirmation that the United States was not proposing to withdraw from Europe.[59] Six months earlier, in September 1946, the Stuttgart speech by Byrnes had been received with 'general approval' by the British and it had been perceived as the first concrete indication that the American troops were going to stay in Europe;[60] and now Bevin saw in Marshall's attitude the confirmation of the permanent turn of the American policy in the Old Continent. In his memoirs the French ambassador, René Massigli, recalls how 'Byrnes transformed the elements of the debate: the European problem became an Atlantic problem.'[61]

The conditions were now in place for a new stage in Western co-operation and the Byrnes treaty was to have once more a part in it. From the summer of 1947 Great Britain was to assume a leadership role in western Europe[62] as the United States moved decidedly to the front of the European scene.

London, November–December 1947

A few days after the end of the Moscow conference the British Foreign Office was discussing the opportunity of signing pacts similar to the Anglo-French one with the Belgians and the Dutch. The issue had been raised by the Belgians and was clearly a direct consequence of the Dunkirk treaty and the outcome of the Moscow CFM.

In fact that same issue had been a lingering subject under the label 'Western group' particularly since the arrival of Ernest Bevin at the Foreign Office, but it had been broached at least as far back as 1944.[63] The idea had been put in store for future use mainly because of the unwillingness of the Foreign Secretary to confront Soviet opposition to it and lately American suspicion about a proliferation of bilateral pacts.[64] This was a sign of the attention Bevin was now giving to American concerns, and of the growing care Bevin was dedicating to nurture the transatlantic link. In any case a common feature of all those discussions had been that the keystone of any Western group or association or whatever else it would be named, had to be the Anglo-French alliance.

At the beginning of May 1947, when the Belgians again raised the issue, the alliance was in place, the gloomy results of the Moscow CFM and the evidence of a close understanding between the Western powers in its aftermath showing a fast-changing scene: no wonder then that the moment could be seen as a favourable one by the small power which had been considering Great Britain as Western Europe's natural leader since the war.[65]

The first reaction at the Foreign Office was to see the alliance with the Belgians (and possibly with the Dutch) as an alternative to be considered only if 'we have given up hope on the Byrnes treaty' – that is, on collaboration with the Russians and on keeping the Americans in Europe.[66] But according to Bevin, after what had happened at the Moscow CFM both the alliances and the Byrnes treaty could be pursued together.[67] So much so that by 17 June, on the eve of his departure for Paris to discuss Marshall's Harvard speech with the French, Bevin had on his desk a draft Cabinet memorandum discussing the proposal to sign alliances with Belgium and the Netherlands and the draft of the treaty of alliance with Belgium on the model of the Dunkirk treaty.[68] But the Foreign Office deemed it necessary to stress the importance of the Byrnes treaty: 'Although the Byrnes treaty is not now under active consideration we feel strongly that our treaty with Belgium should include a reference to it. We are most anxious to demonstrate to the world in general and *to the Americans in particular* that, in spite of the rough handling which the Byrnes treaty received at Moscow, we are still firmly in favour of its conclusion at an early date. At this time our object is to support to the utmost the draft treaty.'[69]

If nothing followed thereafter, it was because all the attention being taken by the Paris conference on American aid, as Bevin 'characteristically... put economy first': Pierson Dixon minuted to Harvey that according to Bevin his proposal 'constitutes a political approach, whereas the present trend of events seems favourable to an economic approach' and that therefore the Secretary preferred to await the outcome of the Paris talks.[70]

'In a way', argues Klaus Schwabe,[71] 'the Marshall plan served as a substitute for the earlier envisioned Four Power Pact' as it was designed to stabilise the political situation in Europe albeit with economic and not with military means. But, one has to add, the west Europeans were more and more anxious to secure also some sort of a 'military leg' to the stabilisation process; since early June Bidault had praised the perspective of an American military presence on the Elbe.[72]

In the meantime the Foreign Office had requested further informal discussions with the Americans on the Byrnes treaty and Washington had accepted the suggestion.[73] Then around the middle of July, probably within the framework of the proposed bilateral discussions, the State Department made known through Charles Bohlen, then counsellor at the Department of State and special assistant to Secretary of State Marshall, its willingness to conclude the Byrnes treaty on a three-power basis leaving the door open for the Soviet Union to join later if she so decided:[74] it was a suggestion which applied the bizone blueprint to security[75] and paralleled the efforts to convince the French to join the Anglo-American zone.

The three-power solution had been considered already by Sargent during the Moscow CFM, but it had been kept within the British delegation on the score that it would not have been accepted by the Americans.[76] In the new situation of summer 1947, at the Foreign Office the comments on Bohlen's proposal were generally positive even if there was full awareness that the consequences of such a choice would have been the possible prejudice of the whole London CFM and the splitting of Germany in two;[77] on the other hand, so the argument went, the French would have obtained a guarantee similar to that gained with the Dunkirk treaty. The question was how the French would react to such a proposal.

It was late October when Jean Chauvel, the Secretary-General of the French Ministère des Affaires Etrangères, then in London with his foreign minister for a round of talks with Bevin and Foreign Office officials,[78] discussed with Sargent the three-power option. For the French diplomat the proposal did not meet the case: if in consequence of the failure of the London CFM the three western zones of Germany were fused, 'what in fact would result would have been a new frontier against Russia in Germany which would have to be policed'. The serious deterioration in relations with Russia that would have ensued was going to project added risks for the countries of western Europe. The French wanted to know what military support they could count upon, not against Germany but in case of a Soviet–American clash involving western Europe.

It was evident that the French were trying to strengthen their bilateral link with the British and wished to give military teeth to the Anglo-French alliance. But according to Sargent the best course was still to insist on the Byrnes draft because even if essentially against Germany 'it had for us the inestimable advantage of keeping the Americans in Europe'. If that treaty could be brought into being on a three-power basis, argued Sargent, then no doubt it could be adjusted to circumstances as they arose. Besides, the French were told that in British opinion it would have been 'unwise in the extreme' to frighten the public by staging Anglo-French military talks 'prematurely and without reference to the United States'.[79]

Once again then it appeared that British support of the Byrnes treaty was one of the keystones of their policy to keep the United States in Europe; besides, for the first time they had directly linked the Byrnes draft to the general problem of security in Europe, which was becoming urgent: 'I believe myself', minuted the Head of the Northern Department on a pessimistic dispatch from the Moscow embassy at the beginning of November,[80] 'that we must now reconcile ourselves to face a trial of strength in Western Europe.'

On 8 December, with the London conference drifting towards a deadlock, Sargent submitted to Bevin three papers which were the result of discussions he had had with General Robertson and other officials involved in German affairs. One paper dealt with the establishment of a provisional German government, a second paper dealt with the methods of handling possible future discussions with the Americans and the French about Germany, and the third document was a draft paper produced by Sargent about the Byrnes treaty on a three-power basis.

Following the Chauvel–Sargent conversations in October, the Foreign Office had decided 'to explore the possibilities' of the Byrnes treaty as Sargent had insisted with the French diplomat. The treaty had to be considered from three perspectives: '(i) we want security against Germany; (ii) we want a sop to the French in regard of security against Russia; (iii) applicability to three zones, in the event of Russia standing out, without any apparent alteration in principle and with room left for Russia to join later'. The Foreign Office suggested a redraft of Article IV of the American draft in a form which could be used against Russian aggression and could be joined by Moscow 'without trouble *if there should be a détente.* 'Yet', it was recognised, that solution 'will not be sufficient to please the French' and at the same time it was difficult to see 'how we can go further within the framework of the Byrnes treaty.'

After the matter was discussed with Sargent and the State Department had been informed, nothing was decided for the immediate future. But when, at the London CFM, Molotov refused to discuss the Byrnes treaty and this was interpreted by the Western powers as a final ominous sign of the Soviet intentions towards Germany, the ready-made solution re-emerged: 'Sargent', observes Anne Deighton, 'wanted to apply the principles of the creation of the bizone, which was still technically open to the Soviets and the French to join, to resolve Western Europe's security problems.' The draft paper was approved immediately by Bevin and was printed to be presented to the Cabinet.[81]

It was the first time that the three-power treaty became a policy option at Cabinet level. But within a week the complete failure of the London CFM was to bring out a thoroughly new perspective.

The new pattern

The breakdown of the London CFM was the decisive turning-point for the freezing of the division of Europe. The American intervention in the recovery of Europe had 'crystallised' the opposition to any closer organisation of the western European countries.[82]

Europe, Bevin told Bidault who had gone to tell him goodbye on the morning of 17 December, 'was now divided from Greece to the Baltic and from Oder to Trieste'; what was needed was 'some sort of federation of formal or informal character' and the Americans had to be brought in. He would tell the Americans that they must now face the situation and that if the British and the French played their part 'it would not be good enough for the Americans to expect us to take action while they themselves were not ready to take any risk until a much later stage.' There would be Anglo-French military talks with American participation coming later, remembering however that the Americans would never agree to military alliances or treaties. It was a matter of building up their confidence and not rushing matters: 'If however the Americans were prepared to take the right steps in Europe', said Bevin, 'it would still be necessary for the French and ourselves to advise them, while letting the Americans say and think that it was they who were acting.'[83]

In the evening of that same day Bevin proposed with more details his 'Western Union' scheme to Marshall.[84] In considering the problem of security the Foreign Secretary said that a three-power version of the Byrnes treaty, which had been considered a possible solution, had been better substituted by 'some treaty or understanding which also brought in Benelux and Italy.' The essential task was to create confidence in western Europe that further communist inroads would be stopped.

It was Bevin then who first discarded the three-power Byrnes treaty option.[85] And he did so only in his conversation with Marshall; when he handed to the French an expurgated copy of the record of his talk with the American Secretary of State, one of the sections omitted was the one concerning the Byrnes treaty option. And yet to his French colleague he said that 'In fact he doubted whether Russia was as great a danger as a resurgent Germany might become.'[86]

The explanation of this attitude of Bevin was in his newly adapted strategy: Germany was to be the object of a 'soft containment' within the framework of the devised western democratic system[87] to which the added participation of North America and the Dominions would have provided the necessary power for a 'hard containment' of the Soviet Union: this seems to have been the meaning of his discourse to the American Secretary of State.

On the other hand, Bevin was convinced that the first step, that is, establishing a joint multilateral economic, political and defensive treaty in Western Europe, had to be realised without any previous guarantee of American backing.[88] But in fact an informal American guarantee had developed and there were indications of growing American interest in the defence of western Europe.[89]

Marshall himself soon got to the conclusion that the Byrnes treaty 'would not go to the heart of the present European security problems'; to increase security of western Europe on behalf of a general German settlement, the United States, cabled Marshall to the embassy in Brussels, would have favoured a widening of the three western powers' cooperation 'to include participation other Western European countries if satisfactory way to do this can be found'.[90] And the day before Bevin's speech at the Commons on the Western Union, the British Ambassador in Washington, Lord Inverchapel, was advised that the four-power treaty clearly 'no longer responds to the present situation and that other means must be found to achieve its objectives, in which the United States is prepared to play its part'.[91]

Yet the French were not inclined to abandon specific measures of security against Germany. But Bérard, counsellor at the French embassy in Washington, who still wondered whether the United States would have been prepared to enter a three-power treaty on the blueprint of the Byrnes/Marshall draft,[92] was told bluntly by Achilles, the Chief of the Division of the Western European Affairs at the State Department, that the Americans 'regarded the draft as a dead duck'.[93] At the tripartite conference on Germany in London in the spring of 1948, the French put forward their proposal again, but they had already had some second thoughts on its suitability: 'The two essential points of the Byrnes draft', said an unsigned 'Note sur le Plan Byrnes'[94] 'were the presence in Europe of the American control forces and the maintaining of a certain level of disarmament of Germany through an agreement of the four powers. *It looks necessary to obtain those same conditions in an agreement with the United States, perhaps by different ways.... To propose to keep the Byrnes treaty on a three power basis seems insufficient'*.

The Byrnes treaty had played its role in the relations between the Western powers. It had fixed the principle of American presence in Europe. It had been an instrument of coordination of Western policy with regard to the Soviet Union and the German question. As a three-power hypothesis, it had prefigured a sort of Western alliance. And finally, it was explicitly substituted for Bevin's 'magnificent'[95] European scheme which was going to ease the second American diplomatic revolution, leading eventually to the Atlantic Alliance.[96] It was true that Britain had adjusted its foreign policy to reality and had 'played second fiddler'[97] in organising western Europe in cooperation with the United States, but the music had been composed at four hands.

Notes

1   D. Sanders, *Losing an Empire, Finding a Role: British Foreign Policy since 1945* (London: Macmillan, 1990), p. 53. D. Dimbleby & D. Reynolds, *An Ocean Apart: the Relationship between Britain and America in the Twentieth Century* (London: Hodder & Stoughton), 1998, p. 176: 'At the centre of the deepening of the Cold War was Germany.'

2   D. Reynolds, *Britannia Overruled: British Policy and World Power in the Twentieth Century* (London: Longman, 1991), pp. 160–61. G. Warner, 'Britain, the United States and Western Europe: Some Reflections on Documents on British Policy Overseas', *Diplomacy and Statecraft*, Vol. 1, No. 1 (March 1990), p. 103.

3   W. Loth, *The Division of the World 1941–1945* (London: Routledge, 1988), pp. 98–9, 123. Dimbleby & Reynolds, cit., pp. 170–1. Carolyn Wood Eisenberg, *Drawing the Line: the American Decision to Divide Germany, 1944–1949* (Cambridge: Cambridge University Press, 1996), pp. 228–9. On the criticisms to Byrnes at home: Robert L. Messer, *The End of an Alliance: James F. Byrnes, Roosevelt, Truman, and the Origins of the Cold War* (Chapel Hill: University of North Carolina Press, 1982), pp. 167–88. *DBPO*, I, IV, Halifax to Bevin, 10 Mar. 1946, No. 49, pp. 155–6.

4   J. Gimbel, *The Origins of the Marshall Plan* (Stanford: Stanford University Press, 1976), pp. 111–13; Gimbel argues that the treaty was meant as Byrnes's 'major effort to bring France around'. Carolyn Wood Eisenberg, *Drawing the Line*, op. cit., p. 228.

5   Ministère des Affaires Etrangères (hereafter MAE), Série Y, 356, Washington à Paris, 23 Mar. 1946.

6   Denise O'Neal Conover, 'James F. Byrnes and the Four-Power Disarmament Treaty', *Mid-America*, Vol. 70, No. 1 (1988), p. 20.

7   On this latter aspect see also: W.W. Rostow, *The Division of Europe after World War II: 1946* (Aldershot: Gower, 1982), pp. 5–6 and passim. John L. Gaddis, *The Long Peace: Inquiries into the History of the Cold War* (Oxford, Oxford University Press, 1989), pp. 52–4.

8   MAE, Série Y, 356, Juin à Bidault, Cabinet, Direction des affaires Politiques, 23 Apr. 1946.

9   MAE, Série Y, 356, Bonnet à Paris, Direction d'Europe, 18 May 1946.

10   MAE, Série Y, 356, Bonnet à Bidault, 4 May 1946.

11   MAE, Série Y, 356, Washington à Paris, 29 Mar. 1946.

12   Annie Lacroix-Ritz, 'Sécurité française et menace militaire allemande avant la conclusion des alliances occidentales: le déchirement du choix entre Moscou et Washington (1945–1947)', *Relations Internationales*, No. 51 (automne 1987), pp. 304–8. Gimbel, *The Origins*, op. cit, p. 115.

13   On the French policy, see: Eisenberg, *Drawing the Line*, op. cit., pp. 166–76; Gimbel, *The Origins*, op. cit., 38. A. Grosser, *Affaires Extérieures. La politique de la France 1946/1984* (Paris: Flammarion, 1984), pp. 33–8.

14   O'Neal Conover, *James F. Byrnes*, op. cit., p. 21

15   Public Record Office (hereafter PRO) CP(46)156, 15 Apr. 1946; Gen 121/1, 11 Mar. 1946; PRO CAB 128/5 CM 36 (46), 17 Apr. 1946 (all quotations from Crown Copyright documents in the Public Record Office are reproduced by kind permission of the Controller of Her Majesty's Stationery Office).

16   PRO CAB 109/8 CP(46)139, cit., COS(46)105(0), 5 Apr. 1946. Julian Lewis, *Changing Direction: British Military Planning for Post-war Strategic Defence, 1942–1947* (London: The Sherwood Press, 1988), pp. 263–4.

17   Anne Deighton, *The Impossible Peace: Britain, the Division of Germany and the Origins of the Cold War* (Oxford: Clarendon Press, 1990), pp. 54–80; J. Fosche-poth, 'British Interest in the Division of Germany after the Second World War', *Journal of Contemporary History*, Vol. 21 (1986), p. 400.

18   Deighton, *The Impossible Peace*, op. cit., p. 74; PRO CAB 129/9CP (46) 156, Policy towards Germany, 3 May 1946.

19   Deighton, *The Impossible Peace*, op. cit., p. 75; the other condition being raising the food ratio in Germany and rendering Western Germany self-supporting. G. Warner, 'From Ally to Enemy: Britain's Relations with the Soviet Union, 1941–1948', in M. Dockrill and B. McKercher, *Diplomacy and World Power: Studies in British Foreign Policy 1890–1950* (Cambridge: Cambridge University Press, 1996), pp. 221–43, p. 236.

20   PRO CAB 129/9, CP(46)186, Policy towards Germany, 3 May 1946, Annex, Survey of present situation in Germany, 24 Apr. 1946; see also Deighton, *The Impossible Peace*, op. cit., pp. 53, 78–9. But for a 'trenchant and outspoken' Foreign Office judgement on the Americans, see Lewis, *Changing Direction*, op. cit., pp. 285 and 363–8.

21   Gimbel, *The Origins*, op. cit., p. 116.

22   Deighton, *The Impossible Peace*, op. cit., chapter 3; P. Cornish, *British Military Planning for the Defence of Germany 1945–50* (London: Macmillan, 1996), p. 15.

23   Deighton, *The Impossible Peace*, op. cit., p. 85. It has to be stressed that the main preoccupation in the Brief for Paris Conference on the Byrnes Treaty for

the British delegation was about clarifying the US attitude and bringing France into the discussions, PRO FO 371/55381, 15 Apr. 1946

24 Eisenberg, *Drawing the Line*, op. cit., p. 239; Deighton, *The Impossible Peace*, op. cit., pp. 81–134, 86. *FRUS*, 1946, II, p. 169–70. In fact Lord Halifax had communicated to Byrnes that the Foreign Secretary had been authorised by the Cabinet to declare that the British Government 'warmly welcom(ed)' the American proposal and that Bevin would have been very happy to discuss it in Paris with Byrnes, *FRUS*, 1946, II, Letter from Halifax to Byrnes, p. 82. Possibly Bevin was thinking of confidential and informal discussions.

25 *FRUS*, 1946, II, p. 172; the report of Bevin to the Cabinet in PRO CAB 129/9, CP(46)207, 23 May 1946.

26 A. Cairncross, *The Price of War: British Policy on German Reparations, 1941–1949* (New York: Blackwell, 1986), p. 159.

27 Deighton, *The Impossible Peace*, op. cit., p.101–2. In fact 'When the Paris CFM reconvened, Secretary Byrnes was prepared for its failure', Eisenberg, *Drawing the Line*, op. cit., pp. 269, 236.

28 O'Neal Conover, *James F. Byrnes*, op. cit., p. 25. For the French attitude in general, see: Anne Lacroix Ritz, 'Sécurité française et ménace militaire allemande avant la conclusion des alliances occidentales: les déchirements du choix entre Moscou et Washington (1945–1947)', Relations Internationales, No. 31, (automne 1987), p. 304 ff; H. Bungert, 'A New Perspective on French–American Relations during the Occupation of Germany, 1945–1948: Behind-the-Scenes Diplomatic Bargaining and the Zonal Merger', *Diplomatic History*, Vol. 18, No. 3 (Summer 1994), pp. 333–52; Gimbel, *The Origins*, op. cit., p. 116. The British had judged the French position as 'reserved', FO 371/ 55382, 27 Apr. 1946.

29 Appendix to CP(46)139, COS(46)105(0), United States proposal for a Four-Power Treaty, op. cit.

30 MAE, Série Y, 356, Ambassadeur à Londres à G. Bidault, 17 May 1946.

31 A. Bullock, *Ernest Bevin, Foreign Secretary* (London: Heinemann, 1983), p. 270.

32 MAE, Série Y, 356, Bonnet à Bidault, 4 May 1946; Gimbel, *The Origins*, op. cit., p. 117.

33 PRO CAB 128/6, CM 68(46), 15 Jul. 1946. PRO CAB 128/6, CM 73(46), 24 Jul. 1946. *DBPO*, Inverchapel to Bevin, 20 Jul. 1946, No. 124, p. 390.

34 PRO PREM 8/662, The Anglo-Soviet Treaty: the Question of an Anglo-Soviet Military Alliance; and Anglo-American standardisation. Memorandum by the Secretary of State for Foreign Affairs, 27 Jan. 1947; CM 15(47), 3.2.47

35 Ritchie Ovendale, *The English Speaking Alliance: Britain, the United States, the Dominions and the Cold War 1945–1951* (London: George Allen & Unwin, 1985), pp. 44–6. Kenneth O. Morgan, *Labour in Power, 1945–1951* (Oxford: Oxford University Press, 1985), pp. 248–9. Later in the year Lambert of the Northern Department will comment that 'one cannot help a feeling that the real Soviet objective in these negotiations has been to separate us from the US and possibly even from France', PRO FO 371/66371, N 12488, minute by A.E. Lambert, 23 Oct. 1947.

36 Cornish, *British Military Planning*, op. cit., Appendix 6, pp. 363–9.

37 Klaus Schwabe, 'The Origins of the United States' Engagement in Europe, 1946–1952', in Francis H. Heller and John R. Gillingham, *NATO: the Founding*

of the Atlantic Alliance and the Integration of Europe (New York: St. Martin's Press, 1992), p. 164.

38 Philip Zelikow, 'George C. Marshall and the Moscow CFM Meeting of 1947', *Diplomacy and Statecraft*, Vol. 8, No. 2, (July 1997), pp. 97–124; Gaddis, op. cit., p. 55. 'On the American and British sides, the forthcoming Moscow conference of Foreign Ministers was viewed as climactic. Either the Allies would find a way to harmonise differences and reintegrate the zones or Germany would be divided', Eisenberg, *Drawing the Line*, op. cit., p. 277. A fact to note: the Truman doctrine seemed to have no immediate impact on the Moscow negotiations, p. 290. On British reactions: Peter G. Boyle, 'The British Foreign Office and American Foreign Policy, 1947–48', *Journal of American Studies*, Vol. 16, No. 3, pp. 376–8.

39 Deighton, *The Impossible Peace*, op. cit., pp. 134 and 138; see chapters 5 and 6. 'The new partnership with the United States was providing the necessary confidence to attempt to exclude the Soviets from Western Germany', Eisenberg, *Drawing the Line*, op. cit., p. 277.

40 Deighton, *The Impossible Peace*, op. cit. p. 157; Bullock, *Ernest Bevin*, op. cit., p. 371–3.

41 G. Warner, 'Ernest Bevin and British Foreign Policy 1945–1951'. Gordon Craig and Francia L. Lowenheim, *The Diplomats, 1939–1979* (Princeton: Princeton University Press, 1994), pp. 106–8.

42 Roy E. Jones, 'Reflections Upon an Eventful Period in Britain's Foreign Relations', *International Relations*, II, No. 8 (October 1973), pp. 524–40. See also A. Adamthwaite, 'Britain and the World, 1945–1949: the View from the Foreign Office', in J. Becker and F. Knipping, *Power in Europe? Great Britain, France and Germany in a Postwar World, 1945–1950* (Berlin & New York: Walter de Gruyter, 1986), pp. 15–16.

43 On the Eastern Mediterranean, see Bruce R. Kuniholm, *The Origins of the Cold War in the Near East: Great Power Conflict and Diplomacy in Iran, Turkey and Greece* (Princeton: Princeton University Press, 1980); Bullock, op. cit., pp. 361–71.

44 D. Reynolds, *Britannia*, op. cit., p. 168. For a reflection on the British situation in those circumstances, see PRO FO 371/62420, UE 678/176/53, Circular no. 028–Secret, 12 Feb. 1947 (on effects of British external financial position on UK's foreign policy).

45 Lord Strang, *Home and Abroad* (London: André Deutsch, 1956), pp. 292–3. Frank K. Roberts, 'Ernest Bevin as Foreign Secretary', in R. Ovendale, *The Foreign Policy of the British Labour Governments, 1945–1951* (Leicester: Leicester University Press, 1984), pp. 21–42, 29.

46 PRO FO 371/67672, 2317, 26.2.47; R. N. Rosecrance, *Defense of the Realm: British Strategy in the Nuclear Epoch* (New York: Columbia University Press, 1968), p. 60.

47 It was Hoyer Millar who used those words in a minute on the draft paper on the Western Group by Mr Ronald, PRO FO 371/59911, 2410, 3 Dec. 1945.

48 John W. Young, *Britain, France, and the Unity of Europe, 1945–1951* (Leicester: Leicester University Press, 1984), p. 51. M. Dockrill, 'British Attitudes towards France as a Military Ally', *Diplomacy and Statecraft*, Vol. 1, No. 1 (March 1990),

pp. 49–70. D. Ardia, *Il patto di Dunkerque. Alle origini dell'alleanza ocidentale* (Padova: Signum, 1983).

49   D. Ardia, *Il patto*, op. cit., pp. 161–2.
50   *FRUS*, 1948, III, p. 14, Inverchapel to Lovett, 27 Jan. 1948.
51   For an historiographical review of the treaty, see Bert Zeeman, 'Britain and the Cold War: an Alternative Approach. The Treaty of Dunkirk Example', *European History Quarterly*, Vol. 16 (1986), pp. 343–67.
52   PRO FO 371/67671, 1777, From Foreign Office to Paris, 15 Feb. 1947; Massigli–Sargent conversation, 18 Feb. 1947. John W. Young, *Britain, France*, op. cit., pp. 48–9.
53   PRO FO 371/676672, 2317, minute by Sargent, minute by P. Dixon, 26 Feb. 1947.
54   Wayne Knight, 'Labourite Britain: America's "Sure Friend"? The Anglo-Soviet Treaty Issue, 1947', *Diplomatic History*, Vol. 7, No. 4 (Fall 1983), p. 280.
55   FRUS, 1947, II, p. 332; FO 800/SU/47/40, Record of conversation at the Kremlin on Friday 25 April 1947. Eisenberg, *Drawing the Line*, op. cit., pp. 294–5.
56   Bullock, *Ernest Bevin*, op. cit., p. 388, Bevin to Attlee, 16.4.47.
57   Marshall cited in Warner, 'From Ally to Enemy', op. cit., p. 241. Murphy in Eisenberg, *Drawing the Line*, op. cit., p. 313.
58   PRO FO 371/67724, 15529, from Brussels to Foreign Office, 11.6.47; it was the opinion of the Belgian Foreign Minister, Paul Henri Spaak, expressed after a conversation he had with his French colleague. Young, Britain, France, op. cit., p. 57. Annie Lacroix-Ritz, 'Vers le plan Schuman: les jalons décisifs de l'acceptation française du réarmement allemand (1947–1950)', i, *Guerres mondiales et conflits contemporains*.
59   PRO CAB 129/9, CM 43 (47), 2.5.47. See also Deighton, *The Impossible Peace*, op. cit., pp. 162–7. After his conversation with Stalin on 15 April, Marshall was optimistic about the Soviets accepting the Byrnes treaty, Eisenberg, *Drawing the Line*, op. cit., p. 307.
60   R. Ovendale, *The English Speaking Alliance*, op. cit., pp. 245–8: the promise to keep American troops in Germany 'had been added to the speech at the last minute, with a view to assuring both the French and Germans that the country would not be abandoned to the Russians', p. 246.
61   R. Massigli, *Une comédie des erreurs, 1943–1956* (Paris: Plon, 1978), p. 86; Ardia, op. cit., p. 124.
62   A. Adamthwaite, *Britain and the World*, op. cit., p. 16.
63   V. Rothwell, *Britain and the Cold War, 1941–1947* (London: Jonathan Cape, 1982), chapter 8. John Bayliss, 'Britain, the Brussels Pact and the Continental Commitment', *International Affairs*, Vol. 60, No. 4 (Autumn 1984), pp. 615–29.
64   G. Warner, 'The Labour Governments and the Unity of Western Europe', in R. Ovendale, *The Foreign Policy*, op. cit., pp. 62–3. Morgan, *Labour in Power*, op. cit., p. 249.
65   John W. Young, *Britain, France*, op. cit., chapter 2 passim and p. 27. PRO FO 371/67724, 5971, J. P. (47) 70 Final, 4 June 1947.
66   PRO FO 371/67724, 4670, Record of conversation with Belgian ambassador, minute by Hoyer Millar, 5 May 1947.

67 PRO FO 371/67724, 4670, Record of the meeting with Secretary of State at the Foreign Office, 7 May 1947. Warner, 'The Labour Governments', op. cit., p. 63.

68 PRO FO 371/67724, 5971, 17 June 1947.

69 PRO FO 371/67724, Z5839, Letter from Harvey to Sir John Stephenson (DO), 23 June 1947 (emphasis added).

70 PRO FO 371/67724, 6791, Telegram from Foreign Office to Brussels, 23 June 1947. Roberts, *Ernest Bevin*, op. cit., p. 29. PRO FO 371/67724, 5971, P. Dixon to Harvey, 25 June 1947. It is worthwhile to note that the British Embassy in Washington informed the Foreign Office that the representative James Wadsworth (Rep., NY) had told a member of the embassy that 'most of his colleagues on Capitol Hill viewed the Marshall Plan from the strategic more than economic standpoint' in so far as it 'might serve to prevent the extension of Soviet power in the direction of the Atlantic seaboard', PRO FO 371/62402, UE5102, from Washington to Foreign Office, 26 June 1947. Peter J. Boyle, 'The British Foreign Office and American Foreign Policy, 1947–1948', *Journal of American Studies*, Vol. 16, No. 3, pp. 373–89.

71 Schwabe, *The Origins*, op. cit., p. 165.

72 Eisenberg, *Drawing the Line*, op. cit., p. 355.

73 *FRUS*, 1947, II, The Ambassador in the United States (Douglas) to the Secretary of State, 2 June 1947, pp. 676–8.

74 PRO FO 371/64511, 9838, from Washington to Foreign Office, Balfour–Bohlen conversation, 20 July 1947. On Bohlen's assessment of the situation by mid-1947 and his suggestions on how to cope with it, see T. Michael Ruddy, *The Cautious Diplomat: Charles E. Bohlen and the Soviet Union, 1929–1969* (Kent and London: The Kent State University Press, 1986), p. 76. In his memoirs Bohlen recalls in general terms the Byrnes proposal and notes how 'By late 1947 positions on both sides had hardened. There seemed to be no basis for compromise, no common ground . . . .', Charles E. Bohlen, *Witness to History, 1929–1969* (New York: W. W. Norton & Co., 1973), pp. 274–5.

75 Deighton, *The Impossible Peace*, op. cit., p. 213; Deighton refers to Sargent but the same can be applied to Bohlen. Since at least April 1947 the Byrnes treaty was seen by the Americans as 'an interim measure to maintain four-power cooperation while the bizone was built up', Eisenberg, *Drawing the Line*, op. cit., p. 308.

76 Deighton, *The Impossible Peace*, op. cit., p. 159.

77 PRO FO 371/64511, C9838, op. cit., Minute by Fraser, 23 July 1947.

78 Bullock, *Ernest Bevin*, op. cit., p. 491.

79 PRO FO 371/67724, 9376, Proposed Anglo-French talks on Germany – Sargent–Chauvel conversation. Top Secret. 21 Oct. 1947. *FRUS*, 1947, II, Hickerson–Strang conversation, 30 Oct. 1947; Annex – UK Paper on recent UK–French conversations, p. 695. See also Deighton, *The Impossible Peace*, op. cit., p. 204.

80 PRO FO 371/66371, N12959, From Moscow to Foreign Office, 8 Nov. 1947; Minute by Hankey.

81 PRO FO 371/64633, 16198, Minute by A.G. Gilchrist on the Three Power treaty, 29 Oct. 1947. PRO FO 371/64250, 16198, 16199, 16200, 8 Dec. 1947; PRO CAB 129/22CP, 326, 10 Dec. 1947. See also Deighton, *The Impossible Peace*, op. cit., pp. 212–13. At the same time, 'the pattern of thinking in Britain

concerning a military involvement in Europe became influenced by two distinct forces: movement towards greater political involvement in Europe; and a similar movement towards a more intimate global strategic relationship with the Americans', Cornish, *British Military Planning*, op. cit., p. 107.

82   PRO CAB 128/12CM (2) 48, 8 Jan. 1949.

83   PRO FO 371/64633, 16397, Anglo-French conversations, 17 Dec. 1947, record by F. K. Roberts.

84   *FRUS*, 1947, II, pp. 815–822.

85   Also in Schwabe, *The Origins*, op. cit., p. 170.

86   PRO FO 371/64633, 16397, op. cit.

87   'Only such a union', thought Kennan, the father of containment, 'holds out any hope of restoring the balance of power in Europe without permitting Germany to become again the dominant power', *FRUS*, 1948, III, p. 7, Memorandum by the Director of the Policy Planning Staff (Kennan) to the Secretary of State, 20 Jan. 1948.

88   Warner, 'The Labour Governments', op. cit., pp. 66–7.

89   PRO FO 371/73047, Inverchapel to Bevin, 12 Feb. 1948.

90   *FRUS*, 1948, III, The Secretary of State (Marshall) to the Embassy in Belgium, 10 Jan. 1948, p. 3. Marshall asked the ambassador to confidentially inform Spaak 'only for present as we have not yet discussed this question with British or French'.

91   *FRUS*, 1948, III, Inverchapel–Hickerson conversation, 20 Jan. 1948, p. 10.

92   Exchanges of new drafts of the treaty had taken place among the three western powers between June and November 1947, MAE, Y, 356, various documents.

93   *FRUS*, 1948, II, Memorandum of conversation by Achilles, 13 Feb. 1948, p. 64. On the French proposal at the London tripartite conference on Germany, see also PRO CAB 129/25, CP 48 (78), Talks on Germany, Memorandum by the Secretary of State for Foreign Affairs, 7 Mar. 1948. At the conference Strang said the British were willing to consider adapting the Byrnes draft to the situation and that it might be a useful idea, *FRUS*, 1948, II, Douglas to Secretary of State, 29 Feb. 1948, p. 105. The British position seemed to be dictated more by their willingness not to isolate France than by a genuine sharing of French fears.

94   MAE, Y, 356, 10.2.1948 (emphasis added).

95   *FRUS*, 1948, III, p. 7, Memorandum by the Director of the Office of European Affairs (Hickerson) to the Secretary of State, 19.1.48.

96   On the Brussels pact see A. Varsori, *Il Patto di Bruxelles (1948): tra integrazione europea e alleanza atlantica* (Roma: Bonacci Editore, 1988); John Bayliss, 'Britain, the Brussels Pact and the Continental Commitment', *International Affairs*, Vol. 64, No. 4 (Autumn 1988), pp. 617–29.

97   PRO PREM 8/1431, Minute by N. Brook on CP (48) 6, 7, 8: 7 Jan. 1948.

5
'But westward, look, the land is bright': Labour's Revisionists and the Imagining of America, c. 1945–64

Steven Fielding

Of the Labour government elected in May 1997, David Marquand wrote that its 'rhetoric is American; the intellectual influences which have shaped its project are American; its political style is American'.[1] Marquand highlighted the transatlanticism of Labour 'modernisers' so as to attack their neo-liberal bias, his own view being that they should, instead, emulate the apparently more collectivist western Europeans.[2] It is ironic, then, that Marquand formed part of a tradition within the Labour Party which beheld the United States with unprecedented favour. It was Marquand, indeed, who, while in temporary exile from the party, bemoaned Britain's failure to produce its own 'Roosevelt coalition'.[3] While the America so admired was, in a number of important respects, another country located in a contrasting context, if Tony Blair and his cohorts are guilty of unduly falling under American influence, then many of their postwar Labour predecessors must also stand in the dock.

This chapter highlights how the first two generations of Labour revisionists viewed the United States during the twenty years or so which followed 1945.[4] The first 'American generation' came to political maturity during the interwar period and embraced Hugh Gaitskell as well as Denis Healey, Roy Jenkins and Tony Crosland. Gaitskell was credited by Arthur Schlesinger, a figure close to Democrats such as Presidential candidates Adlai Stevenson and John Kennedy, with bringing about a 'new view of the United States' in the party.[5] After working at the American Embassy in 1941, Jenkins, normally viewed as the keenest of Europeans, habitually quoted A.H. Clough's line: 'But westward, look, the land is bright' on appropriate occasions.[6] To this group, the United States appeared as something like a revelation, both in terms of its postwar economic development and the extent of its international role, all of which were in sharp contrast to British decline. The second cohort, comprising the likes of Roy Hattersley, David Owen, Shirley Williams and Marquand, took this American role for granted. As Hattersley stated, he was 'part of that Labour Party generation which felt a cultural – if not ideological – affinity with the United States. We were the children of the war, Hollywood movies and current affairs lessons about Roosevelt's New Deal. We felt at home in America.'[7]

The chapter does not investigate the motives and actions of those in the United States who sought to influence the opinions of such politicians. Even before 1939 elements in the US were, for a variety of reasons, keen to establish links with leading Labour figures. With the onset of the cold war this interest only increased: the decades following 1945 were ones defined by the Smith–Mundt programme, Congress for Cultural Freedom conferences, transatlantic journals, most famously *Encounter*, as well as lucrative lecture tours and prestigious university fellowships. Some of these enterprises were orchestrated or subsidised by the Central Intelligence Agency although its influence remains moot, despite some of the wilder assumptions of the left.[8] On the one hand was Jenkins who journeyed to the US for the first time in 1953 on a two-month stay financed by the Smith–Mundt programme for young world leaders. Although thinking the intentions of his right-wing sponsors were not achieved, Jenkins nonetheless thought the trip led to a transformation in his view of America and described the tour as 'a major formative influence in my life'.[9] As another up-and-coming Labour figure, Woodrow Wyatt also benefited from a Smith–Mundt fellowship a year prior to Jenkins. However, instead of encouraging a love of the US, his experience provoked no little resentment. At a fairground in Seattle, he 'looked one night at the stars and wept: this vast country thought my darling England was not worth bothering about, equating her to a poor old aunt out of the mainstream'. Such 'mortification and jealousy', he considered, 'made me anti-American emotionally but not politically'.[10] Yet Wyatt was an exception, in this as in so many other respects: so far as most other social democrats were concerned, the Americans knocked at an open door.

While CIA initiatives might have played an important part in facilitating the revisionists' American connection, they were at least supplemented by less covert, more banal, factors. As plane supplanted ship, aspiring Labour politicians could reach the eastern seaboard with relative ease. Although only making his first trip in 1950 Gaitskell had been trying to get to the United States for years and made five more journeys before his death.[11] After making his first transatlantic journey in 1949, Healey made annual lecture tours until becoming Defence Minister in 1964.[12] Once contact had been made, Americans made a favourable and strikingly similar impact on Labour politicians of various stripes. During the war, the Bevanite Richard Crossman compared their delight in innovation with the reluctance of his British colleagues; the solidly centrist James Callaghan also admired the 'boldness and openness of the [American] national character' as well as their 'can do' attitude. After the conflict, the young and ideologically ambiguous Tony Benn described the majority of American students whom he met as 'natural, unsophisticated and carefree'. In particular, he wrote, the 'girls display just that freedom from stiffness and awkwardness which mars the social behaviour of so many English girls'. Perhaps unsurprisingly, given this view, Benn went and married an American. He was not alone: so did Crosland, Owen and, rather later, Williams. Countless others had affairs. Despite this, not all were impressed. While conceding their 'goodness', Wyatt – an exception again – thought the Americans he met on one tour as 'dull earnest talkers into the night'. Nonetheless, he still managed an amorous, if not necessarily nocturnal, adventure with one US citizen.[13]

The scale of American material plenty also left its mark. Something as simple as food impressed early postwar Labour visitors – understandable, given British austerity. Manny Shinwell suggested that one of the burdens of attending a US conference was the amount of hospitality laid on for delegates.[14] The power of catering probably diminished with time: Hattersley, an acknowledged expert in the field, considered the food on his first visit in 1968 'unexceptional'. Even so, the effects of Britain's economic difficulties remained: also in 1968 Owen was victim of post-devaluation limits on the amount of sterling to be taken out of the country. As a result, he could not afford to pay the bill in the restaurant chosen by his future wife on their first date.[15] Finally, the ability of Hollywood to create powerful and favourable images of America should not be overlooked. When Healey first visited Detroit he was struck by the extent to which it echoed images generated by those films he had devoured as an adolescent.[16] Such movies, according to the young critic and Labour member Gerald Kaufman, gave a more egalitarian picture of American life than their British equivalents. According to him, they reflected the lives and loves of workers as well as the middle and moneyed classes; some, such as *On the Waterfront*, even tackled issues associated with trade unionism.[17]

Despite the significance and historical novelty of the social demo-crats' vision of the United States, little has been made of it in historical accounts.[18] Yet, while not much has been said in detail, Labour's revisionists were commonly defined, at least by hostile contemporaries, by two characteristics. The first was their 'Atlanticism', that is the pro-motion of Britain's alliance with the United States within NATO. The second was their commitment to 'modernisation', to which undertak-ing the United States appeared an archetype. Certainly, in the 1950s, the revisionists' favourable vision of the United States gave them an identity which distinguished them from the Labour left as well as the likes of Clement Attlee and Hugh Dalton on the old right. However, the revisionists' relationship with the United States was more ambiguous than is usually supposed. First, their Atlanticism was a product of Brit-ain's decline and a belief in the Soviet threat: in many ways, this was a reluctant embrace. Second, the extent to which they thought the US could be a model for British development was never fully resolved. Initially, indeed, some suggested Britain mapped out the *American* future. Moreover, by the early 1960s, there was an increasing sense that the peculiarities of American society were too profound to be emulated.

The attitude of the British left to America has rarely been investigated in any depth. Henry Pelling's *America and the British Left* (1956) is the major exception, although, given the author's politics, this work should be seen as largely representing the revisionists' view of America.[19] According to Pelling, many of the origins of modern English radicalism, to which Labour was ultimately heir, lay in the campaign to support the American struggle for independence. Indeed, prior to Labour's return to power in 1964 Tony Benn wrote that 'the deliberate democratisation of British life which is to be undertaken [by Harold Wilson] can be seen as the direct re-import of the spirit of the 1776 revolution'.[20] The vision of an egalitarian and democratic America which emerged from the conflict over independence persisted into the nineteenth century: the US continued to be viewed in a favourable light by both advanced Liberals and Chartists. After the Civil War, however, this image was compro-mised as the US industrialised and annexed overseas territories. By the early 1930s, in fact, the United States was perceived as the citadel of international capitalism. It was, after all, American bankers who, legend had it, brought down the Labour Government in 1931.[21]

Franklin Roosevelt helped restore the United States' radical reputa-tion. Ironically, the New Deal probably made more of an impact after, rather than before, the Second World War. Instead, it was FDR's well-known antipathy for Fascism which led Labour leaders to urge the National Government to promote an Anglo-American agreement in place of appeasement.[22] Even during the later 1930s, however, the party's attitude to the US, according to Christopher Mayhew, remained 'distant and ambivalent'.[23] America's favourable image was, nonetheless, emphasised by wartime Lend-Lease, Roosevelt's advocacy of the Four Freedoms and his support for the Atlantic Charter. In the period prior to Pearl Harbor, Jenkins stated that 'the America of Roosevelt was looked to, not as the arch capitalist country, but as a great progressive force which might redress the reactionary balance of the Old World'.[24] American entry into the Second World War in 1941 further enhanced FDR's reputation, as well as that of other New Dealers such as Henry Wallace, whose *Century of the Common Man* found its way on to an official Labour reading list on socialism. While Roosevelt's death in 1944 was seen as a great blow to the cause of progress, his New Deal cast a long shadow, being cited as evidence, nearly twenty years later, that the United States was not irredeemably hostile to Labour's kind of progress.[25]

When Labour came to power in 1945, it was widely expected that the new government would pursue a foreign policy independent of both the Russians and Americans. The party's formal position was one of scrupulous impartiality.[26] Indeed, Bevin's and Attlee's initial assessment was that Labour Britain stood between the US and USSR in a number of ways. Whereas it held a common conception of political freedom with the former, there remained numerous differences over economics. In contrast, while sharing a similar view of the need for state control over the economy with the latter, Labour was critical of the Soviet conception of democracy.[27] The hope was that, by standing between the two powers, Labour could 'weld together these different approaches and different conceptions into a world organisation to prevent aggression'.[28] Indeed, G.D.H. Cole thought that only by reconciling American capitalism with Soviet communism could a future world war be averted.[29]

The Labour left's view of international relations was broadly similar to that of the leadership. In 1943 Aneurin Bevan called for the party to establish links with other continental socialists to form a 'Third Force' which would be independent of the two major powers.[30] In 1946 about one-third of the Parliamentary Labour Party supported this independent strategy, including unlikely figures such as James Callaghan.[31] The Soviet-inspired Czechoslovak coup caused many to reassess this strategy. In light of such Russian expansionism, most of the Tribunite left at least saw a defensive alliance with the US as a sensible policy. Indeed, during the late 1940s the Americans were viewed in unprecedentedly positive terms by this section of the party.[32]

The leadership's road to an American alliance was similar to that of the left. While Bevin was accused by one 1946 conference delegate as proposing that 'the U.S.A. was everything that was good in the world', this was a distortion of the true situation. It was a faint echo of Denis Healey's earlier intervention at Labour's 1945 conference, that the party should encourage socialist revolution in Europe, that Bevin implicitly supported the Third Force view with his comment, 'Left understands Left'.[33] Indeed, during his initial period in office, Bevin's attitude to the US and USSR was, according to Alan Bullock: 'a plague on both your houses'. Bevin mistrusted the Americans, considering them capable of concluding an agreement with the Russians without any reference to British interests.[34] The Americans, were, moreover, deeply resented over their abrupt termination of Lend-Lease and the consequent necessity of obtaining a loan with its debilitating conditions. As Minister of Fuel, Hugh Gaitskell complained, after being forced to entertain the chair of the Congress Appropriations Sub-Committee: 'It is pretty intolerable to accept patronising comments from people who are quite so odious.'[35] Even more annoyingly, the US was not averse to attacking Bevin's Palestine policy, while it freely encroached on Britain's interests elsewhere in the world.[36]

The Labour leadership changed its position due to an appreciation that Britain could not stand alone in the face of the widely perceived Soviet threat. If the United States reverted to isolationism, Britain would be left to stand alone: the government had no option but to abandon any pretence at neutrality to try and prevent this.[37] In Cards on the Table, published in 1947, Healey, now Labour's International Secretary, described hopes for a Third Force as illusory and portrayed the Russians as intent on confronting a Britain too weak to defend itself. To survive, a temporary 'understanding' with the Americans was required. In the long term, however, Labour, it was said, sought to reduce Britain's dependence on the US and return to a more independent foreign policy.[38] As Christopher Mayhew argued in 1952, if capitalism remained a threat to 'peace and freedom' in the world, 'whether we like it or not, since the war there is this new threat of Soviet Communism': this meant a new attitude to the Americans was required.[39]

By the end of Labour's time in office, therefore, Healey could write: 'Relations with the United States have become the central problem of British foreign policy.' 'Anglo-American unity', he went on, 'is indeed a condition of Britain's survival' while, for the foreseeable future, 'Britain's fundamental interest in unity with the United States will remain supreme.' Yet, the American public was unwilling to have their national interests compromised by the demands of others while the reemergence of Japan and Germany diminished Britain's bargaining power.[40] This meant that 'Britain's influence with the United States will depend largely on her military contribution and on her loyalty to promises already made.'[41] The cost would, then, be heavy, if Britain was to remain a respected, if subordinate, partner.

As he was later to recall, Healey considered that, while it was difficult to live with the Americans, it was impossible to exist without them: this was a very practical Atlanticism.[42] So far as other revisionists were concerned, for the remainder of the Cold War, this pragmatism defined their attitude to the US. Moreover, while they were advocates of the American alliance, they were conscious of its dangers. It was the resolutely right-wing figure of George Brown who feared that Britain in the 1960s was in danger of becoming a mere vassal of the US.[43] Two decades later, another ex-Labour Foreign Secretary, David Owen, considered that Britain required its own nuclear deterrent, if only to remain independent of changes in fickle American policy.[44]

With the outbreak of the Korean war and the rise of McCarthyism, the Labour left reverted *en masse* to its interwar mistrust of the US government. By the early 1950s, it became commonplace within the party to think of the Americans as at least as much of a threat to world peace as the Russians.[45] The revisionists followed the leadership in arguing that this was not the case. Yet, the 1950s were not a good time to be a friend of the American alliance: revisionists found themselves criticising President Eisenhower's foreign policy, which they thought gave credibility to those who espoused anti-Americanism. Secretary of State John Foster Dulles' 'Holy War' was seen as increasing the chances of nuclear war.[46] Despite what Healey described as the 'autocratic tactlessness' of the US at this time, as well as their leaders' 'pharisaism softened only by laziness', the alliance had to be maintained: it remained the best on offer.[47]

The revisionist case for the American alliance was threefold. First, Jenkins among others argued that the United States was not an 'imperialist' power in the classic Marxist sense; in fact, it flouted the laws of Marx. American foreign policy was not motivated by the necessity to find markets to which its capital surplus could be exported: domestic demand was high and gave investors a good rate of return.[48] The revisionist journal *Socialist Commentary* argued that, while Marshall Aid was supported by some business leaders, others opposed it, wanting to return to isolation. In contrast it was 'the American workers' movement which has been the staunchest protagonist of the flow of American capital abroad'.[49] As Bevin assured Labour's 1950 conference, the United States could never be an aggressor as the American labour movement 'would bring down any Government which set out on such a path'. In any case, within the State Department, the 'flower of liberal and progressive thought' had found a privileged place.[50] Healey went further, stating two years later that it was not 'Wall Street that has run America's foreign policy since the war. It has been backed by the 15 million organised workers in the American Labour Movement, and they are our blood brothers.'[51]

Secondly, revisionists believed that the United States was open to the influence of its confederates – in stark contrast to the Soviet Union.[52] Indeed, while Labour was in power it was believed that due to its 'great prestige' across the Atlantic it could decisively influence American public opinion in a more liberal direction both in terms of domestic and foreign policy.[53]

Finally, as *Socialist Commentary* noted, wherever the 'Russian-controlled world expands, democratic socialism and all the values for which it stands are doomed to perish, whilst present-day American capitalism, however deep our misgivings about it, at least leaves room for free institutions to flower and survive.'[54] Consequently, it was asserted, socialists 'have an even keener concern for maintaining the free world than have British Tories or Americans of any party' because they were 'aware that if the Iron Curtain should move further outwards in Asia, the new progressive movements there, now struggling to find their feet, would be the immediate victims. Democratic socialism is a tender growth demanding, above all, conditions of political freedom'.[55]

It needs to be emphasised that when revisionists spoke of America they meant 'Liberal America' or what the MP Fred Peart described as the 'good America'. This America encompassed New Deal and Fair Deal Democrats, friendly academics, the State Department under Dean Acheson and the AFL-CIO.[56] Those with whom social democrats established friendships consisted mainly of radical Democrats: Adlai Stevenson's aides, advisers close to Hubert Humphrey and progressive figures such as J.K. Galbraith and Robert Schlesinger.[57] As *Socialist Commentary* made clear in 1946, liberalism was thought to enjoy a unique hold on Americans, something which gave them a contempt for class and other forms of privilege. It also ensured that administrations 'pledged to preserve equality and liberty and administer justice for all' were the rule rather than the exception. Moreover, it was believed, this liberalism was assuming a social democratic form, familiar to those in Britain.[58] Thus, while a minister, Gaitskell thought he shared the same fundamental economic outlook with his American counterparts.[59]

During the later 1940s and early 1950s, some in the party even believed that the United States was evolving in the direction mapped out by Attlee's postwar government. As late as 1956, Bernard Crick remarked that British socialists found 'it hard not to think of the typical Northern Democrat as an arrested or chronically discreet British socialist'.[60] One of the reasons Jenkins gave for his preference for the United States over the Soviet Union was that the former held the possibility of moving towards welfare socialism; the latter did not.[61] He was not alone. Harry Truman's 1948 presidential victory seemingly confirmed America's march towards a welfare state: the Fair Deal was described by Crossman as a type of democratic socialism.[62] As Bevin had told the 1946 Labour conference: 'America may be a capitalist country. That does not mean she always will be. There are great forces moving in the United States, and when they move they move very quickly.' The Fabian MP John Parker suggested that as the Democrats under Truman shed some of their more radical New Dealers, the chances of an alliance between left-inclined intellectuals and trade unions, along Labour lines, increased.[63] Harold Laski in 1950 certainly considered an American Labour Party was close at hand.[64]

At this time, according to Peart at least, there was a 'growing consciousness amongst American trade unionists of the need to follow the path of social democracy'.[65] The significance of unions was seen as an important point in America's favour. As the social democratic weekly *Forward* noted in 1956: 'unionism plainly constitutes an important force in American life. Indirectly this influence undoubtedly extends beyond the area of union organisation and collective bargaining.'[66] Presumably this influence was thought to extend into politics where, as Patrick Gordon Walker noted, in Michigan the Democratic Party was organised in much the same way as Labour, 'except that Trade Unions support it instead of being in it'.[67]

Due to their view of the United States as inherently liberal, revisionists considered the country's racial problems, much to the fore at this time, could be solved. Firstly, some believed that matters were not as bad as certain critics made out. As Wyatt made clear during his Smith–Mundt visit, 'I went to the South fearful of what I might find. I left encouraged and with something to say in reply to the people who would use the

Negro and his problems to prove a prejudiced case out of preconceived facts.' Secondly, there was, in any case, 'a great lifting process in the air as segregation was challenged.[68] It was conceded that this 'lifting process' was slow and there were occasions when to British eyes it appeared imperilled. This was especially so when, in 1956 a black student was physically prevented from attending a college in Alabama. At this point, Douglas Jay reminded *Forward* readers that a 'very strong, representative and growing body of liberal opinion in the United States is fighting – and gradually winning – the battle of the Negroes for full civil rights'.[69] Indeed, *Socialist Commentary* went so far as to list all nineteen landmarks which showed the extent to which American liberals had fought to end racial discrimination since the abolition of slavery.[70]

Labour's revisionists, then, had a partial and highly partisan view of American domestic politics. *Forward* published numerous complementary profiles of leading liberal Democrats. In 1956 Adlai Stevenson was described as 'a man of exceptionally high intelligence, sincere "liberal" views in the best sense, and a rare breadth of vision and toleration on world problems'. In contrast President Eisenhower, and his Vice-President Richard Nixon especially, were subject to much criticism.[71] The Republicans, described by Douglas Jay as working in 'the reactionaries' and millionaire interests', were seen as the implacable enemy of progress.[72] Any sign of their advance was viewed with trepidation: Labour's object was to give as much help to the Democrats as possible. Yet, with the fall of China and the outbreak of the Korean war, Republican fortunes improved, raising the fear that America would become isolationist or at least shift resources from defending the West to the East. Callaghan claimed he supported the Labour government's deeply unpopular rearmament programme so as to forestall such moves.[73]

The advent of McCarthyism was of obvious concern: its proposed victims were among Labour's closest friends. At first, McCarthy's significance was downplayed: while the US had the Senator from Wisconsin, Britain, it was suggested, had to endure Lord Beaverbrook.[74] Some comforted themselves with the thought that, just as the Americans lived through the Red Scare of the 1920s, they would pass through McCarthyism.[75] Nonetheless, even when Stevenson failed to beat Eisenhower on the second time of asking, *Forward* attempted to make the best of it, stating that the 1956 Congressional elections proved 'conclusively that the majority of US electors are still basically behind the Democratic Party as likely to produce the social and economic reforms that are wanted'. America was still 'good'; remained 'liberal'; and might still resume the road toward a form of social democracy.[76] Despite the resurgence of the Republican right, the revisionist vision of America, therefore, remained positive. Yet social democrats were uncertain of the extent to which the US could be seen as an archetype for British development. While viewing America as, in Francis Williams' phrase the 'benevolent eagle', they did not consider that all of the eagle's attributes should be imitated.[77]

For the most part, initial observers were struck by the two countries' similarities: this was certainly the view of Jay and Evan Durbin in the late 1930s. Both were 'traditional and stable democracies' among that small group of countries which could be described as 'civilised'. In adhering to *laissez-faire* capitalism they were distinct from Nazi Germany and Soviet Russia. Britain and the United States were, however, making a similar journey towards a more controlled economy, in terms of state intervention and private monopoly.[78] After the war, Jay continued to view the US and Britain as possessing analogous economies. Both were examples of the 'Social-Democratic State' which limited *laissez-faire* and increased social justice through combining progressive taxation with spending on social services. If anything, the US tax system was more progressive than Britain's.[79]

The most influential revisionist of the day was, of course, Anthony Crosland. A keen Atlanticist, much of his work appeared in *Encounter*, while in 1954 and 1960 he visited the US 'on a grant'. The former trip allowed him to pursue research which contributed to *The Future of Socialism*.[80] While the New Left critic Perry Anderson once described Sweden as Crosland's 'dreamland', it was the United States which loomed largest in Crosland's mind – or at least in the index to his greatest work.[81] Crosland echoed his less-regarded contemporaries in assuming that Britain and the US shared the same fundamental economic character: social mobility and income distribution were broadly similar. Moreover, due to the 'creeping socialism' of the New and Fair Deals, Americans had lost their faith in unrestrictive free enterprise, thereby compelling employers to accept state intervention. The centre of political gravity had shifted, as in Britain, to the left.

While careful to note that the United States was not necessarily a 'good' or 'superior' society, Crosland identified a crucial American quality which he admired and hoped would be emulated across the Atlantic. This was what he saw as the greater sense of social equality in the US which meant that, while there was an elite, there was no 'elite psychology'. The country lacked those manifestations of class difference commonplace in Britain: public schools, debutantes, Tudor mansions as well as (at least white) domestic servants. The rich were unable to preserve a 'conspicuous consumption gap' between themselves and the rest. Technology and affluence meant that all social groups could buy the same sorts of goods. Crosland cited the example of the Cadillac and Chevrolet whose differences were, he suggested, marginal and would be eradicated by the time the following year's Chevrolet model was unveiled. Even if the rich had been able to flaunt their wealth through consumption, Crosland suggested, they would only win popular disapproval. As a consequence, attitudes between the classes were less subject to deference and class consciousness; social relations were 'fluid and dynamic' whereas in Britain they were 'rigid, static'.

The roots of this happy state of affairs were traced back to the peculiarities of American history and geography. These were, of course, unique; less so was the mass affluence promoted by economic growth. Crucially, however, the most significant American attribute Crosland considered could and should be imitated in Britain was egalitarianism. He conceded that British Conservatives praised the United States for its equal opportunities. Yet, the corollary of this egalitarianism was, he argued, competitive entry into industry; an end to nepotism and favouritism; the virtual elimination of inheritance; abolition of fees in public schools; and the 'extrusion of all hereditary influences in our society'. As Conservatives opposed such reforms, they could not really want to emulate the American model. Thus, Crosland claimed, America's 'restless, egalitarian ideology' was 'much closer' to that of the British left.

One of the important consequences of the American consciousness of social equality was a 'less distinctive working-class psychology, either individually or collectively'; indeed, the American worker had been inoculated against a 'proletarian class outlook'. This meant that industrial relations enjoyed a 'much less underlying, nagging class resentment' than was evident in Britain. This did not mean unions were weaker than in Britain: indeed, the American labour movement was taken to enjoy a greater influence over management decisions. This, in turn, made the firm more efficient.[82] Workers were less hostile to profit or the idea that it was occasionally appropriate to cooperate with employers for the greater good of the firm. Crosland was not alone in noting differences between American and British unions. That the former welcomed new technology as a means of increasing wealth while the latter saw it as a threat to jobs was a revisionist commonplace.[83] As with his contemporaries, Crosland claimed that the most significant result of this weaker emphasis on the inevitability of workplace conflict was higher levels of efficiency which, in turn, led to greater affluence for the workforce. This further undermined any remaining class resentments.

According to Crosland, if Britain was to emulate American egalitarianism, consumption patterns would have to be modified; the redistribution of inherited wealth needed to proceed further; and privilege within industry had to be equalised. Perhaps the most crucial change, however, needed to occur in education. Britain's education system had to be reformed to ensure that the huge majority of the population would share the same educational experience. Crosland was especially struck by the quality of American education and the lack of snobbery in schools.[84] Moreover, by expanding access to technical and higher education on the American scale, Britain would also become more economically efficient and so further encourage the development of egalitarian attitudes.[85]

Crosland's view of the United States was largely based on work done in the middle 1950s. By the early 1960s, the cold war had thawed to such an extent that some revisionists considered the emergence of a more liberal Russia likely. Others thought the command economies of titans such as Bulgaria held the key to future development.[86] Also at this time, some revisionists began to focus their attention on the Common Market and called for Britain to join the Six. While this case was argued in geopolitical terms, there was a simultaneous, and hardly coincidental, emphasis on the extent to which the United States was immutably different to Britain and possibly more dystopian than previously imagined.

In 1960 *Socialist Commentary* argued that Britain's resources were now insufficient to enable it to exert much influence over the US. The balance in the partnership was shifting. 'In a number of respects' it stated, 'our relationship with the US is now less close than that of other European countries.' Britain had to look after itself, especially as nuclear technology and a reorientation in US policy to the Far East might leave the country isolated if it did not enter the Common Market.[87] Healey also noted that the new economic strength of the Six gave them a much stronger bargaining position with the US.[88] This point was developed by Marquand. He thought the postwar revival of western Europe had created a widening gulf between the Six and the US, one which was bound to end American predominance over the rest of the Atlantic world. This shift in power would, he considered, destabilise Britain due to its unique position between the two as 'the only true Atlantic power in existence'. The basic reason for the gulf, Marquand argued, anticipating his later position, lay 'partly because the interests of Western Europe differ, in a number of ways, from those of the United States, and partly because most of Western Europe has a profoundly different political and cultural inheritance from that of the United States'. In such circumstances, he argued, Britain needed to bridge that gulf by joining the Common Market, albeit on terms which did no harm to Atlantic unity.[89]

This shift of emphasis was accompanied by a greater stress on the irreducible distinctiveness of the United States. This sense of difference had always existed, but by the early 1960s, it was increasingly emphasised. Thus, in 1956 *Forward* started what it hoped would be a debate on 'conformity' in the US by publishing an article by a British teacher in a small American town. This described the extent to which those who did not spend their evenings watching TV, had even vaguely liberal ideas and did not attend church on Sundays were considered odd by their neighbours.[90] Despite the editor's hopes, however, his readers did not respond. In 1964 *Socialist Commentary* went further and published an article which castigated the US for its high levels of poverty which induced 'the menace of a whole class being separated from the mainstream of successful American society'. Individualism had dissolved the complex ties of obligation which held society together: all relationships had been commercialised. The Roosevelt years had long gone; in fact, the 'liberals, the progressives, and the left generally, in abandoning any attempt at a general critique of American society have betrayed not only themselves, but America. They have left America bereft of any consistent set of indigenous principles as an alternative to the dominant individualism as a basis for social action. "The Left" in America has been overawed by "affluence".' With little hope of a change in direction, America showed 'every sign of becoming, not the standard bearer of a free individualist society, but a new type of feudalist, class society, masquerading under the banner of enlightenment'.[91]

In conclusion, it is clear that Labour's revisionists, while supporting the Atlantic alliance, did not idealise the arrangement; nor did they view the United States in unqualified utopian terms. Social democrats looked, undoubtedly helped by CIA fronts in this search, for what they took to be the best from the other side of the Atlantic. In so doing they, to some extent, created an America of their own imagining. Seeing what they wanted to, during the middle 1950s especially, they used this distorted picture as a means of judging Britain's and Labour's progress in the postwar world. For some, this was close to a rhetorical tactic, one intended to cajole sceptics to support certain changes; others probably actually believed that the 'good America' *was* America.

Yet, while unique in their optimism, whether real or exaggerated, revisionists also held a number of reservations about the United States. It might be thought that, in the context of a Manichean world conflict such as the cold war, the extent to which they freely aired their criticisms of Britain's dominant ally was surprising. What is clear, however, is – as the cold war thawed and Britain's position degenerated – the alacrity with which certain younger social democrats especially turned to Europe and away from the US. Yet, as Hugh Gaitskell's 1962 Labour conference speech indicated, by no means all revisionists saw Europe as a panacea. Taken as a whole, even in the early 1960s, Labour's social democrats were Americans first and Europeans second. In this, it might be said, they share something with the majority of their New Labour counterparts.

Notes

Place of publication is London unless otherwise stated.

1 D. Marquand, 'The Blair paradox', *Prospect*, May 1998, p. 20.
2 D. Marquand, *The New Reckoning* (Cambridge, 1997).
3 D. Marquand, *The Progressive Dilemma* (1991), pp. 12–13.
4 While appreciating their distinct meaning, this chapter – reflecting contemporary usage – uses 'revisionist' interchangeably with 'social democrat'. Such terms are themselves notoriously ill-defined. For present purposes, revisionists are taken to be those Labour intellectuals, leaders and followers who accepted the mixed economy as a sufficient basis for the achievement of Labour's wider purposes. See G. Foote, *The Labour Party's Political Thought* (1985), pp. 206–34.
5 A. Schlesinger, 'Attitudes towards America' in W.T. Rodgers (ed.), *Hugh Gaitskell* (1964), pp. 146–7.
6 J. Campbell, *Roy Jenkins: a Biography* (1983), p. 17.
7 R. Hattersley, *Who Goes Home? Scenes from a Political Life* (1996), p. 102.
8 F. Hirsch and R. Fletcher, *The CIA and the Labour Movement* (Nottingham, 1977).
9 R. Jenkins, *A Life at the Centre* (1991), pp. 100–1.
10 W. Wyatt, *Confessions of an Optimist* (1985), p. 187.
11 P.M. Williams (ed.), *The Diary of Hugh Gaitskell 1945–56* (1983), p. 201.
12 D. Healey, *The Time of My Life* (Harmondsworth, 1990), p. 194.
13 A. Howard, *Crossman: the Pursuit of Power* (1990), p. 101; J. Callaghan, *Time and Chance* (1987), p. 75; T. Benn, *Years of Hope: Diaries, Papers and Letters, 1940–1962*, R. Winstone (ed.), (1994), p. 111; Wyatt, *Optimist*, p. 189.
14 M. Shinwell, *Conflict Without Malice* (1955), pp. 219–20.
15 Hattersley, *Home*, p. 94; D. Owen, *Time to Declare* (Harmondsworth, 1992), p. 118.
16 Healey, *Time*, pp. 119–20.
17 *Forward*, 12 October 1956.
18 For example, R. Desai, *Intellectuals and Socialism. 'Social Democrats' and the Labour Party* (1994) and I. Crewe and A. King, *SDP: The Birth, Life and Death of the Social Democratic Party* (Oxford, 1996).

19 H. Pelling, *America and the British Left from Bright to Bevan* (1956).
20 A. Wedgwood Benn, *The Regeneration of Britain* (1965), pp. 58–61.
21 Pelling, *Left*, pp. 131–2.
22 Pelling, *Left*, pp. 133–49.
23 C. Mayhew, *Party Games* (1969), p. 53.
24 R. Jenkins, *Pursuit of Progress* (1953), p. 31.
25 R. Pearce (ed.), *Patrick Gordon Walker: Political Diaries 1932–1971* (1991), p. 133; *Forward*, 9 August 1957.
26 Labour Party, *The International Situation* (1944), p. 3.
27 C. Attlee and E. Bevin, *Britain's Foreign Policy* (1946), p. 30.
28 *Labour Party Conference Annual Report, 1945* (1945), p. 115.
29 G.D.H. Cole, *A Guide to the Elements of Socialism* (1947), p. 38.
30 M. Foot, *Aneurin Bevan: Volume 1* (1975), pp. 434–5, 437.
31 J. Schneer, *Labour's Conscience: the Labour Left, 1945–51* (1988), pp. 53, 55, 56, 61–2.
32 A. Bevan, *In Place of Fear* (1952), pp. 120–3; Howard, *Crossman*, pp. 132, 141–2; Pelling, *Left*, pp. 151–2; Schneer, *Conscience*, pp. 64–5, 69, 72, 73; Callaghan, *Time*, pp. 75–6.
33 *Labour Report*, 1945, pp. 114, 115, 119.
34 A. Bullock, *Ernest Bevin: Foreign Secretary 1945–51* (1983), pp. 194–5.
35 Williams, *Diary*, p. 40.
36 J. Parker, *Labour Marches On* (Harmondsworth, 1947), pp. 160–1.
37 H. Nicholson, 'The Labour Government's Foreign Policy', in D. Munro (ed.), *Socialism: The British Way* (1948), pp. 310–11.
38 Labour Party, *Cards on the Table* (1947).
39 *Labour Party Conference Annual Report, 1952* (1952), pp. 122–3.
40 D. Healey, 'Power Politics and the Labour Party' in R.H.S. Crossman (ed.), *New Fabian Essays* (1952, 1970 edn), pp. 176–9.
41 D. Healey, 'Defence of Western Europe', *Socialist Commentary*, October, 1951, p. 237.
42 Healey, *Time*, p. 205.
43 G. Brown, *In My Way* (Harmondsworth, 1972), pp. 201–2.
44 Owen, *Time*, p. 146.
45 Pelling, *Left*, pp. 151–2; Schneer, *Conscience*, p. 75.
46 D. Jay, *Socialism in the New Society* (1962), pp. 97–8.
47 Editorial, *Socialist Commentary*, March 1953, pp. 49–51; D. Healey, 'NATO in a Changed World', *Socialist Commentary*, May 1961, p. 11.
48 Jenkins, *Progress*, pp. 39–41; *Socialist Commentary*, November 1950, p. 13; Editorial, *Socialist Commentary*, April 1952, pp. 73–5.
49 *Socialist Commentary*, November 1950, p. 13 & December 1950, p. 265.
50 *Labour Party Conference Annual Report, 1946* (1946), p. 168.
51 *Labour Party Conference Annual Report, 1950* (1950), p. 146; *Labour Conference Report, 1952*, p. 123.
52 Jenkins, *Progress*, pp. 41–2.
53 K. Martin, 'The Visit of Henry Wallace', in H. Wallace, *Speeches in Britain* (1947), p. 6; *Socialist Commentary*, February 1950, pp. 25, 36.
54 Editorial, *Socialist Commentary*, August, 1950, p. 181.
55 Editorial, *Socialist Commentary*, March 1953, pp. 49–51.
56 *Labour Conference Report, 1950*, p. 144.

57 Healey, *Time*, p. 122–3; Jenkins, *Centre*, pp. 100–1.

58 Anonymous, 'The American Liberal', *Socialist Commentary*, April 1947, pp. 611–15; S. Williams, *Politics is for People* (1981), p. 21.

59 Williams, *Diary*, pp. 190–1.

60 B. Crick, 'All Liberals Now', *Socialist Commentary*, December 1956, pp. 23–4.

61 Jenkins, *Progress*, pp. 38–9.

62 Schneer, *Conscience*, p. 72.

63 Parker, *Labour*, pp. 164–5; *Labour Conference Report, 1946*, p. 168.

64 Pelling, *Left*, p. 159.

65 *Labour Conference Report, 1950*, pp. 144–5.

66 H.M. Doughty, 'How Unions in U.S. Have Grown', *Forward*, 25 August 1956.

67 Pearce, *Political Diaries*, p. 255.

68 *Forward*, 2 May 1953.

69 *Forward*, 18 February 1956.

70 *Socialist Commentary*, March 1956, p. 10.

71 *Forward*, 16 June 1956.

72 *Forward*, 14 September 1956.

73 Callaghan, *Time*, pp. 107–9.

74 Labour Research Department, *Speakers' Handbook, 1949–50* (1949), p. 415; Labour Research Department, *Facts and Figures for Socialists, 1951* (1951), pp. 386–9.

75 A. Fox, 'A Tale without a Moral', *Socialist Commentary*, November 1953, p. 268.

76 *Forward*, 16 November 1956.

77 F. Williams, *The American Invasion* (1962), pp. 11–15.

78 D. Jay, *The Socialist Case* (1937, 1945 edn.) pp. 45–7, 107–8, 136, 177; E. Durbin, *The Politics of Democratic Socialism* (1940, 1965 ed.) pp. 23, 77, 82, 87, 96, 98–100, 113, 123–4.

79 Jay, *Socialism*, pp. 11–13, 24, 52, 199–200.

80 S. Crosland, *Tony Crosland* (1982), pp. 66, 111.

81 This section is based on, C.A.R. Crosland, *The Future of Socialism* (1956), pp. 201–2, 218–19, 223–5, 233, 249–56, 283–4, 335–6; and his notes contained in the Crosland papers, British Library of Political and Economic Science.

82 C.A.R. Crosland, *The Conservative Enemy* (1962), pp. 219–20.

83 M. Stewart, *Life and Labour* (1980), p. 95; D. Jay, 'Automation: a New Policy or Else', *Forward*, 26 May 1956.

84 US notes, Crosland papers, 4/7, BLPES.

85 Crosland, *Enemy*, p. 177.

86 Jay, *Socialism*, pp. 100–3; M. Shanks, *The Stagnant Society* (Harmondsworth, 1961).

87 Editorial, *Socialist Commentary*, June 1960, pp. 2–3.

88 D. Healey, 'NATO in a Changed World', *Socialist Commentary*, May 1961, pp. 8–11

89 D. Marquand, 'The Shape of the West', *Socialist Commentary*, October 1962, pp. 18–20.

90 *Forward*, 5 October 1956.

91 F. Pickstock, 'The Sickness of American Society', *Socialist Commentary*, April 1964, pp. 15–17.

6
'The Number One Reason': McCarthy, Eisenhower and the Decline of American Prestige in Britain, 1952–54

Jussi M. Hanhimaki

In the late summer of 1953 President Eisenhower faced a barrage of reports from his Ambassadors in Europe complaining about the sudden decline in American prestige. It was so bad, in fact, that the National Security Council meeting of 30 July 1953 witnessed a memorandum that boiled down to a simple point: 'U.S. prestige in the world is now lower than ever before.' The question was simple: why? C.D. Jackson, who was in charge of the Eisenhower administration's psychological warfare (read propaganda) campaigns, had a simple answer: 'the Number One reason for this situation is McCarthyism'.[1]

The major point of this chapter is straightforward: to claim that C.D. Jackson was correct and that most of those present at the NSC meeting – including Vice-President Richard Nixon, Secretary of State John Foster Dulles, and President Eisenhower – were too eager to dismiss the influence of McCarthyism in shaping foreign opinion about the United States. In fact, the British, for example, had for quite some time been wondering about the state of play in the United States and the new President's ability to conduct an effective foreign policy. They had had high expectations for Eisenhower, who had played such an instrumental role in the Allied victory in 1945 and in shaping NATO as its first Supreme Commander (SACEUR) in 1950–52. Undoubtedly, a man of Eisenhower's stature would eat a rogue like Joe McCarthy for breakfast.

But he did not. In the first six months of the Eisenhower administration, Joe McCarthy repeatedly made mockery of the executive branch. Not only did he push ahead with the investigations of the State Department and its various branches and oppose several of the President's

104

ambassadorial choices, but McCarthy tried to make both the CIA and the Army subjects of his vigilant 'exposures'. In fact, even his eventual fall from grace in the fall of 1954 had seemingly very little to do with Eisenhower, who refused to criticise the Wisconsin Senator in public.

While McCarthyism was much more than the story of Joe McCarthy's career, I have chosen to focus on him – or views about him – simply because he did, in the early 1950s, manage to command the attention of the nation and, indeed, much of the rest of the world in a way no other 'McCarthyite' could. The anticommunist crusade that he embodied had begun with the search for traitors in the State Department during the late 1940s, but soon extended to Hollywood, higher education, the Defense Department and the Army.[2]

In all the books and articles about McCarthy and McCarthyism, however, relatively little has been said about the reaction to McCarthyism abroad. The impact of McCarthyism among allied countries has been particularly neglected. For example, in the only article on the British reaction, John P. Rossi merely concludes that while McCarthy 'caused the greatest strain in Anglo-American relations of any incident' after the Second World War, the British tended to overestimate McCarthy's influence.[3] While this was, in all likelihood, part of the story – comparing McCarthy to Hitler as some British journals did was surely an exaggeration – the 'bigger' story was the sour impact that McCarthyism had on the Atlantic partnership between London and Washington. By strengthening the longstanding image of an 'irrational' and 'immature' America, and by raising questions about the ability of the White House to conduct an effective foreign policy, McCarthyism served to undermine the trust – not only in Britain but elsewhere in Europe – in the leadership abilities of the Eisenhower administration as the cold war entered a new phase following Stalin's death in March 1953.

I

Joe McCarthy's dramatic publicity stunt in February 1950 had gradually increased European concerns about the ability of the Truman administration to conduct an effective foreign policy. To be sure, McCarthy's early antics initially amused European observers, who dismissed the wild accusations as part of a Republican campaign to capitalise on the 'loss of China' in the upcoming fall 1950 Congressional elections. Indeed, some foreign observers, such as the British Ambassador to the United States, Sir Oliver Franks, thought that McCarthy's antics might even prove beneficial to the State Department. 'It is difficult to believe that the American public can take Senator McCarthy's charges seriously', Franks wrote to London. He added a colossal misjudgement: 'the State Department may benefit by the popular reaction to McCarthy's accusations'.[4]

As McCarthy survived early challenges, however, the British Ambassador became increasingly concerned. To him this irresponsible demagogue from Wisconsin was far too easily terrorising the administration that had been responsible for the launching of the Marshall Plan and the creation of NATO. Already in late March 1950 the British ambassador reported that 'the days of the "Bipartisan Foreign Policy" may well be over' because of McCarthy. Franks also revised his earlier prediction about the impact of McCarthy's charges on the State Department which had, he noted on 31 March, 'suffered from [McCarthy's] attack'. The Ambassador further explained that '[p]ublic esteem for the Department has for years been rather low and the suspicion that it is infested with left-wing sympathisers and even fellow-travellers, especially in its Far Eastern section, is a recurrent theme of its critics'. Communist victory in China, the Soviet atomic bomb and the formation of the Sino-Soviet alliance had created a fertile ground for McCarthy's wild attacks. As Franks concluded: 'The man in the street is predisposed to believe that there may well be some fire behind all the smoke pouring from Senator McCarthy's smudge-pot.'[5]

These concerns were not limited to the confines of the British Foreign Office. Much like Franks, the British press worried over what McCarthy's accusations would do to American foreign policy and the State Department. As *The Times* put it in March 1950: 'it is a matter of universal concern and disquiet that the conduct of American foreign affairs should be subjected to irresponsible political attacks'. The wildest speculations even maintained that McCarthy's clear ambition was 'to be the first Catholic President of the United States'. Few took this seriously, yet the *Economist* suggested with a not-so-veiled reference to George Orwell's book: 'he would be an ideal candidate in 1984'.[6]

In the last two years of the Truman administration the further increase in international tensions allowed Joe McCarthy to expand the scope of his attacks even beyond the United States. The outbreak of the Korean War in June 1950, moreover, gave him a convenient pretext to attack the attitude of the European allies, particularly the British, for their alleged leniency towards the USSR and the PRC. Indeed, one of the turning points regarding British perceptions about McCarthy came with President Truman's dismissal of General Douglas MacArthur in April 1951, which gave McCarthy another reason to rave and rant about the treasonous nature of the Democratic administration's policies. President Truman got his fair share of the verbal abuse when McCarthy told a reporter that: 'The son of a bitch should be impeached.' He added, however, that Truman 'is not important. It's the crowd around him that causes the trouble.'[7]

Although the chief target was usually Secretary of State Dean Acheson, this 'crowd', McCarthy seemed to believe, also included members of the British Labour government. For example, following President Truman's dismissal of MacArthur in 1951 McCarthy argued on the Senate floor that the General's dismissal – 'the greatest victory the Communists have ever won' (apparently the Russian Revolution paled in this regard)[8] – was 'done by the sinister, tentacled monster, conceived in the Kremlin, and given birth by Acheson, with Attlee and [deputy PM Herbert] Morrison as midwives'.[9]

While such attacks were upsetting in their own right, what truly caused concern in Britain was the fact that McCarthy seemed to encounter little opposition, particularly from within his own party. It was 'deplorable', the *Economist* reported on 23 June 1951, 'that no Republican has yet had the courage to repudiate [McCarthy]'. This was even more worrisome, the *Economist* warned, because '[i]n Senator McCarthy's view, the next step in the "conspiracy" is to arrange a cease-fire at the 38th parallel'.[10]

Be that as it may, the fact was that McCarthy carried an adequate amount of public support and senatorial deference to allow him to continue a programme of character assassination as the United States entered another election year. His stature thus appeared magnified beyond what any foreign observer could have envisioned back in early 1950. If not viewed as a potential dictator, he was certainly considered a man whose substantial and growing influence inside the US held serious implications for the conduct of American foreign policy and for US–European relations. 'The only cure', the *Economist* maintained in August 1951, 'is in the hands of the Wisconsin voters.'[11]

The problem was that in November 1952 the Wisconsin voters failed to deliver while McCarthy was influential in handing the White House to Eisenhower. From the British perspective the majority of the Republican party leadership, including Eisenhower, in fact seemed to believe 'that the tactics of McCarthy are necessary and fully endorsed by the [American] electorate'.[12]

That Eisenhower felt that he 'needed' McCarthy became disturbingly clear during the 1952 campaign. To be sure, there was little question of Ike's dislike of McCarthy. Still, following his advisers' suggestions,

Eisenhower agreed not to criticise McCarthy during his campaign tour in Wisconsin. Instead, the future President told a crowd in Green Bay that he shared the objective of getting rid of 'Reds' in the government, but believed that the job should be done by the executive, rather than the legislative, branch. Ike also made numerous statements that were uncomfortably similar to McCarthy's rhetoric. For example, tolerance for communism had, according to Eisenhower, 'poisoned two whole decades of our national life', the communists had made inroads 'into our government', in a way that translated into 'contamination in some degree of virtually every department, every agency, every bureau, every section of our government'.[13]

As the Republican party claimed all the prizes at the polls in early November 1952, the situation looked rather gloomy for those in Britain hoping to see a rapid end to McCarthy's mudslinging. For although he received fewer votes than in 1946, McCarthy was destined to take advantage of the seniority rule and become a head of a Senate committee charged with investigating and 'uncovering the reds' in the government.

II

From the very start of the Eisenhower administration in January 1953 it was clear that the State Department – even when headed by a Secretary of State whose rollback rhetoric left few doubts as to his anticommunist credentials – would continue to be attacked and investigated. With the help of his eager subcommittee staff, in particular his chief counsel, a 26-year-old former US attorney named Roy Cohn, McCarthy wasted no time but commenced a thorough attack on various government organs, with investigations into the Voice of America, the State Department's information centres around the world, the Government Printing Office, and the United Nations following each other in short order in the spring of 1953. He also challenged – or threatened to oppose – a number of Eisenhower's early appointments, including James B. Conant as High Commissioner to West Germany and Charles 'Chip' Bohlen as Ambassador to the USSR.[14]

Although the administration stood its ground on these key appointments, the most important factor in shaping foreign perceptions and concerns about McCarthy's influence was, however, Eisenhower's and Dulles's meek response to McCarthy's antics. While the President, on the one hand, did not ignore the Senator, he refused to acknowledge him in public and instead chose to work behind the scenes. On the other hand, in 1953 Dulles appeared almost willing to cooperate with the Senator in purging the State Department. And while both the President and the Secretary of State were keen on preventing McCarthy from exercising excessive influence over the affairs of the executive branch, they were equally unwilling to risk an open confrontation that might tear the Republican Party apart soon after its historic victories in November 1952.

For example, when McCarthy charged that a number of USIS libraries abroad harboured books by 'communist authors' Dulles tried a pre-emptive strike. On 17 March 1953 the new Secretary of State directed various embassies to remove from their shelves books by 'communist authors, fellow travellers, etc.' While this directive was meant to avoid too much congressional meddling in the affairs of Dulles's new empire, its implementation could only have resulted in ridicule from abroad.

In the spring of 1953 this hunt extended to Europe in the form of the infamous Cohn–Schine mission of April 1953. During their whirlwind tour that lasted about a fortnight, these two young McCarthy aides searched a number of USIS libraries in Europe, in order to verify whether they still harboured 'un-American' (or 'communistic') books. The trip that took Roy Cohn and David Schine to Paris, Frankfurt, Berlin, Bonn, Munich, Vienna and Belgrade invited much ridicule from the local press at each stop.[15]

The last stop of the Cohn–Schine mission, London, was probably the worst for the dynamic duo. The British press was adequately prepared for the last leg of Cohn and Schine's trip. During a press conference reporters chanted 'Positively Mr. Cohn! Absolutely Mr. Schine!' and *The Times* described the two men's tour as an indication that McCarthy was no longer a pure concern for American domestic politics, but 'the direct concern for the United States' allies'. As *The Times* maintained:

> The recent grotesque voyage through Europe of the Senator's two lieutenants, Mr. Cohn and Mr. Schine, provided Europeans with a living example of those qualities of rashness and intolerance which the Communist claim as characteristic of the Administration as a whole. . . . McCarthy has gone a long way to hamstring American propaganda and to make American representatives abroad so cautious in their behaviour that their usefulness is seriously weakened. These are achievements which other countries cannot ignore.

Perhaps more significantly, the article argued that 'Senator McCarthy has set up a challenge to President Eisenhower's Administration which cannot be evaded indefinitely.'[16]

Indeed, a number of questions bothered British observers in 1953 and 1954. Why was President Eisenhower allowing something like this, something that so clearly hurt American prestige, to happen? Why did Secretary of State Dulles allow Cohn and Schine, let alone McCarthy, to terrorise his employees?

A large part of the answer was that in the first half of 1953 the Senator from Wisconsin was at the height of his powers, while Eisenhower did not want to pick a fight with a prominent member of his own party. In Dulles's case, as well as in the case of many members of the administration including Vice President Nixon, some of the effects of McCarthyism were not all that bad. After all, the Republicans had an axe to grind with a State Department run mostly by Democratic appointees.

Viewed from Britain, however, such inaction against McCarthy appeared to be a simple case of cowardice. Some enterprising journalists began making comparisons between Eisenhower (McCarthy) and Hindenburg (Hitler). Yet, more disturbing for the British – as well as for the Eisenhower administration – was the impact that McCarthy seemed to yield over US foreign policy at a crucial time in international relations. This was particularly evident in Anglo-American relations during Eisenhower's first year in office.

III

One of those who felt shunned by McCarthyism was British Prime Minister Winston Churchill. The man who had led Britain through the turmoil of the Second World War and who had in March 1946 coined the term Iron Curtain in a speech delivered at Fulton, Missouri, turned out to be somewhat of a peacemonger during his second premiership. The man who could never be described as soft on communism wanted to, in fact, 'bridge the gulf between the two worlds, so that each can live their life if not in friendship, at least without the hatreds of the Cold War'.[17] The opportunity to push ahead with such an agenda, overtly ambitious though it may have been in retrospect, came after 5 March 1953.

Stalin's death on that day and the speech by Georgi Malenkov ten days later signalled an apparent Soviet interest in, at the minimum, a thaw in East–West relations that could, in turn, act as a building bloc of a permanent détente. True to his words, the British premier had already on 11 March written to Eisenhower about the need to take advantage of Stalin's death in order to improve Western relations with the USSR. After Malenkov's speech he continued to press Eisenhower, referring to the new Soviet leadership's overtures as 'a new hope in the unhappy, bewildered world'.[18] Eisenhower's 'Chance for Peace' speech in mid-April, however, did little to satisfy Churchill's drive for quick action. In 1953 he was, after all, the quintessential 'old man in a hurry'.

Thus, on 11 May 1953 the Prime Minister took matters into his own hands. In a speech to the House of Commons, Churchill called for a summit 'between the leading powers without long delay' and any preconditions. Churchill thus made his bid for the coveted position of a peacemaker. While acknowledging that 'no hard-faced agreements [were likely] to be reached', Churchill insisted that even 'a general feeling [that] those gathered might do something better than tear the human race into bits' made such a summit worthwhile.[19]

Nothing came of Churchill's plans. Indeed, the Prime Minister managed to upset his counterparts in Washington by acting in such a unilateral manner at a time when Washington 'needed' the Soviet threat to justify its support for the plans for German rearmament and the European Defence Community. Eisenhower himself apparently paid little attention to Churchill's call for a summit and maintained his line of demanding of the Soviets 'deeds not words' before any substantial steps towards a détente could be taken. At the top of the list of needed 'deeds' was, not unexpectedly, movement in the deadlocked negotiations over ending the Korean War. Yet, even as the armistice was concluded in June 1953, other events, such as the uprisings in East Germany the same month as well as the American argument that the Soviet 'peace offensive' indicated no change in ultimate Soviet goals of world domination, kept the Eisenhower administration cool to Churchill's unsolicited proposal. In a late olive branch offered to the Prime Minister, the Americans suggested tripartite preliminary talks between Americans, British and French in order to coordinate Western strategy.

The lower house of the British Parliament heard another important speech in May 1953. A day after Churchill had called for an early four-power summit, former Prime Minister and Labour leader Clement Attlee focused his remarks on the United States and, in particular, Senator McCarthy's antics. The opposition leader even questioned who actually was running American foreign policy, McCarthy or Eisenhower. The speech, which John Rossi calls 'tactless', provoked an angry response from McCarthy, set off a 'Hate England' campaign in the

United States, and, although neither of the main participants represented official government views, soured Anglo-American relations at a
sensitive time.[20]

If Attlee may have been somewhat tactless in his remarks, McCarthy
was downright outrageous in his. Calling the former Prime Minister
'comrade Attlee', he released a picture of Attlee receiving a communist
salute during the Spanish civil war. If this was not enough to prove that
the Labour leader was, at best, a fellow traveller, McCarthy also used the
opportunity to attack the British government's trade with China.
Despite evidence to the contrary, McCarthy argued that Great Britain
was clearly contributing to the PRC's war-making potential.[21]

While McCarthy's charges themselves were not taken too seriously,
the issue of trade with China did provide further fuel for European,
particularly British, concern that McCarthy was amassing too much
of a role in the conduct of American foreign affairs. McCarthy's sub-
committee had investigated, since mid-March 1953, the trade between
communist and non-communist countries. But McCarthy had not been
content simply to investigate. On 28 March 1953 he announced at a
press conference (with one of his aides, Bobby Kennedy, at his side) that
he had recently negotiated a deal with Greek shipowners to stop their
deliveries to Chinese and Soviet ports. McCarthy said that he had done
the deal privately so as to avoid any 'interference' and that there was no
reason why the President and the Secretary of State would not be excited
about the positive impact of such 'backchannel' negotiations.

What followed was a series of charges, accusations and, eventually, a
truce between Dulles and McCarthy. The Secretary of State agreed to
acknowledge that McCarthy had acted in 'the national interest', while
the Wisconsin Senator promised that 'if in the future any group of
shippers agrees to withdraw from the China trade, we will report it to
the Secretary'. At the same time Eisenhower, who was privately furious
at McCarthy, refused to publicly criticise him. The administration's
silence was further noticed when McCarthy announced a few weeks
later that he had made yet another agreement with Greek shipowners;
this time they were based in London.[22]

For the British this sort of 'lone ranger' mentality in foreign affairs
was most disturbing because McCarthy got away with it without a
serious reprimand from the president. Indeed, when Harold Stassen,
the Mutual Security Director, criticised McCarthy for 'undermining'
the Eisenhower administration's own efforts, the President – who
excelled in confusing semantics – soon argued in a press conference
that Stassen had meant 'infringed'; a point Stassen quickly conceded.[23]

Based on that exchange, as well as Eisenhower and Dulles's clear and continuing reluctance to criticise McCarthy directly, the British Ambassador to the US, Roger Makins, worried that Ike's 'current policy of conciliation and his determination to avoid open conflict [will] lead to an abdication of leadership and the emasculation of [Eisenhower's] legislative program'.[24]

Throughout the summer of 1953 McCarthy continued to criticise US allies, particularly Great Britain, with vehemence. In a speech to the Marine Corps League in Cleveland, Ohio in August 1953, for example, McCarthy argued that the British had been stepping up their shipments to China. McCarthy further lamented that the British non-compliance with the American trade embargo on China was 'the sort of thing which makes it easier to understand the statement made by that great American – no longer with us – Bob Taft, when he said that we might ultimately have to "go it alone".... We do not want allies who cringe and surrender in the face of an enemy threat, or lick the boots of the enemy and give him weapons of war.'[25]

With statements like this, McCarthy managed to cause severe damage to the Anglo-American relationship. In the spring and summer of 1953, American prestige in Britain was at a postwar low as McCarthy continued to practise his own foreign policy, publicly insult the Labour leader and a former Prime Minister, and attack the British government's trading practices with the PRC. If this was not enough, Eisenhower – who had coordinated the final assault against Nazi Germany, led NATO, and had been elected president the previous year – was either unwilling or unable to do anything to minimise McCarthy's influence. The fact that this coincided with the apparent American lack of interest in Soviet (and British) calls for a three-power summit and a relaxation of international tensions following Stalin's death in March 1953, only added to the belief in Europe that McCarthyism had a stranglehold on US foreign policy and that there would be no room for improvement in East–West relations until McCarthy's power was minimised. It was not a view that Eisenhower and his aides could easily stomach.

III

Although Secretary of State Dulles may have declared at one point that '[i]f I so much as took into account what people in other countries are thinking or feeling, I would be derelict in my duty',[26] in the summer of 1953 the Eisenhower administration was compelled to take such concerns rather seriously. At an NSC meeting on 9 July 1953, Ike said that he was much disturbed and concerned that so many of our allies seemed frightened of what they imagine the United Sates government is up to. It is a sad fact, said the President, that every returning traveller whom he talked to stated that the people of Europe were vastly confused about the objectives and programs of the Republican administration. The name of McCarthy was on everyone's lips and he was constantly compared to Adolf Hitler.[27]

After some discussion, the NSC decided that further study was needed. A few days later Secretary of State Dulles sent a circular telegram to the US embassies in 11 NATO countries, Austria and West Germany, asking for a 'frank confidential estimate and views on how the US is regarded both by government and public'. Among the specific questions Dulles wanted an answer to was the following: 'Have US domestic political events influenced [Allied] attitude[s] toward US leadership?'[28]

The answers poured in within a few weeks and confirmed Dulles's – and others' – worst fears. The first to respond was John O. Bell, the US Ambassador to Denmark, who wrote that 'the Danish people consider [McCarthyism] symptomatic of the uncertainty and unpredictability of the United States'. Bell concluded his telegram by advising that the best way of improving American prestige in Denmark and, he assumed, in Europe in general, was 'a concrete and effective demonstration by the Administration that its policies were not determined by and could not be controlled by Senator McCarthy or "McCarthyism"'.[29] On 12 August 1953 Ambassador Winthrop Aldrich from London wrote in much the same vein that McCarthyism had 'raised doubts as to the integrity of our institutions, the strength of our democracy and our reliability as Free World leaders'.[30]

These were tough words that tell a great deal about the perception that American ambassadors abroad had about McCarthy and his attacks on the State Department. Yet, they also reflected a growing concern about the impact that the junior Senator from Wisconsin had on the allied perception about the United States' and Eisenhower's ability to lead the free world effectively. Hence, McCarthy was making the job of a number of US ambassadors more difficult than before, as they were forced to answer pointed questions about the health of American democracy.

The problem was eventually summarised for the NSC on 11 September 1953 in a 'Prestige Report' by the Psychological Strategy Board (PSB). It noted that 'with all their liking for Eisenhower as a man and as a military leader in war or peace, many Europeans distrusted the

Republican party among other things for the past isolationist tendencies of certain of its leaders'. The PSB maintained that: ' "McCarthyism" is used to justify much of [the Europeans'] dislike and distrust of the United States. Rightly or wrongly many articulate Europeans point to the possibility that the McCarthy philosophy may become dominant in the United States.' What was bound to drive President Eisenhower mad was the assertion that 'Since to many Europeans McCarthy is a symbol entirely incompatible with their image of President Eisenhower, they profess to be particularly bewildered at the apparent deferential treatment McCarthy has received from the administration.'[31]

The inevitable conclusion of all this was that together with latent anti-Americanism, a general resistance to being dominated by and dependent upon a country usually considered as 'politically immature in international affairs', and the Soviet 'peace offensive', 'it is possible that "McCarthyism" will alienate a vital segment of European public opinion and thereby diminish the prospects of maintaining middle-of-the-road coalition governments sympathetic to American objectives and interests'.[32] If that was the problem, the solution to it was also crystal clear. What one should strive for was:

> The achievement of a standard of behaviour in domestic political affairs which would enable the United States to stand forth clearly as an example of political comportment to be respected and imitated by other countries. In particular, this would involve *a convincing demonstration that the philosophy of 'McCarthyism' is not typical of American thinking, governmental or public.*[33]

IV

In 1953 and 1954 such demonstration was slow in coming, however, because the President himself, justifiably or not, took the reports about European reactions to McCarthyism with a bit more than just a pinch of salt. At an NSC meeting on 1 October 1953, Eisenhower in fact came as close as he would to backing up the clean-up of the State Department from potential subversives. As the record indicates:

> [Ike] said that he had nearly blown his top when he first read this report. It was obvious to him that many of the individuals overseas who had sent in the views out of which the report had been made, had only been appointed to their jobs when they thought that the

only way to assure the prestige of the United States overseas was to hand out money. Many of them were New Dealers with the result that the report was badly overdrawn and colored.

In closing, Ike said that 'it might be possible in some fashion to send to these various foreign countries observers who were really loyal to the new Administration to find out what is going on overseas. It would be very helpful to find out who are the traitors in these various missions.'[34]

This was about as close as Eisenhower himself ever came to actually supporting the goals, if not the methods, of McCarthyism. The difference of course was that while Eisenhower wanted the executive branch to be in charge, McCarthy wanted to do the housecleaning in public view by using the legislature and hence enhancing his position as the chief investigator. In late 1953 both men had the same goal at least as far as the State Department was concerned: get rid of the 'New Dealers'. One can thus easily speculate that it was in part as a result of this antipathy towards the State Department that Eisenhower refused to publicly denounce the Senator from Wisconsin. This despite numerous warnings, growing criticism, and all the pressure – from both home and abroad. Without serious opposition from the White House, it was no wonder that according to the polls McCarthy's activities were, in late 1953, approved by 50 per cent of the American public.

To be sure, Eisenhower, Dulles and other key figures in Washington were privately fuming about McCarthy's 'lone ranger' mentality and his ability to embarrass the administration. Yet Ike had no intention to make a public break with the Wisconsin senator. Instead, he unleashed a behind-the-doors campaign against McCarthy, a campaign to undermine McCarthy's support among Republican Senators, to approach various leaders of religious organisations, and to speak out against the methods of McCarthy in public without actually mentioning the dreaded name. A famous example of the last strategy was a speech at Dartmouth College on 14 June 1953 where Eisenhower denounced 'book burners' – a reference to the campaigns in Europe as well as the extension of McCarthyism to many public libraries in the United States where books written by communists, fellow travellers, and the infamous 'etc.' were being called into question and at times pulled off the shelves.[35]

Why did Eisenhower not take McCarthy on, head to head? The President explained his rationale in a letter to Philip Reed, Chairman of General Electric, on June 17, 1953:

There is one thing to be remembered. The President of the United States has a position that gives his name a terrific headline value. Therefore, if he points his finger at any particular individual – meaning to name anyone specifically – he automatically gives to that individual an increased publicity value. This is exactly what many people are seeking and I decline to be a party to it.[36]

In other words, Ike believed that by not openly criticising McCarthy he, in fact, was undermining the Senator.

Whether the strategy was as great a success as many Eisenhower revisionists argue, it certainly did little to change the European view of McCarthyism's impact on US foreign policy. That is, while Europeans expected a show of force, Eisenhower delivered silence. While Ike may have been involved in a subtle, secret and eventually effective campaign to get rid of McCarthy, Western Europeans could only observe a President who seemed unable or unwilling to take a firm stand against a demagogue with a large following. In fact, although opinion surveys in late 1953 indicated that Eisenhower remained 'the most admired man in America' (followed by Winston Churchill), Joe McCarthy was the only new member in the 'top ten' list of this kind. At number seven, McCarthy ranked higher than the Pope![37] In the words of the British Ambassador, Sir Roger Makins, the key issue was that 'Above all, "McCarthyism," as it is interpreted abroad, is having a damaging effect on the prestige of the United States in foreign countries and particularly among its Allies.'[38]

That this was the case in Great Britain was made clear to the readers of one of the United States' most distinguished journals in early 1954. Clement Attlee's article in *Foreign Affairs* picked up his former theme, noting that not only was McCarthy way off the mark when he spoke of communism and equated the British Labour Party with it, but he had no business instructing him and his colleagues about how to fight communism. After all, '[t]he Labour Party has had nearly 40 years of fighting Communism in Britain and, despite the war and economic depression, the Communists have utterly failed. We are pardonably annoyed at being instructed by a beginner like Senator McCarthy.' In the same article Attlee also complained about the US allying itself with such 'undemocratic reactionaries as Chiang Kai-Shek, Syngman Rhee and General Franco [because] there is a danger lest there should be disregard for the fundamentals of the democratic alliance'.[39] In late February of 1954 Attlee's Deputy leader, Herbert Morrison, wondered in a speech 'whether the US is aware of what a serious liability Senator McCarthy is to America in the eyes of the world?'[40]

V

Most American officials, including President Eisenhower, were by this time well aware of the prestige problem and the calls for direct action by the White House. Ike even acknowledged this in his own diary in late February 1954, writing that McCarthy was 'grabbing the headlines and making the people believe that he is driving the administration out of Washington'.[41] At the same time, however, Eisenhower was no closer to publicly criticising McCarthy. Happily for the President, McCarthy, with his hubris in overdrive or with too much whiskey in hand, had already plunged into a disastrous confrontation with the US Army. As a result, Eisenhower did not need to do much at all to speed up McCarthy's demise as America entered another election year.

As early as the summer of 1953 McCarthy's investigators had begun to unearth some 'shocking' evidence about security risks while investigating an Army research site placed at Fort Monmouth, NJ. Although he temporarily backed away from a confrontation with the administration in late 1953 due to pressure from the White House and from his fellow Senators, McCarthy could not help his instincts and proceeded with his investigation. Thus, in early 1954 the search uncovered that an army dentist who had been identified as a security risk – he had invoked the fifth amendment when filling in the loyalty questionnaire in 1952 – had been promoted to major due to a number of mix-ups and eventually granted an honourable discharge. When General Ralph Zwicker, the commander of Camp Kilmer in New Jersey where Major Peress had served, refused to reveal any names – i.e. the identity of those who had been responsible for the promotion – McCarthy went ballistic. Although General Zwicker was simply following an executive order from 1948, McCarthy told him that he was 'not fit to wear that uniform'. When the Secretary of the Army, Robert Stevens, issued a critical statement following this episode, McCarthy was able to bully him into submission.[42] On 24 February *The Times* of London accordingly editorialised that 'McCarthy [has] achieved what General Burgoyne and General Cornwallis never achieved: the surrender of the American Army.'[43]

As events in the next few months proved, however, McCarthy had reached the end of his spectacular career as the 'chief prosecutor'. In fact, he seemed to have gone a touch too far even for the President. After all, McCarthy had not only crossed the line by challenging the US Army, the very institution that had given Eisenhower his claim to fame, but he was clearly challenging the executive branch. From the British

Embassy's perspective it seemed that the Army–McCarthy controversy 'has brought the issue closer than it has ever been to a direct contest between the President and the Senator'. And while the public generally sympathised with Eisenhower's refusal 'to name names' (or *the* name), 'there is a more general feeling of regret that he did not express himself more forcefully or reply more directly to McCarthy's charges'. The event had, at a crucial time, exposed Ike's 'political weakness'.[44]

Rather than further advancing McCarthy's power, however, the Army–McCarthy controversy turned the tide against the Senator. Ironically, it was McCarthy's right-hand man, Roy Cohn, who handed the White House the perfect tools to use in attacking him. In March 1954 the administration, with Eisenhower's consent, began releasing documents that proved that McCarthy had abused his power by allowing his staff members, particularly Roy Cohn, to make demands for special privileges of a recently recruited G. David Schine. In fact, it emerged that Cohn had even called the Secretary of the Army at one point to demand that his friend – Cohn's chief counsel who had accompanied him on that tragicomic trip to Europe in the spring of 1953 – be allowed to get off the base for leave on weekends and most evenings. An investigation into this particular Cohn–Schine farce and hence McCarthy's committee's abuse of power inevitably followed.[45]

The so-called Army–McCarthy hearings proved to be the Senator's undoing. For about two months in April–June 1954 McCarthy's irrational and aggressive behaviour was exposed to the public on television. Whereas his tough manner and readiness to clean up the mess in Washington had previously attracted followers around the country, McCarthy, once put on the defensive, came across as merely abusive. His eagerness to obstruct the procedures by frequent calls for a 'point of order' that resulted in efforts to shift the subject no longer sent heads nodding, it only provoked disgust. As T.W. Garvey of the Foreign Office wrote already in March 1954: 'there is no doubt that the overt opposition to Senator McCarthy is stronger and more articulate than ever before and appears to be growing'.[46]

In fact, McCarthy's star fell faster than expected. By the late summer of 1954 Roy Cohn had resigned, while Joe McCarthy himself no longer grabbed the headlines. Senate hearings over his conduct began on 31 August. In November 1954 Republicans lost control of both houses of the Congress. Finally on 2 December 1954 the lameduck Senate (still controlled by the Republicans) condemned McCarthy for 'conduct contrary to Senatorial traditions' by 67–22 votes. Two-and-a-half years later he was dead.

VI

While the fall of McCarthy was likely to improve the battered prestige of the United States and shatter doubts about who actually was in charge of US foreign policy, the episode had left a severe stain on Eisenhower's image in Europe. Ike's silent campaign – his backroom pressure on Republican senators to distance themselves from McCarthy, his persistence that domestic communism was not an issue in the 1954 elections – may have been successful in shaming McCarthy and, perhaps, even in driving him into an early grave. But it was, in the end, the secrecy that mattered to most observers; to them it was McCarthy himself, rather than anything Eisenhower did or said, that was responsible for the fall from grace.

In this context the *Economist*'s assessment of McCarthy's censure is worth noting. 'Americans are conscious now, as in the past they were not, of the vast impact of their internal arrangements on the opinions of the outside world; the integrity of American institutions is an issue in the cold war', as the issue of 11 December 1954 put it. The article also maintained that 'in the struggle against communism [McCarthy] has always been a liability abroad; now, because of his acutely divisive effect on a nation united on the Communist issue, he has been officially recognised as a liability at home'. Optimistically, the *Economist* anticipated that McCarthy's fall would make the Republican party at large 'more responsible' and would allow Ike to finally grow *'into a real President'*.[47]

What McCarthy had managed, though, was to label a widespread paranoia that would colour the European image of the United States long after he was politically and – after 2 May 1957 – physically dead. In fact, Europeans paid scant attention to the obituaries of the man who so recently had commanded headlines in the most powerful country on earth. But despite McCarthy's demise, the 'ism' that carried his name was to live on. For after all, while the junior Senator had given the era his name, he was but one exponent of 'the blind haunting fear' that ran amok in the United States in the early 1950s. As T.W. Garvey of the Foreign Office had predicted already a year before the censure of the Senator, the great fear 'will probably long outlive him. America will not easily or quickly regain her confidence and cease to be the prisoner of her fears, even though McCarthy himself should disappear.'[48]

In June 1954 Ambassador Makins, in the aftermath of the Army McCarthy hearings, wrote in a very similar vein. While reaffirming that the exposure of McCarthy's behaviour on television 'has reduced his appeal outside the hard core of his supporters', Makins stressed that:

> the long-term effect of the hearings on the basic issue of McCarthyism can not yet be assessed. McCarthyism is a complex phenomenon which has its roots not only in the endemic fear of Communism but in features of the American scene which will necessarily remain unaffected by any passing event no matter how dramatic and well publicised.[49]

It was no wonder, therefore, that the term 'McCarthyism' and the name McCarthy – no matter who was in the White House, no matter what the issues of the day were – would remain a useful euphemism in Britain, as in America, for decades to come.

Notes

1 Memorandum of the 156th meeting of the NSC, July 30, 1953, *Foreign Relations of the United States, 1952–1954* (hereafter *FRUS*), vol. I, part 2, 1467–1469.
2 The most recent comprehensive account of McCarthyism in the United States is Ellen Schrecker, *Many are the Crimes: McCarthyism in America* (Boston, 1998). The following is a sample of earlier McCarthy literature: John G. Adams, *Without Precedent: the Story of the Death of McCarthyism* (New York, 1983); Edwin R. Bayley, *Joe McCarthy and the Press* (Madison, WI, 1981); Donald F. Crosby, *God, Church, and Flag: Senator Joseph R. McCarthy and the Catholic Church, 1950–1957* (Chapel Hill, NC, 1978); William B. Ewald, *McCarthyism and Consensus* (Lanham, MD, 1986); William B. Ewald, *Who Killed McCarthy?* (New York, 1984); Richard M. Fried, *Nightmare in Red: the McCarthy Era in Perspective* (New York, 1990); Richard M. Fried, *Men against McCarthy* (New York, 1976); Marjorie Garber and Rebecca Walkowitz, eds, *Secret Agents: The Rosenberg Case, McCarthyism and Fifties America* (London, 1995); Robert C. Goldston, *The American Nightmare: Senator Joseph R. McCarthy and the Politics of Hate* (Indianapolis, 1973); Robert K. Griffith, *The Politics of Fear: Joseph R. McCarthy and the Senate* (Amherst, MA, 1987); Robert Griffith and Athan Theoharis, eds, *The Specter: Original Essays on the Cold War and the Origins of McCarthyism* (New York, 1974); Mark Landis, *Joseph McCarthy: the Politics of Chaos* (London, 1987); David M. Oshinsky, *A Conspiracy so Immense: the World of Joe McCarthy* (New York, 1983); Thomas C. Reeves, *The Life and Times of Joe McCarthy* (New York, 1982); Michael P. Rogin, *The Intellectuals and McCarthy: the Radical Specter* (Cambridge, MA, 1967).
3 John P. Rossi, 'The British Reaction to McCarthyism, 1950–1954', *Mid-America* 70:1 (1988), 5–18 (citation on page 6).

4   Franks to Foreign Office, Weekly Political Summary (hereafter WPS), March 18, 1950, FO 371/81611, Public Record Office, Kew, Surrey (hereafter PRO).

5   Franks to FO, March 25 and 31, 1950 (WPS), FO 371/81611, PRO.

6   'Washington Loyalties', *Economist*, 25 March 1950, p. 653; 'Atlantic Council', *Economist*, 25 April 1950, 922; 'Mr. Acheson's Send-Off', *Economist*, 6 May 1950; *Times*, 28 March 1950.

7   Reeves, *The Life and Times*, p. 370.

8   Quoted in Stephen J. Whitfield, *The Culture of the Cold War* (Baltimore, 1991), p. 59.

9   Quoted in Rossi, 'British Reaction', p. 8.

10   'MacArthur in Texas', *Economist*, 23 June 1951, p. 1507.

11   'Censuring McCarthy', *Economist*, 18 August 1951, p. 398.

12   Foreign Office minute, September 17, 1952, FO 371/97581, PRO.

13   Reeves, *Life and Times*, pp. 438–9.

14   Schrecker, *Many are the Crimes*, pp. 256–8; Reeves, *The Life and Times*, 459–85. McCarthy dropped his opposition to Conant after a meeting with Vice President Nixon, but did bitterly, albeit unsuccessfully, oppose Bohlen. See Ambrose, *Eisenhower*, p. 59; Fred I. Greenstein, *The Hidden-Hand Presidency: Eisenhower as a Leader* (New York, 1982), pp. 167–8. On Roy Cohn, see Nicholas von Hoffman, *Citizen Cohn* (New York, 1988).

15   This particular episode is covered in, for example, Richard Pells, *Not Like Us: How Europeans Have Loved, Hated, and Transformed American Culture since World War II* (New York, 1997), pp. 80–2; Reeves, *Life and Times*, pp. 489–91.

16   *The Times*, 29 April 1953.

17   Cited in John W. Young, 'Cold War and Detente with Moscow', in *The Foreign Policy of Churchill's Peacetime Administration 1951–1955*, ed. by John W. Young (Leicester, 1988), p. 55. See also Young's *Winston Churchill's Last Campaign: Britain and the Cold War 1951–1955* (Oxford, 1996), pp. 123–5.

18   Churchill to Eisenhower, 7 April 1953. In Peter G. Boyle, ed., *The Churchill–Eisenhower Correspondence* (Chapel Hill, 1990), p. 42.

19   Cited in Young, 'Cold War and Detente with Moscow', pp. 60, 61.

20   Rossi, p. 13.

21   Cited in Rossi, p. 13.

22   Reeves, *Life and Times*, pp. 485–8 (citations on pp. 486, 487).

23   Ibid.

24   Makins to FO, 4 April 1953 (WPS), FO 371/103495, PRO.

25   *Time*, 22 August 1953.

26   Cited in Thomas C. Sorensen, *The Word War: the Story of American Propaganda* (New York, 1968), p. 82.

27   Memorandum of Discussion, 153rd Meeting of the NSC, 9 July 1953, *FRUS, 1952–1954*, I:2, p. 1463.

28   Dulles circular telegram, July 23, 1953, ibid., p. 1465.

29   Bell to State, July 23, 1953, ibid., p. 1763.

30   Aldrich to State, 12 August 1953, *FRUS, 1952–54*, VI:1, p. 998.

31   'Reported Decline in US Prestige Abroad', 11 September 1953, *FRUS, 1952–1954*, I, pp. 1484, 1486, 1487.

32   Ibid., p. 1537.

33   Ibid., p. 1542. Emphasis added.

34 Memorandum of Discussion, 156th Meeting of the NSC, 1 October 1953, *FRUS, 1952–1954*, I:2, pp. 1546–8.

35 The story of Eisenhower's silent campaign to remove McCarthy is detailed in Ewald, *Who Killed McCarthy?*. For more on Eisenhower's tendency to work out of the limelight, see Greenstein, *Hidden-Hand Presidency.*

36 Eisenhower to Reed, 17 June 1953, Eisenhower Papers, Diaries, Reel 2/28.

37 This was of some concern to Makins, who included the information in one of his last dispatches of 1953. Makins to Foreign Office, 31 December 1953 (WPS), FO 371/109100, PRO.

38 Makins to Foreign Office, 29 September 1953, FP 371/103499, PRO.

39 Clement Attlee, 'Britain and America: Common Aims, Different Opinions', *Foreign Affairs* 32:2 (January 1954, pp. 201–2.

40 Aldrich to State, 4 March 1954, *FRUS, 1952–54*, I:2, p. 1549.

41 *Eisenhower Diaries*, 26 February 1954.

42 E.g. Schrecker, *Many Are the Crimes*, pp. 261–2.

43 *The Times*, 24 February 1954.

44 Makins to FO, 6 March 1954 (WPS), FO 371/109100, PRO.

45 Schrecker, *Many Are the Crimes*, pp. 262–3.

46 Foreign Office minute by T.W. Garvey, 19 March 1954. FO 371/109100, PRO.

47 'McCarthy Hits Back', and 'A Republican Rump?', *Economist*, 11 December 1954, pp. 906–7.

48 T.W. Garvey, Foreign Office Minute, 13 October 1953, FO 371/103499, PRO.

49 Makins to Foreign Office, 19 June 1954 (WPS 6/12–18), FO 371/109161, PRO.

7
A Very Considerable and Largely Unsung Success: Sir Roger Makins' Washington Embassy, 1953–56

Saul Kelly

Introduction

Sir Roger Makins' embassy has tended to be overshadowed by that of his predecessor in Washington from 1948 to 1952, Sir Oliver Franks. Various accounts of Franks' embassy have shown that he played a not inconsiderable role in keeping Britain and the United States together in these critical years, which saw Marshall Aid and the formation of NATO, and how he conciliated in times of strain and crisis, particularly during the Korean War. These accounts have emphasised how his sterling qualities and his extraordinary personal relationship with the US Secretary of State, Dean Acheson (which was embodied in their regular, off-the-record talks) gave him an unusual amount of influence for an ambassador in Washington. By contrast, these accounts have stated or implied that Makins had only a formal relationship with Acheson's successor, John Foster Dulles, and therefore not the same degree of influence as Franks.[1]

According to the veteran *Sunday Times* journalist, Henry Brandon, Makins had to keep notes of his conversations with Dulles because the latter was so tricky that he often 'brazenly denied having said something...'.[2] Apart from the fact that it is normal diplomatic practice to record such conversations, and even Franks conveyed the gist of his informal talks with Acheson to London, this is to misunderstand the way that Dulles developed his thinking on a subject. Moreover, if Makins had had only a formal relationship with Dulles, it is unlikely that the latter would have regarded the former's return to London during the Suez Crisis as a personal betrayal by the British Prime Minister, Anthony Eden. On the contrary, it would seem to indicate the high esteem in which the Secretary of State held the British Ambassador and how much he valued him as a link with London.

This chapter will reassess the nature of Makins' relationship with Dulles and the role he played as British Ambassador during the period of the first Eisenhower administration from 1953 to 1956 when, as Professor Watt has pointed out: 'American hegemony was asserted in a manner which made it open for all to see.'[3]

Appointment to Washington

The question has to be asked why it was decided to appoint Makins to the Washington embassy, after Franks let it be known in the spring of 1952 that he wanted to return to the UK at the end of the year? Makins later surmised that, after three political appointments (Lothian, Halifax and Franks) and the unfortunate Inverchapel performance, Eden, who was then Foreign Secretary, wanted to appoint a competent professional from the diplomatic service. The Prime Minister, Winston Churchill, would have preferred a public figure, like Mountbatten, but agreed to Makins after looking him over on 20 July.[4]

But why Makins and not the other candidates for the job (Pierson Dixon, Gladwyn Jebb and Ralph Stevenson)? In later years, Makins speculated that it might have been because Eden knew him better than the other candidates,[5] although it should be pointed out that Bob Dixon had been Eden's Principal Private Secretary during the latter years of the war and Stevenson had been one of the League of Nations advisers in the Foreign Office when Eden had been Minister for League Affairs and then Foreign Secretary in the period from 1934 to 1938. As an assistant League adviser, Makins had worked closely and harmoniously with Eden in Geneva during the same period. Makins had been Eden's man in the Mediterranean from 1942 to 1944, first at AFHQ at Algiers and then at Caserta in Italy, where Churchill became aware of the high calibre of his work as the principal assistant to Macmillan.[6]

When Eden returned to the Foreign Office in late 1951, Makins was an influential Deputy Under-Secretary who had been dealing with all the major issues in Anglo-American relations in the previous four years. In particular, Makins had been familiar since 1945 (first as Joint Secretary of the Combined British Policy Committee in Washington, and then as Chairman of the Official Committee on Atomic Energy in London) with the vexed question of atomic energy and had demonstrated his commitment to the revival of cooperation.[7] The Press on both sides of the

Atlantic were to dub him 'Britain's Atomic Ambassador' and 'Mr Atom', a sobriquet which he always disliked.[8]

Certainly, he had more experience of the United States than the other candidates, having worked in the American Department of the Foreign Office from 1928 to 1931, and being posted to Washington from 1931 to 1934 and 1945 to 1947. Moreover, his American wife, Alice, was an obvious asset to him on the social side. As the daughter of Dwight Davis (the former Secretary for War in the Coolidge administration and then Governor-General of the Philippines, as well as the founder of the Davis Cup tennis tournament) she provided him with an entrée into American political and social circles and gave him an insight into American life which the other candidates lacked.[9] He was quite simply the best qualified professional diplomat for the post at the time. Like Franks, he was a confirmed Atlanticist, convinced of the need for close cooperation between Britain and the United States in order to protect British interests and guarantee world peace.

First impressions

Makins' arrival in Washington in January 1953 coincided with the visit of Churchill. Much has been made by historians of the President-elect, Dwight Eisenhower, rebuffing Churchill's attempt to re-establish the old wartime Anglo-American intimacy and not giving more than token encouragement to Churchill's idea of an East–West summit meeting.[10] What they have not mentioned is that Eisenhower and the Republican Party were still at this time in election-mode and thinking in terms of the next day's headlines and how they were going to establish their internal political position (the Republicans had been out of power for 20 years). The Under-Secretary of State in the new administration, Bedell Smith, confirmed to Makins that he could not get Eisenhower to pay any attention to pressing foreign policy issues. And Churchill observed to Makins that the Republicans seemed mainly to be concerned to take a line different from that of their Democrat predecessors, who had worked closely with Britain. Makins informed Eden that Churchill's visit had had a salutary effect on Eisenhower 'in heading him off one or two dangerous plunges, or at least in making him look before he leaps'. Makins predicted that Britain could be in for a period of 'rough weather' with the new administration and that 'we should not expect early favourable results. Much patience will be needed.'[11] He set out to win the confidence of the new President and the new Secretary of State in order to promote British policies as effectively as possible.

Makins had first met Eisenhower during the war, when they had worked closely together in Algiers. When they met again in Washington in January 1953, Eisenhower exclaimed: 'Christ, Roger, what are you doing here?!'[12] Makins regarded this as an important greeting, since it indicated that he would be able to gain access to the new President whenever it was necessary to do so, as proved to be the case. If he had started well with Eisenhower, he was not at all sure how he would get on with Dulles. They had never met, the new Secretary of State was a good deal older than the new British Ambassador and, according to Makins' later recollection, he was already regarded as a bit of a bogeyman by Eden and the Foreign Office.[13] When in London in late 1952, Makins had himself certainly expressed reservations about Dulles' appointment as Secretary of State.[14] But he was soon reassured after meeting him in Washington in mid-January 1953.

As Makins has written in his memoirs:

I found him accessible and easy to work with, he thought for himself and expressed his thought at some length. He also developed it over time, and this gave him a reputation for inconsistency with some of my colleagues who did not see him as often as I did. He was certainly ponderous and rather clumsy, particularly in his statements to the Press, and he was badly advised by his press Secretary, McCardle. Out of the office, he was friendly and genial and a good companion who took his bourbon with the best of them. My main problem was that he travelled a great deal and I never quite knew what had passed in his dealings with Anthony Eden, Selwyn Lloyd, and others in London, Geneva or elsewhere. Reports were sent, of course, but it is only if one is actually on the spot that it is possible to know what winks or nods have been exchanged. One thing I quickly learned was that Dulles never took an important step or replied to representations on major issues, without first consulting the President. It was an advantage too that Foster's brother Allen, the head of the C.I.A. and his wife Clover were old friends and, in addition, sister Eleanor in the German Section of the State Department. The Dulles trio was an important element to have on one's side.[15]

This later testimony, which is confirmed by the contemporary documents, conclusively shows that Makins had early on established a close working relationship with Foster Dulles and his siblings and that he was under no illusions as to the nature of the relationship between the President and his Secretary of State. Moreover, he was greatly helped at the outset in establishing close contacts with the new Republican administration by the fact that the Under-Secretary of State was Bedell Smith, Eisenhower's former Chief of Staff in the Mediterranean, whom Makins had known well in Algiers. He and Bedell Smith, who knew Churchill and Eden well from the war, were almost always able to clear up the frequent misunderstandings which later arose between Dulles and Eden. Makins had many old friends in the State Department, and was soon *persona grata* there. He never had any trouble communicating with them, except on occasion with the right-wing Assistant Under-Secretary for the Far East, Walter Robertson (who inadvertently sported an Old Etonian tie) and more frequently with the deaf, stubborn and anti-British Herbert Hoover, Jr, who succeeded Bedell Smith as Under-Secretary in October 1954.[16] Makins' inability to establish a rapport with Hoover was to have serious consequences, particularly over the Middle East, in that it closed down that vital channel of communication which had existed with Bedell Smith for dealing with the disagreements and tensions between Eden and Dulles.

Anglo-American relations, 1953–56

As Ambassador in Washington, Makins had to deal with that series of problematic issues which plagued Anglo-American relations during 1953–56, culminating in the great rift in the transatlantic alliance during the Suez Crisis. This chapter will be concerned with this aspect rather than Makins' monitoring of the US domestic scene and his charting of the progress of Eisenhower towards the Presidency.

'Trade not Aid'

Given Makins' primary concern with economic matters in the FO from 1947 to 1952, it is ironic that he was only peripherally involved in the first major Anglo-American talks during his embassy, namely the Chancellor of the Exchequer, 'Rab' Butler's abortive 'Trade not Aid' discussions with US Treasury Secretary, Humphrey, and Commerce Secretary, Weeks, in Washington in March 1953 (instead he accompanied Eden in his political talks with Dulles, which narrowed Anglo-American differences on the European Defence Community (EDC), China, Egypt and Iran). But he was subsequently to monitor closely and sympathetically Eisenhower's uphill and partially successful struggle with the protectionist elements in the Congress to liberalise US trade restrictions.[17]

On the matter of East–West trade, however, and particularly trade with Communist China, Makins made a direct intervention on 20 May when he publicly denied Senator McCarthy's unfounded allegation that British-owned ships, operating out of Hong Kong, had carried communist troops or that there had been a great increase in British trade with China in the first quarter of 1953 (there had, in fact, only been a small increase). Despite official denials by the British Embassy in Washington and the Foreign Office in London, Makins thought these repeated charges did great damage to relations between Britain and the United States. He believed that if the Korean War had continued, the problem would have become more dangerous for Anglo-American relations than any question since the dispute over the First World War debts.[18]

The end of the Korean War

The ending of the Korean War was the Eisenhower administration's greatest achievement in its first year of office, and it eased the strain in Anglo-American relations. But Dulles' conduct of the armistice negotiations came in for considerable criticism in the House of Commons and the British press. This disturbed the Secretary of State, who felt that the UK should show some appreciation for American efforts and sacrifices. Makins conveyed Dulles' feelings to London and explained that allowance had to be made for his rather clumsy and tactless public statements, since he was, in Makins' judgement, 'possibly the most sincere and genuine advocate of close Anglo-American cooperation in the United States today. But it will in the long run sour even the most long-suffering man to be told that yesterday was "Anti-Dulles Day" in London.'[19] At Makins' request, the FO sent suitable messages of appreciation to Dulles which smoothed his ruffled feathers. But the bad press which Dulles received in Britain, and which offended him, was to be a complicating factor in Anglo-American relations and was to lead Makins again and again to stress to the FO the need to mitigate press criticism in order not to alienate Britain's potentially greatest ally in Washington.

The Middle East – the next 'sore point'

With the end of the Korean War, Makins identified the Middle East as the next 'sore point' in Anglo-American relations. The issues which had the potential to disrupt relations in the region were:

(1) Britain's failure to reach agreements with Egypt over the Canal base, with Saudi Arabia over the Buraimi Oasis and with Iran over oil, with

which the State Department, and Makins, had progressively less sympathy;

(2) the independent activities of some US representatives in the Middle East, particularly Ambassador Jefferson Caffery in Cairo;

(3) the feeling among US officials in Washington that the British government wanted to have American cooperation in the Middle East on their terms and did not fully recognise US interests there, and what the Americans were doing towards building up barriers against Soviet penetration;

(4) the suspicion in London that the Americans were consciously trying to oust Britain from the Middle East, by assuming a dominant position in Saudi Arabia and the Northern Tier countries (military aid agreements were signed with Turkey on 2 April 1954, with Iraq on 21 April and with Pakistan on 19 May).[20]

In a submission that went to the Cabinet in February 1954, Makins denied that the Americans were trying to oust Britain from the Middle East (he had already pointed out that any desire to dominate in the State Department was kept in check by the US military and the Congress, who were against assuming major commitments in the region). The question of whether Britain stayed in the Middle East would be dependent largely on its own efforts and how the British government adjusted to the American presence as a new factor in Middle Eastern politics. Makins thought, rather optimistically as it turned out, that as long as a proper understanding existed between London and Washington, disruptive officials such as Caffery in Cairo could be restrained. He was correct in thinking, however, that the conclusion of the agreements with Egypt and Iran in October 1954 (for which he had pressed) would, at least temporarily, increase British freedom of action in the Middle East and lead to greater American respect for the British position in the region (though it was limited by the failure to reach an agreement over Buraimi). Certainly, it encouraged the Americans to enlist British support in trying to solve the Arab–Israeli dispute. But Makins was aware of the potential which policy differences over the Middle East had to disrupt Anglo-American relations. He realised that Britain would always have to contend with certain innate American feelings and prejudices about the British position in the Middle East, which stemmed from their anti-colonialism and economic rivalry. He thought that with a little luck and perseverance, 'we had a good chance of building up American confidence in us and their desire to cooperate with us'.[21]

Indo-China, Guatemala, and SEATO

There continued to be the usual ups and downs in the transatlantic relationship. In the spring and summer of 1954, the circumstances surrounding the convening of the Geneva Conference on Korea and Indo-China and the discussion of the South-East Asian security pact combined with lukewarm British support for the Eisenhower administration's policy towards Guatemala, to put considerable strain on Anglo-American relations. At one time this threatened to develop into a crisis of confidence, while the media highlighted the splits and tensions between London and Washington.

Makins' role in all this was to try to defuse the tensions, heal the splits and prevent a breakdown in mutual confidence. He sought to persuade a reluctant Churchill government to work with the Eisenhower administration on these issues, in order to exert influence on US policy and to protect British interests not only in the Far East and Central America, but further afield in the Pacific (where Britain had been shut out from ANZUS), the Middle East and Europe (where Dulles threatened an agonising reappraisal of the American commitment to NATO).

Thus, he advocated British support for the US proposals for 'united action' on Indo-China and for starting talks on South-East Asian security before the Geneva Conference, only to be slapped down by Eden, who refused to contemplate such actions on the grounds that it would not save the French position in Indo-China, would be opposed by the British public and the Colombo powers, would prejudice the chances of reaching a peaceful resolution to the problem at Geneva, and might provoke a global war. The British government's refusal to follow the American lead over 'united action' put Anglo-American relations under great strain which, as Makins predicted, did not bode well for the Geneva Conference.[22]

Makins did not participate in the Geneva Conference and could only observe from afar the Anglo-American disagreements over Indo-China. He warned Eden that the Americans were 'working slowly towards a historic decision to accept far-reaching commitments on the mainland of Asia' and that Britain's refusal to open negotiations on a security organisation before any agreement was reached at Geneva might endanger Anglo-American relations. But this made little impact on Eden.[23]

The visit of Eden and Churchill to Washington in June 1954, which Makins had pressed for since he believed in the value of personal and informal contacts, did much to restore confidence between them and Eisenhower and Dulles. This was partly due to Makins' efforts since

before the conference he had urged on Churchill and Eden the importance for British interests of their being seen by the US public to reach
agreed lines of action with the Americans on the Middle East, Europe
and particularly the Far East (where the Americans were likely to be
faced with a settlement in Indo-China which they would find unaccept-
able but would not be able to prevent). The purpose of Makins' advice
was to try to reverse 'the incipient trend' which he had detected in
the United States against intervention in the Far East and involvement
in Europe and the Middle East and towards a powerful nationalistic,
anti-colonial and hemispheric, but not isolationist, stance. Makins
advised Eden to expend some effort on Dulles, that 'old buster with
pachydermatous tendencies', who was in 'a pet' at being outshone by
Eden at the Geneva Conference, but who was deep down in favour
of close cooperation with Britain.[24] Both Makins and Churchill also
tried during the conference to blunt the differences between Dulles
and Eden.

Agreement was indeed reached on the terms of a negotiated settlement for Indo-China which was to be presented to the French, on how
to proceed in the negotiations with Egypt, on the EDC, on Guatemala,
atomic energy and East-West détente.[25] The Geneva agreements of 21
July on Indo-China (partitioning Vietnam along the 17th parallel, providing for all-Vietnamese elections in 1956, which were never held, and
the independence of Cambodia and Laos as a buffer with China) and the
Manila Treaty of 8 September, setting up SEATO, temporarily resolved
Anglo-American differences in the Far East, although they failed to solve
the long-term problems in the region, as subsequent American and
North Vietnamese policies were to show. The conclusion of the Anglo-
Iranian and Anglo-Egyptian agreements, the triumph of America's man,
Armas, in Guatemala, and the passing by the Congress of the Atomic
Energy Act, which opened up the prospect of greater Anglo-American
atomic cooperation, all removed obstacles in the way of better Anglo-
American relations. Makins noted that Eden's leadership during the
EDC crisis increased the general respect in which British diplomacy
was held in Washington and drew the Churchill government and the
Eisenhower administration closer together.[26]

East–West relations

It is interesting to note that in the latter half of 1954, Makins and his
embassy advisers picked up on the change of attitude in the United
States towards relations with the Soviets and to a lesser extent with
China (through the British Embassy's extensive contacts with the

administration, the Congress and the press). In a November letter to Eden, Makins correctly attributed this to the realisation (partly due to British influence and Churchill's visit) that in the atomic age there was no alternative to peace; the administration's desire for a more peaceful, less expensive and less engaged foreign policy; some flexibility in the Soviet negotiating position and the desire of America's allies to pursue the path towards peaceful co-existence. But he was aware that the Joint Chiefs of Staff were sceptical about Soviet intentions and reluctant to defer to Allied caution. Even if they were defeated by the realists (like the US Ambassador to Moscow, Charles Bohlen), Makins believed that this would have serious implications for the British position in the world. For the realists

> almost always had somewhere in their minds the idea that there will eventually have to be an understanding between Washington and Moscow, a deux, as the strongest powers in the world. This thought, along with the prospect of withdrawals of United States troops and reductions in military and economic aid to the rest of the free world, raises an interesting question about the effect on British interests, should the trend of American policy which I have suggested gather momentum.[27]

Makins admitted that this was an old bugbear of his. He believed that 'the loss of American interest in Europe and, above all, in what is sometimes called here the "British complex", is the main thing we have to fear within the western world'.[28] It was in order to keep the United States engaged in Europe and supporting Britain's continued role as a global power, that Makins urged Eden to keep in step with the United States in the Far East and, as will be seen, the Middle East. This was to run like a leitmotif through Makins' Washington embassy. Whereas Eden shared Makins' concern, he found it more problematic to make the concessions necessary to align British and US policies in the Middle East and the Far East.

The first Quemoy/Matsu crisis

This was seen clearly during the first Quemoy/Matsu crisis when, as before over Korea and Indo-China, Eden and the Foreign Office were keen to restrain the Americans (this time in their support for continued Nationalist Chinese possession of the offshore islands against the Communist Chinese) and Eden and the Foreign Office exaggerated the threat of a general war in the Far East. Eden's attempt to broker a settlement came to nothing because, as has been pointed out, 'Britain's dependence on the United States, particularly in Europe, was too great for its proposals to carry any weight in Peking or for its pressure to have any influence in Washington.'[29]

The situation only eased in April 1955 when, following the US threats to use tactical nuclear weapons in the Formosa Straits to resolve the crisis, the Communist Chinese Foreign Minister, Zhou En-Lai, declared that Communist Chinese pressure on the islands would be reduced. Makins' approach to the Quemoy/Matsu problem was consistent with the line he had followed on the Korean War and during the Indo-China crisis. He did not want it to be the cause of a rift in Anglo-American relations, which would prejudice more important British interests elsewhere in the world. He believed that the only way that the British government could exert any influence on US policy would be if it acted with the United States (e.g. over Operation Oracle), particularly since it was clear that the Americans would not force Chiang Kai-Shek to evacuate the islands. But he could not overcome the distrust which Eden and the Foreign Office had of Dulles' intentions in the Far East.[30]

In the event, the independent line which Eden took only succeeded in irritating Dulles and Eisenhower. Fortunately, the situation was defused by the Communist Chinese desire to negotiate. For, as John Charmley has surmised, 'Had the Americans pushed further on the offshore islands issue, a breach might well have come in Anglo-American relations – but it would not have been over an issue where vital British interests were concerned.'[31] This was Makins' particular concern throughout this crisis.

Atomic energy

The first Quemoy/Matsu crisis illustrated just how little influence the British could have over their own fate, and how shallow the Anglo-American relationship could be. This helped to strengthen the case of those in London who argued that Britain needed nuclear weapons in order to exert sufficient influence in Washington to protect its interests. In fact, Britain had by 1955 (at great expense because of the limited American help) built up a stockpile of atomic bombs, was building a hydrogen bomb, and had a nuclear power plant programme under way. The atomic energy information which Churchill sought and partially gained from Truman and then Eisenhower was of less importance, though it did lead to a greater exchange of information in the late 1950s. The records of the Official Committee on Atomic Energy show clearly that Makins was intimately involved in the various attempts to secure closer Anglo-American cooperation in the decade following the end of the Second World War. It would be no exaggeration to say that he was perhaps the single most important individual on the British side in the period from 1945 to 1952 and, as Ambassador in Washington from 1953 to 1956, he continued to have a great say in the nature of any approaches to the Americans on atomic matters. Makins played a key role not only in interpreting American thinking on atomic energy for London, but in negotiating the new atomic agreements of 15 June 1955 with the United States. It was Makins who warned the Official Committee in March 1955 that they faced the choice of an agreement on the lines of an American–Canadian draft (the Canadians being the other party to atomic cooperation) or no agreement at all. The Official Committee seems to have followed Makins' advice and the Ambassador hammered out the text of a bilateral agreement which gave the British a great deal, if not all, of what they wanted.

But Makins and his advisers warned London that it was British insistence on excluding power reactors, including Calder Hall (the first power plant in the world to supply electricity to a national grid) from the exchange of information and failure to give sufficient security assurances, which threatened to prejudice the chances of an agreement. These points were eventually resolved by agreeing the exchange of information on a strictly reciprocal basis and British security guarantees. Consequently, a civil bilateral agreement, providing for exchange of information, and for transfer of fissile materials and equipment was signed on 15 June 1955. The same day another bilateral agreement, in the military field, provided for the exchange of information on defence plans, training of personnel on the use of and defence against nuclear weapons, and the evaluation of enemy nuclear capabilities. These agreements were a small but significant step forward in cooperation between Britain and the United States and were to lead to further British requests for increased collaboration.[32] As has been observed: 'Although the major breakthrough did not come until 1958, the 1955 agreements did at least provide an improved atmosphere which contributed to greater intimacy between the scientific communities of each country.'[33] Makins himself played a significant part in bringing about this improved atmosphere, by smoothing the path of cooperation during the negotiations for the 1955 agreements.

The Middle East

Makins' attempts to keep the Eisenhower administration and the new Eden government working together were to be tested to the limit over the Middle East. His efforts, on instructions from London, to get the United States to join the Baghdad Pact came to nought. In a revealing aside to Herbert Hoover, Jr, he said that London did not seem to be getting his message that there was considerable Congressional opposition, inspired by the Jewish lobby, to the USA joining a defence pact with Arab states without a compensatory security guarantee for Israel. The division between Britain and the United States over the Baghdad Pact was somewhat mitigated by their cooperation in Operation Alpha, the top-secret Anglo-American effort to broker a settlement between Egypt and Israel. But even here, cooperation was complicated by Eden's last-minute objections to a general speech by Dulles on Alpha and a supporting statement by the Foreign Secretary, Harold Macmillan, in late August 1955. Makins later commented that this 'was a good example of the petulance to the point of unreason to which he [Eden] was always prone and which became intensified after his illness and when he became Prime Minister'.[34] As he admitted in his memoirs: 'It was this sort of petulant intervention which had the potential to disrupt Anglo-American relations.'[35]

Eden's lack of understanding of the American position was again demonstrated over the negotiations in late 1955 on the financing of the Aswan High Dam. It took much effort by Makins to convince Eden that if the British government wanted 'to get into the poker game it had to put up the ante'.[36] In other words, the British government had to agree to contribute 20 per cent (i.e. $15 million) of the first-stage grant of $70 million to help cover the foreign exchange costs, as well as conceding competitive bidding, in order to secure American participation in the dam project. Makins also had to work hard to get Hoover and Humphrey to change their minds and back US funding of the dam. Hoover and Makins then put the deal to the Egyptians in Washington, which was followed by the World Bank offer, which the Egyptians then considered. This was a good example of Makins' ability to overcome entrenched attitudes and differences of approach in London and Washington in order to secure an agreement on a particular issue. But it could only succeed if the principal players had common and overriding objectives, in this case their mutual desire to prevent the Soviets following up their arms deal with Egypt by financing the Aswan High Dam.[37]

Makins had to deal with flak from Dulles over the British government's attempt to force Jordan into the Baghdad Pact in contravention of its assurance that it would not expand the pact; a move with which Makins had no sympathy. He had also to contend with Eden's refusal to help the Americans to split the Saudis from the Egyptians by making concessions in the dispute with Saudi Arabia over the Buraimi Oasis (which were favoured by Makins). There were differences over Britain's support for Nuri Said in Iraq and over Cyprus, where Britain's head-on clash with the Greek Cypriots and the mainland Greeks over Enosis threatened NATO.[38]

Moreover, what has been called the 'unprecedented Anglo-American concord on Middle Eastern policy', namely the Omega Plan (the long-term programme to cut Nasser down to size) was soon threatened by Eden's desire for a 'quick-fix' solution to Britain's problems in the Middle East and his impatience with the American reluctance to be seen to be cooperating with the British in the region, which he claimed under-mined Western influence.[39] Makins had been involved in the drawing up of the Omega Plan and had been careful to relay to London the American preference for a political and economic, rather than a military response to the Egyptian problem.[40]

The Suez Crisis

The opening gambit in Operation Omega was the decision to let the Aswan High Dam project 'wither on the vine'.[41] Makins was privy to the deliberations in the US government which led up to the withdrawal on 19 July of the offer to finance the dam. He gave London adequate warning of what was coming, despite what Eden and Lloyd later said.[42] When the British government followed suit, and the World Bank offer automatically lapsed, Makins' French colleague in Washing-ton, Couve de Murville, predicted that Nasser would hit back by nation-alising the Canal.[43] During the ensuing crisis, Makins drew heavily not only on his reserves of strength but on his personal friendships with the principal players on both sides of the Atlantic, in order to reduce the tension in the Anglo-American exchanges on how to proceed against Nasser and to secure a degree of cooperation on the imposition of economic sanctions against Egypt and on contingency planning on oil supplies.[44]

More significantly, his warnings to London throughout the summer and early autumn of 1956 against Britain's use of force, coupled with those from Eisenhower and Dulles, were part of that pressure exerted from Washington which delayed matters long enough for other factors to exert an influence and nearly end the Suez Crisis, namely the caution of the FO which led it to push for a diplomatic solution in New York (the 'Six Principles' Agreement) and the need to revise the military timetable because of the onset of winter.[45] When Makins returned to

London on 11 October, to take up his new post of Joint Permanent Secretary of the Treasury, he could have, if he had been so inclined, taken some comfort from the fact that the Anglo-American 'alliance' was still intact.

The main thrust of Makins' advice as Joint Permanent Secretary of the Treasury throughout the rest of the Suez Crisis was the need to secure US support for an International Monetary Fund (IMF) loan for Britain and other financial and economic measures (including access to Western hemisphere oil) to avert the looming disaster for sterling and the economy. Without US support any British approach to the IMF was bound to fail and the Governor of the Bank of England, Kim Cobbold, wanted this guarantee before he would agree to any such approach.[46]

But once official communications at the top between Eden and Eisenhower were cut off, following Anglo-French military intervention in Egypt, it was clear that it would be no easy task to obtain US support. But Makins' knowledge of the Washington scene and his extensive transatlantic contacts (particularly his friendships with the Economic Minister at the British Embassy, Lord Harcourt, and the US Treasury Secretary, George Humphrey) offered Macmillan and the Lord Privy Seal, R.A. Butler, a way around this, an opportunity of informal contacts or, as Makins put it, for 'neighbours to talk over the garden fence'.[47]

As a result of these contacts, Harcourt and the new British Ambassador in Washington, Sir Harold Caccia, reported that Humphrey and the Eisenhower Administration shared the British government's concern at the desperate plight of sterling and said that if Britain and France withdrew from Egypt, the US would supply loans and oil. It was Makins who kept Macmillan and Butler supplied with the necessary information (especially on the reserve figures) which enabled them to convince the Cabinet to agree to a withdrawal.[48]

Makins did not exaggerate the dangers of the financial crisis. He did not believe it was a repeat of the 1949 devaluation crisis. But drawing on the experience he gained in the 1949 devaluation talks, Makins ensured that the momentum was kept up in the negotiations with the Americans. The importance of this was demonstrated on 4 December when, following the announcement the day before of the withdrawal of British troops from Egypt, Macmillan was able to balance the news that the reserves had fallen dangerously low (i.e. near the level at which devaluation had occurred in 1949) with the announcement of US backing for a British loan with the IMF and a waiver on the US loan. Sterling had been narrowly saved, although confidence in the currency had been weakened.[49]

Conclusion

What can we say about Sir Roger Makins' Washington embassy and his role in the Suez Crisis? It has been pointed out that on the British side, much of the misfortune which was to strike Anglo-American relations in 1956 can be blamed on Eden's tenure of the Foreign Office and 10 Downing Street. His 'ability to understand the Americans *was* as limited as his ability to convince himself of American respect *was* unbounded'. In part, he attributed this to 'the very considerable and largely unsung success Sir Roger Makins enjoyed in establishing relations of confidence with the State Department and Dulles'.[50]

This enabled Makins, as has been shown in this chapter, to help prevent a breakdown in Anglo-American relations over the series of crises in the Far East, the Middle East and Europe which occurred during the period of the first Eisenhower administration. Following his return to London in October 1956, the Anglo-American 'alliance' did break down over the Anglo-French intervention against Egypt and he played an important behind-the-scenes role in restoring it. He did not believe that Suez was an important enough issue for Britain and the United States to break over. It would have been interesting to have seen whether Anglo-American relations would have ruptured in the way they did or would have been restored any quicker if Makins had remained in Washington.

Notes

1 Peter Boyle, '"The Special Relationship" with Washington', in J.W. Young (ed.), *The Foreign Policy of Churchill's Peacetime Administration, 1951–1955* (Leicester University Press, 1988), p. 32; Alex Danchev, *Oliver Franks – Founding Father* (Oxford, Clarendon Press, 1993), pp. 109–35.
2 Henry Brandon, *Special Relationship* (London, Macmillan, 1988), p. 93.
3 D. Cameron Watt, *Succeeding John Bull* (Cambridge University Press, 1984), p. 127.
4 Bodleian Library: Sherfield Papers, MS Memoirs, Washington Embassy, pp.1–4. I am indebted to Virginia and Christopher Makins for according me unrestricted access to all relevant material in the Sherfield Papers.
5 Ibid., p. 1.
6 Sherfield Papers, MS Memoirs, chapters on Geneva, Foreign Office, North Africa and Italy.

7   Saul Kelly, 'Sir Roger Makins and Anglo-American Atomic Relations, 1945–55.' Paper delivered to the Ninth Annual Conference of the British International History Group, University of Ulster at Coleraine, 11–13 September 1997.

8   Sherfield Papers, MS Memoirs, Washington Embassy, pp. 4–5; see also Jill Edwards, 'Roger Makins: "Mr Atom"', in John Zametica (ed.), *British Officials and British Foreign Policy, 1945–50* (Leicester University Press, 1990), p. 8; Kelly interview with Sherfield, May 1994.

9   Sherfield Papers, MS Memoirs, The Foreign Office: 1928–31, Washington: April 1931–April 1934, Washington: 1945–47.

10 John Charmley, *Churchill's Grand Alliance, the Anglo-American Special Relationship, 1940–57* (London, Hodder and Stoughton, 1995), p. 241; C.J. Bartlett, 'The Special Relationship', *A Political History of Anglo-American Relations since 1945* (London, Longmans, 1992), pp. 59–60.

11 University of Birmingham, Avon Papers, AP 20/16/23, Makins to Eden, 9 January 1953.

12 Sherfield Papers, MS Memoirs, Washington Embassy, pp. 19–20.

13 Ibid., p. 21.

14 John Young, *Winston Churchill's Last Campaign: Britain and the Cold War, 1951–1955* (Oxford, Clarendon Press, 1996), p. 111.

15 Sherfield Papers, MS Memoirs, Washington Embassy, pp. 22–3.

16 Ibid.

17 PRO, PREM 11/431, Eden–Butler Visit to US, 4–9 March 1953; CAB 128/26, CC(53)20th Mtg., 17 March 1953; Sherfield Papers, MS Memoirs, Washington Embassy, pp. 34 and 43.

18 Sherfield Papers, MS Memoirs, Washington Embassy, pp. 48–9.

19 Ibid., pp. 50–5; PRO, FO 371/103499/AU1016/41, Makins to Salisbury, 29 September 1953; FO 371/103497/AU1015/16, Makins to Salisbury, 10 August 1953.

20 Sherfield Papers, MS Memoirs, Washington Embassy, pp. 60–2; FO 371/ 103497/AU1015/21, Makins to Salisbury, 3 September 1953.

21 Sherfield Papers, MS Memoirs, Washington Embassy, pp. 92–5; CAB 129/66, C(53)58, 15 February 1954; *Foreign Relations of the United States, 1952–1954, Vol. IX, Pt 1* (Washington, USGPO, 1986), pp. 1683–4; W.S. Lucas, *Divided We Stand* (London, Hodder and Stoughton, 1991), pp. 32–4.

22 Sherfield Papers, MS Memoirs, Washington Embassy, pp. 99–104; PREM 11/645, Makins to FO, tel. 524, 27 March 1954, tel. 548, 30 March 1954, tels 579–580, 3 April 1954, tel. 588, 4 April 1954, tels 595 and 596, 5 April 1954, tels 679 and 680, 10 April 1954; Geoffrey Warner, 'Britain and the Crisis over Dien Bien Phu, April 1954: the Failure of United Action', in Lawrence S. Kaplan, Denise Artaud and Mark R. Rubin, *Dien Bien Phu and the Crisis of Franco-American Relations, 1954–1955* (Wilmington, SR Books, 1984), pp. 55–77.

23 Sherfield Papers, MS Memoirs, Washington Embassy, p. 105; PREM 11/649, Makins to FO, 21 May 1954; PREM 11/666, Makins to FO, 15 May 1954; FO 800/841, Makins to Eden, 29 May 1954; FO 800/842, Makins to FO, tel 1094, 4 June 1954.

24 Sherfield Papers, MS Memoirs, Washington Embassy, pp. 107–13; PREM 11/666, Makins to FO, 16 June 1954; PREM 11/667, Makins to FO, tels

1257–59, 24 June 1954; PREM 11/683, Makins to FO, tel. 1260, 24 June 1954; FO 800/842, Makins to Eden, 18 and 21 June 1954.

25 Sherfield Papers, MS Memoirs, Washington Embassy, pp. 113–20; FO 371/ 108933/AE 1015/99, Makins to Kirkpatrick, 4 August 1954; *FRUS, 1952–1954, Vol. VI, Pt 1, Western Europe and Canada* (Washington, DC, USGPO, 1987), pp. 1079–96, 1100, 1104–7, 1112–25; *FRUS, 1952–1954, Vol. VIII, Eastern Europe, Soviet Union, Eastern Mediterranean* (Washington, DC, USGPO, 1988), pp. 709–48.

26 Sherfield Papers, MS Memoirs, Washington Embassy, p. 126; *FRUS, 1952–1954, Vol. V, Western European Security, Pt 2* (Washington, DC, USGPO, 1983), pp. 1154–5, 1234–5.

27 Sherfield Papers, MS Memoirs, Washington Embassy, pp. 136–9; Avon Papers, AP 20/17/30, Makins to Eden, 2 December 1954.

28 Ibid.

29 Michael Dockrill, 'Britain and the First Chinese Offshore Islands Crisis, 1945–55', in Michael Dockrill and John W. Young (eds), *British Foreign Policy, 1945–56* (London, Macmillan, 1989), p. 190.

30 See correspondence on PREM 11/867 and 879; FO 371/110237/110239/ 110240/115031/115035/115049/115054.

31 Charmley, *Grand Alliance*, p. 302.

32 Kelly, 'Atomic Relations', pp. 22–4.

33 John Bayliss, *Anglo-American Defence Relations, 1939–1984* (New York, St. Martins Press, 1984), p. 71.

34 R. Lamb, *The Failure of the Eden Government* (London, Sidgwick and Jackson, 1987), pp. 166,169,180; Lucas, *Divided We Stand*, pp. 40–57.

35 Sherfield Papers, MS Memoirs, Suez Crisis, pp. 3, 16–17.

36 Ibid., p.10; FO 371/113738/JE 1423/253, Makins to FO, tels. 2885–7, 27 November 1955; FO 371/113739/JE 1423/270, Makins to Eden, 29 November 1955.

37 Sherfield Papers, MS Memoirs, Suez Crisis, pp. 7–11; FO 371/113742/JE 113739/JE 1423/270, Makins to FO, 29 December 1955; *FRUS, 1955–1957, Vol. XIV, The Arab–Israeli Dispute* (Washington, DC, USGPO, 1989), pp. 849–51, 860–5, 868–70.

38 Sherfield Papers, MS Memoirs, Suez Crisis, pp. 11–16; Evelyn Shuckburgh, *Descent to Suez: Diaries 1951–6* (London, Weidenfeld and Nicolson, 1986), pp. 320–3; *FRUS, 1955–1957, Vol. XIII. The Near East, Jordan–Yemen* (Washington, DC, USGPO, 1988), pp. 285–6, 303–4, 317–24.

39 Lucas, *Divided We Stand*, pp. 89–90.

40 Sherfield Papers, MS Memoirs, Suez Crisis, pp. 16–21.

41 Sherfield Papers, Lord Sherfield, MS 'Sidelights on Suez', Part 1, p. 2.

42 Keith Kyle, *Suez* (London, Weidenfeld and Nicolson, 1991), pp. 128–9; Sir Anthony Eden, *Full Circle* (London, Cassell, 1960), p. 422; Selwyn Lloyd, *Suez* (London, Jonathan Cape, 1978), p. 71.

43 Sherfield Papers, MS Memoirs, Suez Crisis, p. 24.

44 Ibid., pp. 24–5.

45 Ibid., pp. 30–3; PREM 11/1101, Makins to FO, tels 1845–7, 9 September 1956, Makins to Eden, 5 October 1956.

46 Ibid., pp. 42–5.

47   Sherfield Papers, A. Gorst and W.S. Lucas Interview, p. 8; MS Memoirs, Suez
     Crisis, pp. 46–7; PRO, T236/4189, Makins to Macmillan, 16 November 1956;
     T236/4190, Makins to Macmillan, 22 November 1956.
48   Sherfield Papers, MS Memoirs, Suez Crisis, pp. 48–9.
49   Sherfield Papers, Green Box 41, notes for speech for Monday Luncheon Club,
     10 December 1956.
50   D. Cameron Watt, 'Demythologizing the Eisenhower Era', in W.R. Louis and
     H. Bull, *The Special Relationship: Anglo-American Relations since 1945* (Oxford,
     Clarendon Press, 1986), p. 76.

8
Anglo-American Relations and Diverging Economic Defence Policies in the 1950s and 1960s

Alan P. Dobson

At the end of the Second World War Anglo-American relations deterior-ated badly, but by 1950 economic interdependence and the cold war reversed this decline and forged a new special relationship.[1] It was not as comprehensive or special as in the war, but it counted over a range of changing policy areas until the 1960s when sterling devaluation and British military withdrawal from east of Suez diminished its value. In the meantime it empowered, but also restrained, both countries and this may be clearly seen in the field of cold war economic defence policies.[2]

Anglo-American relations and the cold war

After the war the British needed US help to repair their economy, to secure Western Europe, and to bolster their world position. In contrast the USA was both an economic colossus, with 50 per cent of the world's manufacturing capacity, and the most potent military power that had ever existed and so its needs were understandably less; but it valued Britain as an ally in the cold war and for fostering a liberal world economic order. Although they generally agreed about overall strategic goals, each had its own interests of state and different ideas about how best to safeguard wider Western interests. One area where different priorities arose was the cold war itself. An early clash here resulted from Britain's refusal to comply with US demands that it should lead European integration. In the end the USA decided against coercion, for, as one senior State Department official observed: 'There was deep conviction [in Washington] that the U.S. needed Great Britain above everything else.... All these things must be taken into consideration

143

when studying the problem of how far to press Britain in . . . European integration.'[3]

At the outset, Britain waged the cold war vigorously, but soon saw the confrontation in less pressing terms than the USA. In weighing up both domestic economic factors and the Soviet atomic threat as potentially more immediate and more devastating to Britain than to the USA, the British came to favour less provocative strategies than those of its ally. A Foreign Office official in December 1951 noted US 'impatience with the more cautious British approach to . . . containment of Communism. . . . This contrasts with British anxiety that the impetuous "all or nothing" tendencies in the United States will prematurely expose this country to the first onslaught of Communist aggression.'[4] However, these differences did not diminish the importance of the special relationship for the British. In fact they sought to formalise it to increase their influence, but the Americans resisted that for a variety of reasons including reluctance to offend other important allies, a desire not to be too closely associated with British colonialism for fear of alienating newly independent countries from the Western camp, and fear that it might tie US hands too tightly in policymaking. The British suffered their first rebuff in 1950 during a series of allied conferences in London where British and US officials agreed on the vital importance of their relationship for NATO and the West in general, but the Americans cautioned that by strengthening each other they must take care not to weaken other members of the alliance.[5] The second came in the Truman–Churchill talks of January 1952, when the Americans again refused to formalise things, though they acknowledged *de facto* special relations in some policy areas and with this the British had to be content.[6]

In preparing for allied talks in London in early 1950 the complexity of economic relations and their far-reaching effects were central to British thinking. 'Although British and American political interests coincide in most parts of the world they rest on the assumption in American minds that the United Kingdom is the principal partner and ally on whom the USA can rely.'[7] But to sustain this Britain would have to prove itself and remain useful by maintaining its world role and that involved 'sustained political, military and economic effort' and running its policies in tandem with and not too strongly in opposition to the USA's. Foreign Secretary Bevin agreed with this, but others, in particular the Chancellor of the Exchequer, Sir Stafford Cripps, regarded the implied subservience with distaste. An important feature of Britain's postwar foreign policy is the growing importance of the Treasury in policymaking. Economic constraints necessarily empowered the Treasury, which often spoke against matching British with US policy if it meant more expenditure or sacrificing British economic and commercial interests for the sake of broad Western interests as defined by the USA.[8]

Concern about British economic dependency continued when Churchill and the Conservatives returned to power in 1951. They resented the way economic weakness compromised their autonomy, but they also felt that their economic health and great-power status in the world depended on good relations with the USA. Comments reflecting these not-easily-reconciled positions came from British Ambassador to the USA Sir Oliver Franks. He wrote of the Churchill–Truman talks of January/February 1952 that 'the success of the visits will ripen into a closer partnership and renewed mutual trust in proportion as in the near future we show ourselves masters of our own economic destiny'.[9] Meanwhile Foreign Secretary Eden said that he had returned from the USA 'with a renewed conviction of our need to do everything possible to re-establish our economic and financial independence'.[10]

On a number of grounds, therefore, there were tensions between the two countries and in London deep concern about the overall economic position. London wanted to work closely with Washington and guide affairs in ways which would benefit British interests. At the same time the British resented having to play second fiddle. For their part the Americans looked to the British for help but were often exasperated at their stubbornness and resented having to compromise on specific issues for the sake of overall relations. By the early 1950s those relations had implications for the strategic embargo because of different emphases about the importance of trade and about how the two countries perceived and sought to deal with the Soviet threat.

The fall of China to communism and the explosion of the Soviet atom bomb in 1949 changed American cold war thinking. The review of policy Truman commissioned in the wake of these events produced NSC-68, which identified a danger of war with the Soviets in four to five years' time and advocated a more militarised and globalised containment policy. The outbreak of both the Korean War and McCarthyism pushed the USA into implementing NSC-68 and into a more aggressive stance towards the Soviets. Similar changes happened in Britain, but not to the same extent and policies and attitudes mellowed more quickly. Before Korea, British and US assessments varied. The USA thought that the Soviets had 'somewhat increased their [military] lead on the West' and that that might 'make them more provocative and bolder'. 'There was, therefore, a considerable risk of some incidents arising from a Soviet miscalculation of Western reactions developing into war.'[11] In contrast, the British believed that 'it was unlikely that they [the Soviets] would take serious risks'.[12] For a while after the outbreak of the Korean War, the US position moved even further from Britain's; however, by 1952 their policies appeared to be converging again.

In March 1952 Foreign Office Soviet experts noted: 'The official United States estimate of the likelihood of war, set out in NIE-48 [National Intelligence Estimate] of 3rd January, 1952, is very similar to ours.... But Her Majesty's Embassy, Washington, report that senior American officials are by no means unanimous in their views; the most influential opinion seems to be that the Soviet Government will not allow themselves to be diverted from their planned strategy (which the Americans also believe to exclude total war) by any provocation short of a general Western attack. It may be assumed, at least, that the Americans are likely in general to estimate the safe degree of Western pressure considerably higher than we do.'[13] It was largely this 'estimate [of] the safe degree of Western pressure' fed by the strength of American anti-communism that caused difficulties with Britain over the strategic embargo. But that was a subset of broader cold war strategies and it was there that problems originated which then fed into economic defence policy.

In 1952 the British Global Strategy Paper argued for more reliance on nuclear deterrence. At first this was received rather critically in the USA, but with the coming to power of Eisenhower in 1953 and the development of the New Look strategy, NSC 162/2, it seemed to many that the Americans had adopted a very similar position to the one articulated by the British the previous year. The New Look adopted massive nuclear retaliation to deter communism, supplemented by demands for more conventional rearmament by allies, more psychological, covert and economic warfare, and a complex alliance system. In nuclear terms this looked like the British Global Strategy Paper but reliance by both countries on nuclear deterrence disguised different needs and policies as to how to use nuclear weapons.[14] As we shall also see with the strategic embargo, the Americans, while using the same sort of language as the British to describe broad aims, actually had a more aggressive and forward policy.

This, then, was the backdrop to the development of the strategic embargo. Britain and the USA had a junior–senior interdependent relationship, complicated respectively for the British by their economic weakness and for the Americans by their inability to use coercion. It was a relationship pledged to resist communism and promote liberal democracy, but also one in which there were different appreciations of the cold war.

The strategic embargo – the first phase

By March 1948, after much internal debate, the USA established the principles for a strategic embargo to be implemented against the Soviet bloc and they soon sought multilateral Western action in order to make it effective. There was never any dispute between the USA and her allies over embargoing core military items (nuclear materials and finished high-technology weaponry), but there was over virtually everything else. Whether or not a country decided to embargo non-military items depended upon which of five basic tactics it favoured. These were about using trade controls: to damage communist economies and restrict their military and economic potential; to weaken the orbit of Soviet satellites; to relax or restrict trade as a tactical bargaining ploy; to send messages about resolve and moral positions; and to 'seduce' communist countries with Western consumerism. Britain, unlike the USA, emphasised the less aggressive tactics and came to rely almost exclusively on seduction.

The job of engaging West European cooperation was assigned to Averell Harriman. The guiding principles he had to sell were that the embargo would be selective; that it would be sensitive to the concept of relative gain; the embargo lists should be the same for the USA and her allies or else there would be a form of *de facto* discrimination against US exporters; and, finally, the multilateral embargo had to be voluntary.[15] The Americans realised there might have to be a trade-off between the value of cooperation and the length of the embargo list and so Harriman was instructed to refer matters back to Washington if changes were necessary to secure 'substantial voluntary agreement by the European countries'.[16] Despite the importance of achieving a voluntary agreement, the USA pressed its allies and later congressional legislation exerted hard leverage, in fact in excess of what the administration actually thought was wise.[17] However, there were limits to what the Americans could do and it is also important to remember that the British needed no persuading about the wisdom of the embargo in principle, but only over its extent. The Americans kept out of early talks and it was the British who took the lead in bringing the other allies together in 1949 to a policy consensus, but one that was not quite what the Americans might have hoped for. As one British official explained: 'it would be most important that all the countries concerned should have definitely accepted the policy before the Americans come in since a large part of the discussions of the present stage is inevitably concerned with the extent to which American pressure can be resisted.'[18]

These negotiations very much set the pattern for the future. There was agreement on an embargo and a ministerial level Consultative Group and a working party, the Coordinating Committee (COCOM), were set up, but there was compromise from the start. It had to be a cooperative venture. The very same reasoning which had prevented the Americans from coercing the British into leading European integration applied here as well. So, the USA always found itself with a more extensive national embargo list than the multilateral COCOM list and always with far less trade with the Soviet bloc than its European allies.

The general disposition of the USA to a more combative style towards the Soviet Union and China meant that they were more willing than their allies to put pressure on Soviet 'sore spots', one of which involved 'depriving Soviet Russia of key materials'.[19] During the Korean War the British were not far from the Americans on this. They saw an intensive economic blockade as a positive policy to 'compress and disrupt' and possibly change the Soviet regime: 'This may come about by a process of evolution, or cracks may appear in the apparently monolithic structure and the whole system, carrying within itself the seeds of its own destruction, may disintegrate.'[20] Americans used a similar type of language to this, but in practice exercised a more rigid embargo than the British, hoped for early and more tangible results and were more prepared to aggravate this sore spot than the British. Looking at broad principles it seemed as if there were a community of Anglo-American interests (just as there seemed to be later between the British Global Strategy Paper and NSC 162/2), but specific needs and the implementation of policy revealed substantial differences in the way the two countries conceived of and justified their economic defence policies. During the Korean War the differential between the US and COCOM lists narrowed and there was less allied friction, but as the war wound down renewed controversy arose, which was soon fuelled by the death of Stalin.

The announcement of his death on 5 March 1953 opened the curtain on what British Prime Minister Churchill saw as a stage of opportunity to bring about a new postwar settlement. According to one interpretation he hoped to achieve 'the reunification of Germany and a German–Soviet non-aggression treaty guaranteed by Great Britain', through summit talks with the Soviets.[21] Just how clear Churchill was about this peace initiative remains contested, and we shall never know what might have transpired, because Churchill's desire for an early version of détente was opposed by the Foreign Office and torpedoed by the Americans for fear that the Soviets might exploit Western divisions, especially over the unresolved problem of how to rearm West Germany.

However, this episode highlighted cold war differences which soon had impact on the strategic embargo.

In the summer of 1953 the New Look review embraced the economic embargo and decided that it should be used: 'a. To control selectively exports of commodities and supply of services from the free world which contribute significantly to the war potential of the Soviet bloc. b. To obtain the maximum net security advantages...from economic intercourse.... c. To decrease the reliance of the free world countries on trade with the Soviet bloc. d. To increase the political and economic unity of the free world. e. To decrease, through skilful flexibility in applying controls, the political and economic unity of the Soviet bloc.'[22] This was NSC 152/2. By the autumn, after further consideration, modest liberalisation proposals were formulated for the multilateral COCOM embargo lists.

Lincoln Gordon, US Minister for Economic Affairs in London, outlined the new US thinking to Foreign Office officials. The USA did not envisage 'a wholesale downgrading of the program'.[23] Some items could be removed from the COCOM embargo lists or placed under quantitative control and these changes would create new direction and emphases. But Gordon also explained US concern that since the death of Stalin 'trade is playing an increasing role in Soviet strategy' and that this warranted: 'Full multilateral consideration [of] problems and shifts in Soviet trade tactics which affect the movement of strategic goods to the Soviet Bloc.'[24] The British were reluctant to do anything immediately as they were also in the midst of a policy review, but they said that: 'The UK does not feel that the recent changes in trading patterns and tactics by the Russians are to be viewed primarily as a tactic in the Cold War, but are rather inclined to view them as primarily reflecting a Soviet desire for trade motivated by internal economic and political factors.'[25]

There were divisions of opinion in both Washington and London about the embargo, but the division was sharper in the latter and the faction that prevailed there favoured more liberalisation than anyone contemplated in Washington. Foreign Secretary Eden was well disposed to US policy (i.e. NSC 152/2, or NSC 152/3 as it became after minor amendments on 6 November) and firmly opposed getting out of step with it. In contrast, the economic departments led by Peter Thorneycroft, President of the Board of Trade, wanted radical changes and the abolition of the quantitative control and surveillance lists. Eden, the Defence Department and the Chiefs of Staff opposed this. On 17 November the Cabinet, nevertheless, decided it would be a good bargaining ploy to put Thorneycroft's proposal to Washington.[26]

American reaction was one of 'profound concern' at the 'serious divergence' in policies.[27] This was the very thing that Eden had wanted to avoid because he was well aware 'of the serious dangers of political dispute which it contains'.[28] However, Churchill, ironically the great champion of the special relationship, stated in Cabinet on 18 January that 'increased trade with the Soviet bloc would mean, not only assistance to our exports, but greater possibilities for infiltration behind the Iron Curtain. Determined efforts should be made to persuade the United States Government to accept a new policy on this matter. The policy which he suggested was that we should in future deny the Soviet bloc only goods of direct military value....'[29]

Churchill made sure that his views were carried forward into the formulation of policy by chairing the Cabinet Committee set up to deal with the review. Eden was sidelined, but nevertheless he and the Minister of Defence, Lord Alexander, managed to effect a criteria change to reinstate items of 'significant indirect military importance'.[30] Even with this, however, the COCOM lists would still be halved and Churchill, determined to push liberalisation, made a pre-emptive strike before Anglo-US talks started by stating in Parliament that 'a substantial relaxation would undoubtedly be beneficial in its proper setting'.[31]

On 1 March detailed British proposals were handed to the Americans and there followed a lengthy series of discussions. They moved forward in three stages: the American response and exchanges between Eisenhower and Churchill; talks in London with Harold Stassen, Director for Mutual Security; and talks in Washington between him and Thorneycroft.

During the first stage Eisenhower wrote to Churchill on 19 March indicating a willingness to move towards the British position, but not so far or so quickly as they wanted: 'To do so would be, I think, to go beyond what is immediately safe or in the interest of the free world.'[32] On 24 March, after discussion in Cabinet, Churchill replied, arguing that the opportunities to infiltrate the communist bloc would be increased by trade liberalisation and also that his government had to feed over fifty million people 'on these small islands' and thus more trade was vital.[33] Eisenhower replied that the British seemed to want to go 'a bit further than seems wise or necessary' and that Harold Stassen would come to London to try to sort things out.[34] Stassen, first at Chequers and then in Washington with Thorneycroft, did manage to sort things out, but it was a major compromise on the part of the

Americans. They agreed that in return for new transhipment and trans-action controls the embargo list could be reduced to 176 items, with another 24 to be quantitatively controlled and 55 on the watch list. Stassen thought that this was very satisfactory all things considered: the British were delighted. '...we have secured acceptance by all participating countries of a very substantial reduction in the International Lists. This must be regarded as a major achievement, bearing in mind the difficulties we faced.'[35] The Americans felt obliged to give way because of the value of allied unity and the basic fact that COCOM could only operate on a cooperative basis. However, just as important as the changes themselves was the development of American thinking. The British had quite clearly downgraded the danger of conflict with the Soviets, regarded their new trade initiatives as promising rather than threatening, and were determined to place more emphasis on the need to expand British exports to an extent that often overrode cold war considerations. This latter decision reflected the growing power of the economic departments of state and the limits of Foreign Office influence. The Americans on the other hand, while they had been pushed into a compromise by the British that produced a reduction in the embargo lists that not even the most liberal within the US administration would independently have willingly conceded, they had also begun to change the way they thought about the embargo. And it was not a change that would always be helpful for allied unity in the future.

In the American Cabinet and on the NSC, there was only one person who consistently favoured liberalisation and that was the President, Dwight D. Eisenhower. There has been much scholarly debate about his influence. To what extent was liberalisation facilitated by Eisenhower and to what extent was it forced on to the Americans by their allies, most notably Britain? This is an important issue here because answers to these questions have impact on the analysis of the nature of interdependence and the direction and velocity of influence in Anglo-US relations.[36]

Eisenhower frequently showed exasperation and irritation with his colleagues over their refusal to relax the embargo, but part of the exasperation was because he did not think that the embargo issue was worth such costly man-hour consideration. This makes one wonder just how important the issue was for Eisenhower and may go some way towards explaining why he did not push his views in the face of opposition by colleagues and why he did not always ensure that when liberal policy decisions were made that they were fully carried out. However, when embargo issues threatened Western unity, or when he engaged with the idea of weaning the satellites away from the Soviet Union, or when he thought of the relative gains from embargo policy and the problem of the West European economies and the fact that their standard of living 'was too damn low', then the issues did become important and he argued for compromise and liberalisation.

Unfortunately for Eisenhower, some of his ideas about the embargo were inconsistent with the findings and recommendations of his admin-istration's overall strategic policy and this blunted their impact on the shape of the embargo (for example, intelligence estimates rated the likelihood of separating the satellites from the Soviet Union as extre-mely low, but Eisenhower continued to nurture such hopes). Also, while he recognised the difficulty of distinguishing between strategic and non-strategic goods he was not always sensitive to the full implications of these distinctions. In one NSC meeting he said that he would 'fight the British to the death to keep electronic equipment on the embargo list, but in any event let us pare this strategic list down to its funda-mentals'.[37] But his 'fundamentals' were different from the British and logically led to a more expansive view of the embargo. Finally, Eisenhower was caught up, along with the rest of his administration, with what we have identified as the fourth embargo strategy, which heavily involved the importance of symbolism. In the spring of 1957, when a relaxation of the China trade controls had been forced on to the agenda by the European allies, Eisenhower said 'there is another factor to be considered, the factor that Admiral Radford (Chairman of the JCS) was continually emphasising – namely, that if there is relaxation of the controls on trade with communist China, then all our friends and allies in the Far East [i.e. the Nationalist Chinese and the South Koreans] will conclude that we are abandoning them.... The President confessed that he was much puzzled as to what we were going to say about this remarkable change of policy on trade controls, both to our Congress and to our Far Eastern Allies.'[38] Thus while Eisenhower helped to push liberalisation along it is important to note that his views were sometimes at odds with intelligence findings, that he was not always sensitive to the implications of his own views of strategic fundamentals, and that he placed great importance on the symbolic impact that a drastic change in embargo policy might have. These factors either limited his natural inclination to relax the embargo or compromised, or confused, and thereby weakened, his arguments for liberalisation. From time to time he was helped by Humphrey, Dulles and Stassen, though they were less consistent and committed than the President. The

Americans were thus always several steps behind the Europeans in terms of liberalising the embargo.

The radical British proposals were discussed in the NSC where the overwhelming majority was vehemently against acceptance. Only Eisenhower and Humphrey were critical of current US embargo policy and seemingly inclined to at least some change. But, while the President displayed 'great impatience and exasperation' even he eventually concluded that 'at the present moment... for tactical reasons, we could not agree with the British proposals'.[39] An irony that ran through the meeting was the fact that intelligence reports summarised by Allen Dulles, Director of the CIA, and the opinion of the Defense Department expressed by Secretary Wilson indicated that 'a relaxation of controls even on so drastic a scale as the British were proposing, would result in only a limited amount of additional trade between Eastern and Western Europe'.[40] Relaxing trade would not produce substantial advantages for the West, but neither would the effect of 'relaxation on the Soviet economy... be very significant except in a certain number of key strategic items. In the latter case, ability to purchase these items would break certain bottlenecks in the development of the Soviet war potential.'[41] Clearly this latter point was not without importance, but was its significance such as to warrant a major rift with allies, and to what extent was British policy different to US policy under NSC 152/2? At the outset of the meeting National Security Adviser Robert Cutler explained that the 'essence of the difference between the U.S. and British positions... was the U.S. view that a number of strategic items should be subject to control when they contributed indirectly to Soviet war potential, even though such items were not themselves actual munitions of war'.[42] But the British, under pressure from their own defence people, had reinstated items of 'significant indirect military importance'.[43] So the problem amounted to different judgements as to what fell into that category: a matter that one would not have thought would have caused such consternation among the Americans. But there was more to it than that.

The problem was that US policymakers took a number of other factors into account which affected how they defined the category in question, and determined them against both slashing the embargo list by 50 per cent and abolishing the quantitative and watch lists. The Americans were suspicious of Soviet trade policy. They feared Congressional criticism, especially of the potential for large transhipments to China if controls on Soviet trade were relaxed. They thought that relaxing the embargo before a resolution of the Korean and Indo-China situations at the Geneva Conference would weaken the West's bargaining hand. They believed that the USA had to maintain a more aggressive stance towards China than her allies were prepared to and they felt that relaxing trade with the Soviets would send out the wrong message and would be a preliminary for a relaxation of trade with China. Thus as much for political, psychological and symbolic as for economic and strategic reasons, the Americans fought radical liberalisation.

Intense negotiations with the British now took place, following the schedule and achieving the compromise that strongly favoured the British position described earlier. The Americans had been pushed, against their will, by their allies into a substantial relaxation of the embargo. This had forced the Americans to reconsider their own position and to think about the way that they justified their embargo policy. It was here that in some ways the most radical transformation was underway and which was accelerated during 1953–54 and continued thereafter as the British mounted pressure to abandon multilaterally the China Differential (a stricter embargo on China than on Soviet trade), something they abandoned unilaterally in 1957.

The shift to a different basis for justifying US embargo policy was by no means complete in 1954, but it was gathering momentum and picked up even more pace during the discussions about the China Differential from 1956 onwards. The embargo was now no longer justified primarily in economic terms. Economic benefits for the West and restricting the economic growth and the military potential of the Soviets and the Chinese became minor concerns because the embargo was judged to have only minor effects on these matters. Thus the USA was waging an embargo without expecting even modest, never mind substantial, economic or military gains.

So, what were its objectives? First of all the very existence of the embargo was a factor. Once there it would involve political repercussions to remove it. The USA was partly a prisoner of the policy it had established. To reduce the embargo could not be done without domestic political repercussions particularly in the Congress and, more importantly, without sending messages to the communists, to allies and to uncommitted nations. These considerations became paramount. In addition, the USA did not wish to give things away unilaterally. If it were to reduce the embargo lists then it wanted something tangible in return from both allies and communists. All this is not to say that there were no economic aspects left. There were worries about communist trade penetration of the free world which the US thought that it could control and limit through using the embargo as a negotiating tactic.

Also, because estimates of the effects of the embargo could never be precise and exact there were always opportunities for hard-line anti-communists to argue that the embargo was effective. The favourite arguments here were to do with communist short-supply problems and production bottlenecks. The potential to argue along these lines gave the Defense Department and the Chiefs of Staff ammunition to argue for a strict embargo because even a marginal benefit could not be blithely ignored if there were a danger of war. However, even they came to emphasise most of all the psychological effects of the embargo as a justification for keeping extensive controls.

The strategic embargo – the second phase

The 1960s opened inauspiciously. The West felt intimidated by Soviet pressures on Berlin, it feared that they had taken the lead in ICBMs, there was deep concern about communist advances in the Third World, and there were worrying divisions within the Western camp itself. Kennedy's extravagant rhetoric committed his administration to get America moving again and to re-take the initiative from the communists. His strategy was 'flexible response', which involved a massive expansion of conventional and unconventional forces, a diversification of nuclear capabilities, and a review of economic defence policies. All this was with a view to meeting communist challenges in kind. In the strategic field the USA met most of its goals, though with rather unforeseen consequences, but in the field of economic defence policy little happened because of differences within the Kennedy administration and because of other matters which were accorded higher priority. However, the change of thinking that got under way during Eisenhower's time now became more lucidly and comprehensively articulated. Simultaneously in London the emphasis moved towards an expansion of trade with the Soviets for its own commercial sake as well as seeing it as a means to help change Soviet society in positive ways. In terms of the core and the five tactics of the embargo the British and the Americans still adhered to the core, but Britain had abandoned the tactic of trying to restrict Soviet military and economic potential, had severely downgraded the idea of disrupting the Soviet bloc through manipulating trade, shied away from using carrot-and-stick trade measures to pressurise them, and avoided either using the embargo as a means of expressing moral disapproval or as a means of sending messages about resolve. British concern to expand trade, logically led to emphasis on the cold war tactic of seduction. In contrast the Americans were somewhat ambiguous in their own thinking about using the embargo to restrict the military and economic production of the Soviets, but they believed trade could be used to lessen the dependence of the satellites on the Soviets, emphasised the importance of trade restrictions as bargaining chips in the cold war game, and were almost obsessed with the potency of the embargo to convey messages. With regard to the idea of seduction by consumerism there was less emphasis on this and less unanimity about the beneficial effects of trade. Not all believed a 'fat Russian is a happy Russian'. Emphases on different tactics were again the outcome of different assessments of the nature of the cold war.

US policy in the early 1960s changed in important respects after the Cuban Missile Crisis of October 1962. In its wake came significant moves towards détente and a stabilisation of the superpower nuclear relationship. This began with the Partial Atomic Test Ban Treaty of 1963 and progressed through the SALT and Helsinki agreements. However, this was not the end of the cold war. The nature and focus of the conflict changed, but economic warfare was still a weapon to be used. Kennedy edged towards some liberalisation of the embargo during 1963, but it was modest and still couched in terms of a strategy that would bring the USA cold war advantages. In July 1963 Walt Rostow, Director of the State Department Policy Planning Staff, wrote a seminal paper on the embargo; among his conclusions was that

> For a number of years now, we have attempted to maintain, virtually in isolation, a posture tantamount to economic warfare. A change in this stance would therefore carry considerable meaning.... The major issues in our trade control policy are political not strategic, economic or commercial. Neither full access to, nor complete denial of, trade with the U.S. can affect Soviet capabilities to wage war – either hot or cold war. Nor can either trade situation affect in any meaningful sense the performance or potentialities of the Soviet economy. And from the U.S. side, the economic and commercial significance of trade with the USSR, whether free or restricted, is negligible.[44]

The key for Rostow, and many others within the administration, was the psychological fall-out that might occur if changes were not timed carefully because the system 'has become intricately interwoven into our overall strategic thinking'.[45] In a static cold war situation, which is what Rostow believed the USA to be in, 'there can be no question of giving quarter, psychological or otherwise, to the enemy'.[46] But, in a fluid situation, i.e. one in which the Soviets made the first concessions, he believed that the USA could move to a position where only core items would be controlled. Controls on everything else could be bargained away for concessions from the USSR. These bargaining chips, Rostow explained, were largely psychological in nature. 'Trade denial has come to be an important symbol of our cold war resolve and purpose and of our moral disapproval of the USSR. The trade controls issue has an important place in our continuing efforts to arouse the free world to common action and policies against the communist threat. We have sought to induce non-communist states to hold trade to a minimum, not only on grounds of denying help to the Communists to build their power, but on the grounds that increased trade would carry real and immediate dangers to free world participants in that trade.'[47] This paper was produced during widespread debate about the embargo in Washington. In the end Kennedy, while he saw the situation as more fluid than Rostow and favoured more vigorous moves than the interdepartmental report which resulted from the policy review, nevertheless, decided against radical action. He only called for vigour in pursuing liberalisation within the existing legal framework.[48]

In contrast, the British had arrived at a much more liberal and non-cold war view of trade with the Soviets. In the spring of 1963 a paper for Foreign Secretary Lord Home explained that 'Our stated policy is an expansion of trade subject to the embargo list, no excessive dependence on Soviet supplies and no dumping. With these qualifications, we see both political and commercial advantage in expansion.'[49] A similar résumé was given to the President of the Board of Trade, Sir Frederick Errol, prior to his September 1963 visit to Moscow with the more strongly worded note that 'we enforce strictly the strategic embargo'.[50] But the British now only embargoed items of direct military use and the main preoccupation was not to restrict, but to expand trade and in particular how to close the negative trade balance with the Soviets. In May 1963 after a lengthy investigation and the discovery that other European countries bilaterally controlled their trade to ensure a balance or a surplus, the British considered making threats or offering inducements to push the Soviets into buying more British goods. In the end, they decided against this because inducements would cause difficulties with allies and pressures might be counter-productive. The Soviets were simply told that when renewing the Anglo-Soviet trade agreement in 1964 the imbalance would have to be considered.[51]

The British were committed to expanding exports to help their faltering economy. In addition their attitude towards the Soviets was less aggressive than the Americans'. The British were not naive, but they thought that the Soviets were genuinely in favour of détente, which was also in their interests because 'a) it reduces the risk of nuclear war, and b) if agreement can be reached on some collateral measures (e.g. anti-surprise attack) it might pave the way for progress with measures of real disarmament, and c) detente helps the prospects of evolution within the bloc and provides more fruitful ground for the West to increase its contacts and so further the process'.[52]

Thus the British looked more favourably on détente than the Americans and wanted to expand trade as part of the overall process of improving East–West relations and, equally importantly, to help the British economy. They had neither the leadership responsibilities nor specific commitments in sensitive areas such as Vietnam which often tied US hands and propelled them into more inflexible stances. In any case, as Macmillan had made clear to Kennedy over Laos, the British favoured a negotiated settlement of problems in South-East Asia. The British also did not have past hardline anti-communist rhetoric to live with or such a virulently anti-communist legislature or significant sections of strongly anti-communist public opinion as the Americans. The US was hoist on its own petard of virulent anti-communism and in the foreign trade field the Administration was particularly vulnerable because constitutional control of foreign trade lay in the hands of Congress and, while it had delegated many of its powers to the executive branch since 1934, it retained much influence and ultimately what it delegated it could always recall. It was in this context that the controversy over wide-diameter steel pipes arose in the early 1960s.

In the autumn of 1962 the Americans were disturbed by the sale of wide-diameter steel pipe by Western countries to the Soviet Union to help in its construction of the CMEA pipeline that would bring oil into eastern and central Europe. They feared that it could be useful for the Red Army and that West European countries might become dependent upon Soviet oil supplies, to the detriment, among other things, of US oil companies. This type of piping had been removed from the COCOM lists some time earlier, but on 21 November the Americans brought the issue before the NATO Council and invited members to prohibit further sales to the Soviets. Agreement was unanimous, except for Britain.

More or less at the same time the Nassau meeting in December between Prime Minister Macmillan and President Kennedy showed that the special relationship was still alive, if deeply troubled and not as well as it used to be. It declined rapidly in the 1960s, but there was still enough life left in it to enable Macmillan to persuade Kennedy to sell Britain the Polaris missile system. Unfortunately that special relationship was something that President de Gaulle resented and used as part of his reasoning to deny Britain entry into the EEC. His veto meant, at least temporarily, the end of Macmillan's favoured strategy to deal with British economic problems.[53] Exports now became an even more important matter for Britain.

By this time there were rumours that the Soviets were making overtures to British steel-pipe manufacturers. On 8 January when the Lord Privy Seal with special responsibility for Europe, Edward Heath, was asked about the pipe embargo in Bonn by the Germans he gave them a '... completely negative response with respect to willingness UK cooperate in enforcing embargo decision'.[54] This was a particularly sensitive issue for the Germans because prior to the embargo they had sold 700 000 tons of piping to the Soviets and stopping a flow of exports of that magnitude was no small matter and, in any case, was constitutionally questionable. Britain was not only standing against the decision taken by all other NATO members, but its actions were also now further threatening allied harmony. A further problem arose with rumours that Britain was seeking a deal to exchange ships for Soviet oil. This prompted an angry note by US Ambassador to NATO's Thomas Finletter: 'Regret have to say this latest in a series of HMG actions which imply UK seeming give priority to its short range commercial interests over basic interests of the Atlantic Alliance. Others are large diameter pipe embargo, credits to Sov Bloc, Viscount sales, economic countermeasures, Cuban shipping. If Soviet deal consummated, UK will have achieved almost perfect score of opposition to us in NATO on all E/W trade issues. I am very disappointed....'[55]

As in the dispute over liberalisation in 1954, the Foreign Office favoured a conciliatory line. In Cabinet on 14 February the Foreign Secretary said that 'following the failure of our attempt to join the European Economic Community we must expect pressure for an increase in East–West trade; and this would be liable to raise contentious issues...'.[56] Although increased trade might improve relations in the long term, in the short term it might lead to embarrassing Soviet diversions of resources to military production. 'We should therefore seek an opportunity to discuss with the United States Administration the whole issue of economic policy towards the Sino-Soviet bloc and should attempt to persuade them not to press us on those issues such as oil and large diameter steel pipe, on which public opinion in the United Kingdom was easily roused.'[57]

A week later Kennedy wrote directly to Macmillan: 'We hope that it may be possible to arrange affairs so that Soviet oil penetration is not encouraged. I am asking David Bruce [US ambassador in London] to report the breadth and gravity of the concern which is felt over here on this particular point. On the wide diameter pipe, our concern derives from the danger that if any one of us sells such pipe to the Russians, there may be considerable political damage in other countries where Soviet offers have been rejected.'[58] Kennedy's appeal was ineffective even after Under-Secretary of State for Economic Affairs George Ball followed up the matter in London, arguing that Anglo-German relations would suffer if Britain sold pipes to the Russians.[59]

The business of the wide-diameter pipes had been raised in Cabinet on more than one occasion and the Strategic Exports Committee looked into it in some detail. On 25 March it made a unanimous recommendation that it would be wrong to stop any contracts going forward. 'A decision in this sense would be ill-received by the Governments of other countries (NATO); but it would be consistent with our declared opposition to measures of economic warfare, save in the face of an imminent threat of specific character.'[60]

On 28 March Errol explained to Ball that the British resented being dubbed 'the bad guys' by the Americans in this situation. He told Ball that the Soviets were not even 'nibbling' at a contract, but if they did he would review the situation on its merits.[61] He also 'emphasised present mood in country to maintain independence of action and resentment at US pressure.'[62] That same day he made Britain's position plain in the House of Commons: 'I have told manufacturers that there are no restrictions on the export from the United Kingdom to the Soviet Socialist Republic of steel pipe of any diameter. In the discussion in NATO on this subject, the United Kingdom Representative made it clear that Her Majesty's Government did not support the recommendation and reserved Her Majesty's Government's freedom of action.'[63] Eventually the dispute fizzled out as British prices were too high for the Soviets, but the episode clearly demonstrated differences about the strategic embargo and conceptions of the cold war both of which troubled Anglo-American relations and reveal much about their character.

Conclusion

Throughout the period in question there was a special quality to Anglo-American relations in a number of policy areas connected with the cold war and the management of the international economy. This created interdependence and tension between the power to influence and vulnerability to be influenced. In the field of economic defence policy, and specifically with regard to the strategic embargo, the result was a tense and troublesome relationship because the USA always favoured more aggressive cold war strategies than the British. This was partly because of conviction, partly to do with being caught by its own harsh anti-communist rhetoric within the public and congressional domains, and partly to do with the responsibilities of Western leadership and, for example, its inability to ignore what seemed to be dangerous communist advances in Third World countries. If the leader of the Western Alliance did not react to such challenges then it was feared that the communist world might seriously miscalculate Western responses to threats elsewhere. Britain had the luxury of knowing that the USA would respond to defend Western interests and so could take a more disinterested cold war view and a more interested commercial one. In addition the British tended to see the cold war in less aggressive terms out of conviction. At the same time they realised how vulnerable Britain was to a Soviet nuclear attack and that led Britain towards less provocative policies and to try to diminish the dangers of escalation. Finally, in a long-haul competition with the Soviet Union success depended on the health of the British economy, and its reliance on exports logically inclined it towards more trade whenever it was judged to be prudent.

Britain throughout the 1950s and 1960s held to the embargo of the core, but soon rejected the idea of trying to restrict the growth and overall military potential of the Soviets by embargoing items of indirect military utility. They also placed little emphasis on manipulating trade as a bargaining counter or as a means of levering the satellites out of orbit, or as a means of moral condemnation or a symbol of resolve. Trade for its own sake was the main priority by the 1960s and if that had a seductive effect on the Soviets then that was an added bonus.

The Americans stuck to the core, but wanted to cast the embargo net wider: for them there was little direct cost involved because only a tiny amount of trade was at issue. As the years passed and evidence mounted that the embargo did not restrict either economic growth or Soviet military potential the Americans became rather ambiguous about these as reasons for the embargo. They never abandoned them entirely as a partial justification, but they came to emphasise other factors, namely disrupting the unity of the bloc and using trade restrictions as bargaining counters in the cold war game. Most important of all, the strategic embargo came to be seen as a means of expressing moral condemnation and as a symbol of US resolve and determination to continue the battle against communism. By the 1960s sending messages through the medium of the embargo was seen as more important than inflicting economic pain or restricting the Soviet military potential. The intense psychological and symbolic importance of the embargo weighed on American minds in a way that hardly touched their allies.

Thus by the 1960s the USA and Britain found themselves in different positions regarding the waging of the cold war and the use of the strategic embargo. British policy in early 1963 was such that, as Ambassador Finletter pointed out with some anger, the British had opposed every sensitive embargo issue that had arisen over the previous months. But, there was little the Americans could do. As in 1954 and 1957 they had largely to go along with policies pushed by the British for the sake of allied unity, because the multilateral embargo would only work on a voluntary basis and because of the wider constraints that still had some, though diminishing power, because of the special relationship. In 1962–63 their view of the value of trade was such that they opposed US policy on wide-diameter pipes, credits to the Soviet Bloc, the stringency of the embargo on Cuba, and on trading ships for oil. This was clearly not a hegemonic relationship. It was one of senior and junior partners, but the partnership was too valuable for the USA to try to coerce its ally, especially when there was still agreement on embargoing the core items. Also, the fundamental philosophy of the USA involved notions of independent sovereignty and respect for (at least democratic) nation-states and it had to work within those guiding principles in the Western Alliance or be false to itself. This meant very complex calculations about US national interests and the extent to which the USA could tolerate opposition to its policies. In the field of the strategic embargo one has to conclude that the USA had to stretch its tolerance a long way.

Notes

1 For details of the rise, decline and revival of the special relationship see: Alan P. Dobson, *Anglo-American Relations in the Twentieth Century: Of Friendship,*

Conflict and the Rise and Decline of Superpowers (Routledge, London, 1995), ch. 4.

2 For analyses of Anglo-American relations in both a more general and a more specific focus, see Alan P. Dobson, 'The USA, Britain, and the Question of Hegemony', in Geir Lundestad (ed.), *No End to Alliance: the United States and Western Europe, Past, Present and Future* (Macmillan, London), 1998, pp. 134–67; and Alan P. Dobson, 'The USA, Hegemony and Airline Market Access to Britain and Western Europe, 1945–96', *Diplomacy and Statecraft*, 9(2), 1998, pp. 129–60.

3 Harry S. Truman Library (HST Lib.), PSF box 163, subject file conferences, Sept. 1947–Dec. 1950, folder: subject file conferences, Paris Conference, Oct.–Nov. 1949, US ambassadors' meeting, 21 Oct. 1949.

4 Public Record Office (hereafter all Foreign Office and Cabinet papers cited are from the PRO unless otherwise indicated) FO 371/90932, minute by Robin Cecil, 8 Dec. 1951.

5 R. Bullen and M.E. Pelly (eds.), assisted by H.J. Yasamee and G. Bennett, *Foreign and Commonwealth Office Documents on British Policy Overseas*, Series 2, Vol. 2, 1950 (HMSO, London, 1987), p. 94, first bipartite official meeting, 24 April 1950.

6 Alan P. Dobson, 'Informally Special? The Churchill–Truman Talks of January 1952 and the State of Anglo-American Relations', *Review of International Studies* (1997), 23, pp. 27–47.

7 Bullen and Pelly, *Docs*, p. 87, extract from a memo. for the PUSC, 22 April 1950.

8 Ibid., p. 87; for a consideration of some of the broader implications of these matters, see Alan P. Dobson 'Anglo-American Relations and the Cold War' in Alan P. Dobson (ed.) with Graham Evans and Shahin Malik (assistant eds), *Deconstructing and Reconstructing the Cold War* (Ashgate, Andover, 1999), pp. 69–88.

9 FO 371/97593, Franks to Eden, 27 Jan. 1952.

10 Ibid., CAB 128/24, CC(52)4, 17 Jan. 1952.

11 Bullen and Pelly, *Docs*, pp. 91–2, first bipartite official meeting, 24 April 1950. Analyses of NSC-68 in the context of US and British thinking may be found in Beatrice Heuser, 'NSC 68 and the Soviet Threat: a New Perspective on Western Threat Perception and Policy Making', *Review of International Studies*, 17, 1991, pp. 17–41; and Michael Cox, 'Western Intelligence, the Soviet Threat and NSC-68: a Reply to Beatrice Heuser', *Review of International Studies*, 12, 1992, pp. 75–84.

12 Bullen and Pelly, *Docs*, pp. 91–2.

13 FO 371/100840/6, 'Soviet Reactions to Western Pressure on "Sore Spots"'. All references and quotes from above and PUSC(51)16, and its annex A, FO 371/125002/4, 17 Jan. 1952, are taken from John Young 'The British Foreign Office and Cold War Fighting in the Early 1950s: PUSC(51)16 and the 1952 "Sore Spots" Memorandum', *University of Leicester Discussion Papers in Politics*, P95/2, 1995.

14 Andrew M. Johnston, 'The British Global Strategy Paper and the New Look', *Diplomatic History*, (1998), 22(3), pp. 361–98.

15 *Foreign Relations of the United States (FRUS)*, 1948, vol. 4, pp. 564–68, Marshall and Hoffman to Harriman, 27 Aug. 1948.

16   Ibid.
17   Mutual Defense Assistance Control (Battle) Act, *US Statutes at Large vol. 65*, statute 644; CAB 128/24, 1(5201, 3 Jan. 1952; *FRUS*, 1952–54, vol. 1, pp. 816–17, Penfield to State Department, 4 Jan. 1952.
18   FO 371/77799, UK OEEC delegation to Foreign Office, 24 June 1949.
19   FO 371/125002/4, PUSC(51)16, 17 Jan. 1952, annex A.
20   Ibid., PUSC(51)16, 17 Jan. 1951.
21   K. Larres, 'Eisenhower and the First Forty days After Stalin's Death: the Incompatibility of Detente and Political Warfare', *Diplomacy and Statecraft* (1995), 6(2), pp. 431–70, p. 435.
22   *FRUS*, 1952–54, vol. 15, p. 1012, NSC 152/2, 31 July 1953.
23   Ibid., p. 1043, Gordon to State Department reporting on British response to US proposals, 10 Nov. 1953.
24   Ibid.
25   Ibid.
26   CAB 128/26, CC(53)67, 17 Nov. 1953.
27   *FRUS*, 1952–54, vol. 1, pp. 1062–4, Aldrich to British Government, 3 Dec. 1953.
28   FO 371/106008, Coulson to Scott, 23 Nov. 1953.
29   CAB 128/27, 3(54)5, 18 Jan. 1954.
30   Ibid., 9(54)6, 17 Feb. 1954.
31   *Hansard*, 25 Feb. 1954, 524, pp. 582–91.
32   *FRUS*, 1952–54, vol. 1, pp. 1108–20, NSC 188, 11 March and Eisenhower to Churchill 19 March 1954.
33   CAB 128/27, 22(54)3, Churchill to Eisenhower 24 March 1954.
34   *FRUS*, 1952–54, vol. 1, pp. 1132–3, Eisenhower to Churchill 27 March 1954.
35   FO 371/111214, UK delegation Paris to Mutual Aid Department FO, 24 July 1954.
36   For more detailed discussion of this see Dobson, 'The USA, Britain and the Question of Hegemony'; T.E. Forland, 'Selling Firearms to the Indians: Eisenhower's Export Control Policy, 1953–54', *Diplomatic History*, 15, 1991, pp. 221–44; R.M. Spaulding, 'A Gradual and Moderate Relaxation: Eisenhower and the Revision of American Export Control Policy, 1953–54', *Diplomatic History*, 1993, 17, pp. 223–49; John W. Young, 'Winston Churchill's Peacetime Administration and the Relaxation of East–West Trade Controls, 1953–55', *Diplomacy and Statecraft*, 7(1), 1996, pp. 125–40; I. Jackson, 'Co-operation and Constraint: Britain's Influence on American Economic Warfare Policy in COCOM, 1948–54', PhD thesis, Queen's University of Belfast, 1997.
37   *FRUS*, vol. 1, p. 1220, 205th NSC meeting, 1 July 1954.
38   Ibid., vol. 10, p. 425, 315th NSC meeting, 6 March 1957.
39   Ibid., vol. 1, pp. 1108–16, 188th NSC meeting, 11 March 1954.
40   Ibid.
41   Ibid.
42   Ibid.
43   CAB 128/27, 9(54)6, 17 Feb. 1954.
44   John F. Kennedy Library (JFK Lib.), NSF box 305–10, folder: Trade East–West, US Policy on Trade with the European Soviet Bloc 7/8/63, Policy Planning Council Paper, 8 July 1963.
45   Ibid.

46 Ibid.
47 Ibid.
48 Ibid., NSC meetings box 1, folder: vol. 1, tab 8, 4/16/64, East–West trade, Kennedy memo. for ECRB, 19 Sept. 1963.
49 FO 371/171957, Trevelyan to Home, 25 April 1963.
50 Ibid., Brief on Anglo-Soviet Trade, 6 Aug. 1963.
51 Ibid., FO July 1963 unsigned for despatch to Moscow; see also FO 371/171956
52 FO 371/171957, Northern Department FO brief for President of the Board of Trade for his visit to the USSR Sept. 1963.
53 Wolfram Kaiser, *Using Europe, Abusing the Europeans: Britain and European Integration, 1945–63* (Macmillan, London, 1996); John W. Young, *Britain and European Unity, 1945–1992* (Macmillan, London, 1993).
54 JFK Lib., NSF box 223–31, folder: NATO pipe embargo 11/62 – 1/63, US Bonn embassy to Rusk, 12 Jan. 1963.
55 Ibid., NSF box 171–3, folder: UK general 2/12/63 – 3/5/63, Finletter to Rusk, 12 Feb. 1963.
56 CAB 128, CC(63)11, 14 Feb. 1963.
57 Ibid.
58 JFK Lib., NSF box 223–31, folder: NATO pipe embargo 2/63, Kennedy to Macmillan, 21 Feb. 1963.
59 Ibid., 3/63, memo. of conversation between Ball and Erroll, 28 March 1963.
60 CAB 128, CC(63)18, 25 March 1963.
61 JFK Lib., NSF box 223–31, folder: NATO pipe embargo 3/63, memo. of conversation between Ball and Erroll, 28 March 1963.
62 Ibid.
63 Hansard, 674, col. 192, 28 March 1963.

9
Eisenhower, Eden and the Suez Crisis

Peter G. Boyle

Eisenhower's historical reputation has fluctuated widely. During his two terms in office, 1953–1961, he was very popular. He was re-elected by a landslide in 1956, and, if the Constitution had not prohibited it, he could have been easily re-elected for a third term in 1960.[1] Although his standing among the general population was very high, however, Eisenhower was heavily criticised and constantly derided by intellectuals and sophisticated commentators, especially supporters of his urbane political opponent, Adlai Stevenson. The first books dealing with Eisenhower's presidency, written in the 1960s, reflected the views of such critics, who portrayed Eisenhower as a president of limited intelligence and vision who delegated authority to powerful subordinates such as John Foster Dulles, while Eisenhower spent as much time on the golf links as in the Oval Office.[2] In a poll of historians in 1962 rating the 33 US presidents up to that time in order of merit, Eisenhower was placed twenty-second, between Andrew Johnson, who was Abraham Lincoln's disastrous successor in the 1860s, and Chester Arthur, an obscure, lacklustre Republican who served for a few years in the 1880s.[3] In 1967, an article by Murray Kempton began the process of revision of Eisenhower's historical assessment, which gathered pace with the opening of archives in the Eisenhower Library in Abilene, Kansas. A flood of books in the 1970s and 1980s supported the revisionist view that Eisenhower was a shrewd, intelligent, effective chief executive, who made sensible use of delegation along the lines of his military experience and who deliberately and rather deviously cultivated an image of a non-political amateur, since this had broad popular appeal in America, with its strong tradition of suspicion of professional politicians. Thus, Jeff Greenfield wrote of 'The Hidden-Hand Presidency', while Stephen Ambrose, in the most authoritative biography of Eisenhower, praised him extremely highly, with only a few reservations.[4]

In the 1990s, a new, post-revisionist school of historians began to view Eisenhower a little more critically. While post-revisionists totally rejected the earliest caricatures of Eisenhower, they suggested that revisionists had given too much weight to Eisenhower's unexpected political skills and had placed too much emphasis on process rather than upon substance and policy. The current consensus on Eisenhower reflects the influence of these post-revisionists, such as Elmo Richardson and Chester Pach.[5]

The Eisenhower–Eden correspondence on the Suez Crisis provides interesting evidence as a test case with regard to Eisenhower's ability as a statesman. The tradition of correspondence between the prime minister of Britain and the president of the United States was begun by Winston Churchill and Franklin Roosevelt in 1940.[6] It was not continued by Clement Attlee and Harry Truman after 1945, but, following Eisenhower's election in 1952, Churchill suggested that he and Eisenhower should engage in a regular correspondence. Eisenhower agreed to the suggestion and letters were regularly exchanged, from Eisenhower's inauguration in January 1953, until Churchill's retirement in April 1955. Letters were exchanged at intervals of approximately every two weeks, often raising wide issues in a more philosophical manner than the exchanges of messages through the normal machinery of government or in the Churchill–Roosevelt letters, which had tended to be more cryptic, immediate wartime messages.[7] Following Churchill's retirement, Eden continued this tradition of regular correspondence with Eisenhower.[8] The correspondence during the Suez Crisis is particularly fascinating, while it also provides important evidence with regard to Eisenhower's handling of the crisis and thereby contributes to the ongoing debate on Eisenhower's historical reputation.

When the Suez Crisis broke out on 26 July 1956, with the nationalisation of the Suez Canal by the Egyptian government of Colonel Gamal Abdel Nasser, Eden immediately wrote to Eisenhower, informing him that 'This morning I have reviewed the whole position with my Cabinet colleagues and Chiefs of Staff. We are all agreed that we cannot afford to allow Nasser to seize control of the Canal in this way, in defiance of international agreements.' Eden outlined his view of the situation and stated his conclusion that 'My colleagues and I are convinced that we must be ready, in the last resort, to use force to bring Nasser to his senses. For our part we are prepared to do so. I have this morning instructed our Chiefs of Staff to prepare a military plan accordingly.'[9]

Eisenhower assumed from Eden's letter that the British intended to pursue diplomatic negotiations in the first instance, with the use of force a distant last resort. Eisenhower therefore replied to Eden that he would send the American diplomat Robert Murphy, an experienced troubleshooter, to London for talks with the British and French.[10] On 31 July 1956, however, Eisenhower received a message from Murphy, as well as a message from Chancellor of the Exchequer Harold Macmillan, informing Eisenhower that Britain planned to employ force without delay. This led Eisenhower to write an urgent letter to Eden, warning him in unequivocal terms 'of my own personal conviction, as well as that of my associates, as to the unwisdom even of contemplating the use of military force at this moment'. Eisenhower wrote that

> I cannot over-emphasize the strength of my conviction that some such method must be attempted before action such as you contemplate should be undertaken. If unfortunately the situation can finally be resolved only by drastic means, there should be no grounds for belief anywhere that corrective measures were undertaken merely to protect national or individual investors, or the legal rights of a sovereign nation were ruthlessly flouted. A conference, at the very least, should have a great educational effect throughout the world. Public opinion here and, I am convinced, in most of the world, would be outraged should there be a failure to make such efforts. Moreover, initial military successes might be easy, but the eventual price might become far too heavy.

Eisenhower also pointed out to Eden the constitutional requirement in the United States for Congressional support for the deployment of American military forces. Eisenhower wrote that for such deployment 'there would have to be a showing that every peaceful means of resolving the difficulty had previously been exhausted. Without such a showing, there would be a reaction that could very seriously affect our peoples' feeling toward our Western Allies.' Eisenhower therefore urged Eden 'that the step you contemplate should not be undertaken until every peaceful means of protecting the rights and the livelihood of great portions of the world had been thoroughly explored and exhausted'.[11]

Eden replied to Eisenhower agreeing that diplomatic means should be the first step, particularly, the 18-nation conference which had been arranged to meet in London. But Eden did not disguise his scepticism that diplomacy could attain the objective of producing an acceptable system of control and operation of the Suez Canal or of removing Nasser from power. If this proved to be the case, Eden made it clear that, given the danger which he felt that Nasser posed, resort must be had to force. Eden wrote to Eisenhower that 'Nasser has embarked on a course which is unpleasantly familiar. His seizure of the Canal was undoubtedly designed to impress opinion not only in Egypt but in the Arab world and in all Africa too. By this assertion of his power he seeks to further his ambitions from Morocco to the Persian Gulf.' Eden wrote that

> I have never thought Nasser a Hitler; he has no warlike people behind him. But the parallel with Mussolini is close. Neither of us can forget the lives and treasure he cost us before he was finally dealt with. The removal of Nasser, and the installation in Egypt of a regime less hostile to the West, must therefore also rank high among our objectives.

Eden agreed that a peaceful settlement should be attempted by means of the forthcoming conference. But Eden noted ominously that 'we must prepare to meet the eventuality that Nasser will refuse to accept the outcome of the conference; or, no less dangerous, that he, supported by the Russians, will seek by stratagems and wiles to divide us so that the conference produces no clear result in the sense we both seek. We and the French Government could not possibly acquiesce in such a situation. I really believe that the consequences of doing so would be catastrophic'. Eden concluded that 'our people here are neither excited nor eager to use force. They are, however, grimly determined that Nasser shall not get away with it this time, because they are convinced that if he does their existence will be at his mercy. So am I.'[12]

Eisenhower replied a few days later that 'What you say is very much in our thoughts and we are devoting the major part of our time to this important problem.'[13]

When the London conference produced a formula for a possible solution to the Suez Crisis, Eden wrote to Eisenhower, expressing appreciation of Dulles' role at the conference and of the American contribution to the relatively successful outcome of the conference. Nevertheless, Eden made clear his scepticism as to whether Nasser, with Soviet support, would respond constructively to the proposals emanating from the conference. Eden wrote that 'I have no doubt that the bear is using Nasser, with or without his knowledge, to further his immediate aims. These are, I think, first to dislodge the West from the Middle East, and second to get a foothold in Africa so as to dominate that continent in turn.' Elaborating on the opportunities which would be presented to the Soviets if Nasser's ambitions went unchecked, Eden wrote that 'All this makes me more than ever sure that Nasser must not be allowed to get away with it this time. We have many friends in the Middle East and in Africa and others who are shrewd enough to know where the plans of a Nasser or a Mossadeq would lead them. But they will not be strong enough to stand against the power of the mobs if Nasser wins again.' Eden concluded that the situation was 'certainly the most hazardous that our country has known since 1940'.[14]

Eisenhower replied to Eden on 3 September that he agreed that the united stance of the 18 nations at the London conference created the possibility of a peaceful settlement and that the Suez Committee, which was established by the conference and headed by Australian Prime Minister Robert Menzies, should be given full support, with the possibility also of referral of the matter to the United Nations. But Eisenhower wrote with unequivocal candour that 'I am afraid, Anthony, that from this point onward our views on this situation diverge. As to the use of force or the threat of force at this juncture, I continue to feel as I expressed myself in the letter Foster carried to you some weeks ago.' Eisenhower warned that there was no support within the United States for the use of force. 'I must tell you frankly', Eisenhower wrote, 'that American public opinion flatly rejects the thought of using force, particularly when it does not seem that every possible peaceful means of protecting our vital interests has been exhausted without result.' Eisenhower reiterated that 'I really do not see how a successful result could be achieved by forcible means. The use of force would, it seems to me, vastly increase the area of jeopardy.' Eisenhower spelled out specifically the immense damage to Western interests which would result from the use of force. 'I do not see', he warned, for example, 'how the economy of Western Europe can long survive the burden of prolonged military operations, as well as the denial of Near East oil.' Furthermore, he wrote that 'the peoples of the Near East and of North Africa and, to some extent, of all of Asia and all of Africa, would be consolidated against the West to a degree which, I fear, could not be overcome in a generation'. Eisenhower noted with regard to moderate Arab leaders who were anti-Nasser that they had indicated that in the face of the use of force against Nasser, 'Under those circumstances, because of the temper of their populations, they say they would have to support Nasser even against their better judgement.'[15]

Eden replied to Eisenhower on 6 September with a history lesson on appeasement and containment. Eden agreed that the Suez Committee must be given a chance to fulfil its mission. 'But if the Committee fails,' Eden wrote, 'we must have some immediate alternative which will show that Nasser is not going to get his way.' Eden wrote that

> In the 1930s Hitler established his position by a series of carefully planned movements. These began with the occupation of the Rhineland and were followed by successive acts of aggression against Austria, Czechoslovakia, Poland and the West. His actions were tolerated and excused by the majority of the population of Western Europe. It was argued either that Hitler had committed no act of aggression against anyone or that he was entitled to do what he liked in his own territory or that it was impossible to prove that he had any ulterior designs or that the covenant of the League of Nations did not entitle us to use force and that it would be wiser to wait until he did commit an act of aggression.

Eden observed how the postwar policy of containment had been so much more successful than the prewar policy of appeasement. 'In more recent years Russia has attempted similar tactics', Eden wrote. 'The blockade of Berlin was to have been the opening move in a campaign designed at least to deprive the Western powers of their whole position in Germany. On this occasion we fortunately reacted at once with the result that the Russian design was never unfolded.' Eden argued that

> The seizure of the Suez Canal is, we are convinced, the opening gambit in a planned campaign designed by Nasser to expel all Western influence and interests from Arab countries. He believes that if he can get away with this and if he can successfully defy eighteen nations his prestige in Arabia will be so great that he will be able to mount revolutions of young officers in Saudi Arabia, Jordan, Syria and Iraq. These new Governments will in effect be Egyptian satellites if not Russian ones. They will have to place their united oil resources under the control of a united Arabia led by Egypt and under Russian influence. When that moment comes Nasser can deny oil to Western Europe and we here shall all be at his mercy.

Eden concluded that 'we are conscious of the burdens and perils attending military intervention. But if our assessment is correct and if the only alternative is to allow Nasser's plans quietly to develop until this country and all Western Europe are held to ransom by Egypt acting at Russia's behest it seems to us that our duty is plain. We have many times led Europe in the fight for freedom. It would be an ignoble end to our long history if we tamely accepted to perish by degrees.'[16]

Eisenhower replied on 9 September that 'Whenever, on any international question, I find myself differing even slightly from you, I feel a deep compulsion to re-examine my position instantly and carefully.' But Eisenhower concluded that, after due reflection, he maintained his view that 'the result you and I both want can best be assured by slower and less dramatic processes than military force'. Eisenhower suggested the use of such measures as economic pressure against Egypt, the exploitation of Arab rivalries and the construction of more tankers and a new pipeline through Turkey, which would lessen dependence on the Suez Canal as an oil lifeline. Eisenhower stressed that 'Nasser thrives on drama. If we let some of the drama go out of the situation and concentrate upon the task of deflating him through slower but sure processes such as I described, I believe the desired results can more probably be obtained.' Eisenhower conceded that 'eventually there may be no escape from the use of force.' But Eisenhower insisted that 'to resort to military action when the world believes there are other means available for resolving the dispute would set in motion forces that could lead, in the years to come, to the most distressing results'.[17]

Eden was prepared to support diplomatic efforts to bring about a resolution of the crisis, particularly the formation of a Suez Canal Users' Association which could take over the operation of the Canal. But, especially after he received a threatening letter from Soviet prime minister Nikolai Bulganin, Eden was more convinced than ever that Nasser constituted a grave danger which must be met with resolute action.[18] 'There is no doubt in our minds', he wrote to Eisenhower on 1 October, 'that Nasser, whether he likes it or not, is now effectively in Russian hands, just as Mussolini was in Hitler's. It would be as ineffective to show weakness to Nasser now in order to placate him as it was to show weakness to Mussolini. The only result was and would be to bring the two together.'[19]

In early October, the prospects of a peaceful settlement grew. The Suez issue was referred to the United Nations, and the foreign ministers of Egypt, France and Britain, namely, Mahmoud Fawzi, Christian Pineau and Selwyn Lloyd, held negotiations in New York on 9–12 October. The outcome was a six-principles agreement, which seemed to be a possible basis for a settlement. The agreement accepted the principle of unrestricted transit through the Suez Canal, while the sovereignty of Egypt would be respected and tolls would be agreed between Canal users and

Egypt. After the completion of the negotiation of the six-principles agreement, Eisenhower said to Selwyn Lloyd that 'it looks like here is a very real crisis that is behind us.'[20]

Eden, however, was dissatisfied with a settlement which would not only leave Nasser in power but which would enhance Nasser's reputation. The French government, which regarded Nasser as a dangerous source of aid to the rebels in Algeria who were struggling for independence from France, were likewise dissatisfied. Consequently, on 14 October two representatives of the French government met Eden at Chequers, the Prime Minister's country house in Buckinghamshire. The French proposed a plan whereby Israel would attack Egypt and this would give Britain and France the opportunity to intervene and to occupy the Suez Canal, under the pretext of separating the Israeli and Egyptian combatants and preventing damage to the Canal. Secret negotiations ensued between Britain, France and Israel over the next two weeks, while British military preparations were made for the bombing of Egyptian airfields and the landing of British troops in Egypt. These plans were kept absolutely secret from the Americans, who were aware from intelligence sources, however, of the military preparations.[21]

On 29 October, the plan was put into operation. The Israelis advanced across the Sinai desert towards the Suez Canal. On 30 October, French Prime Minister Guy Mollet and Foreign Minister Christian Pineau flew to London to give the appearance of consultation in face of a surprise. The British and French governments then issued an ultimatum to Israel and to Egypt to withdraw their forces ten miles back from each side of the Suez Canal and to consent to a temporary occupation of the Canal by an Anglo-French force.

On 30 October, Eisenhower wrote to Eden, stating, that 'I address you in this note not only as head of Her Majesty's Government but as my long time friend who has, with me, believed in and worked for real Anglo-American understanding.' Eisenhower requested that 'Without bothering here to discuss the military movements themselves and their possible grave consequences, I should like to ask your help in clearing up my understanding as to exactly what is happening between us and our European allies – especially between us, the French and yourselves.'[22]

Eden replied that he was 'sending you this hurried message to let you know at once how we regard the Israel–Egypt conflict'. Eden stated that 'We have never made any secret of our belief that justice entitled us to defend our vital interests against Nasser's designs.' Nevertheless, Eden argued that Britain had attempted to seek a negotiated settlement by means of the London Conference, the Suez Canal Users Association and discussions at the United Nations. But, Eden wrote, 'Now this has happened.' Feigning surprise over the Israeli attack, Eden wrote that 'We have earnestly deliberated what we should do in this serious situation. We cannot afford to see the Canal closed or to lose the shipping which is daily on passage through it. We have a responsibility for the people in these ships. We feel that decisive action should be taken at once to stop hostilities.' Eden wrote that Britain preferred a peaceful solution through the United Nations but he was sceptical that this was attainable. He wrote that 'We have agreed with you to go to the Security Council and instructions are being sent this moment. Experience shows that its procedure is unlikely to be either rapid or effective.'[23]

After meeting Mollet and Pineau, Eden wrote a further letter to Eisenhower, attempting to justify the British and French action. He tried to assure Eisenhower that there was no question 'of a harking back to the old Colonial and occupational concepts. We are most anxious to avoid this impression. Nothing could have prevented this volcano from erupting somewhere. But when the dust settles there may well be a chance for our doing a really constructive piece of work together and thereby strengthening the weakest point in the line against Communism.'[24]

Before Eisenhower received Eden's letters, however, he was given through the press the news of the Anglo-French ultimatum. Eisenhower sent a cold and formal statement to Eden, which he released to the press, stating that 'I must urgently express to you my deep concern at the prospect of this drastic action even at the very time when the matter is under consideration as it is today by the United Nations Security Council. It is my sincere belief that peaceful processes can and should prevail to secure a solution which will restore the armistice condition as between Israel and Egypt and also justly settle the controversy with Egypt about the Suez Canal.'[25]

Britain and France accepted that a United Nations force should be sent into the Middle East to keep the Israelis and the Egyptians apart. Eden argued, however, that, since a United Nations force would be slow to arrive, an Anglo-French force should meantime take action by landing at Port Said. The Americans put great pressure on Britain to work through the United Nations rather than acting independently. On 31 October, however, Britain bombed Egyptian airfields and on 5 November British troops landed at Port Said. Eden wrote that 'It is a great grief to me that the events of the last few days have placed such a strain on the relations between our two countries.' Eden defended the

Anglo-French actions, writing that 'I know that Foster thought we could have played this longer. But I am convinced that, if we had allowed things to drift, everything would have gone from bad to worse. Nasser would have become a kind of Moslem Mussolini and our friends in Iraq, Jordan, Saudi Arabia and even Iran would gradually have been brought down. His efforts would have spread westwards, and Libya and all North Africa would have been brought under his control.' Eden argued that

> this is the moment to curb Nasser's ambitions. If we let it pass, all of us will bitterly regret it. Here is our opportunity to secure an effective and final settlement of the problems of the Middle East. If we draw back now, chaos will not be avoided. Everything will go up in flames in the Middle East. You will realise, with all your experience, that we cannot have a military vacuum while a United Nations force is being constituted and is being transported to the spot. This is why we feel we must go on to hold the position until we can hand over the responsibility to the United Nations.

Eden wrote that he was 'sending you this message in the hope that you will at least understand the grievous decisions which we have had to make'. He concluded that

> I believe as firmly as ever that the future of all of us depends on the closest Anglo-American cooperation. It has of course been a grief to me to have had to make a temporary breach into it which I cannot disguise, but I know that you are a man of big enough heart and vision to take up things again on the basis of fact. If you cannot approve, I would like you at least to understand the terrible decisions that we have had to make. I remember nothing like them since the days when we were comrades together in the war. History alone can judge whether we have made the right decision, but I do want to assure you that we have made it from a genuine sense of responsibility, not only to our country, but to all the world.[26]

Eden's hope that, when presented with a *fait accompli*, Eisenhower would support Britain was quickly dashed. Eisenhower made unequivocally clear his opposition to the use of force, and the United States applied brutal pressure to bring about an immediate ceasefire, especially financial pressure against the pound and refusal to export oil from the Western hemisphere to make up for the loss of Middle Eastern supplies.[27]

After Eden's capitulation to this American pressure, Eisenhower wrote to Eden on 6 November that he was 'delighted at the opportunity to talk with you on the telephone and to hear that the U.K. will order a cease-fire this evening'. He stated he would be 'delighted to have you call me at any time'.[28]

On 7 November Eden wrote to Eisenhower suggesting that Eden should come to Washington for discussions. He wrote that

> I should feel much more confidence about the decisions and actions which we shall have to take in the short term if we had first reached some common understanding about the attitude which we each intended to take towards a long-term settlement of the outstanding issues in the Middle East. I have for a long time felt that some at least of our troubles there derived from the lack of a clear understanding between our two countries, ever since the end of the war, on policy in the Middle East. And I doubt whether we shall ever be able to secure stability there unless we are working towards common objectives.

He concluded that 'On matters such as this it is difficult to come to considered conclusions by correspondence.' He therefore expressed the hope that 'it may be possible for us to meet within the next few days, as soon as your immediate preoccupations are over'.[29]

Eisenhower enthusiastically responded to Eden's proposal, writing that 'I want you to know that I welcome the suggestion you made in our telephone conversation today regarding early consultation on many of our mutual problems, and that I agree we should meet at an early date.'[30] Eisenhower, however, quickly cooled to this idea, since, not only was he in the throes of activity following his re-election victory on 6 November, but he was also confronted with the issues arising from the Hungarian Revolution, and also, above all, since an early visit by Eden might give the impression to Arab countries that Eisenhower's position had been more supportive of British policy than in reality it had been. Eden's visit to Washington, therefore, did not materialise. Instead, Eisenhower saw that Eden's domestic political position had deteriorated, while at the same time his health had failed. Eden went on holiday to Jamaica, and Eisenhower wrote to him there on 29 November, stating that 'I understand you are recuperating in Jamaica. This short note brings you my very best wishes for an enjoyable and restful vacation, and a complete return to health.'[31]

Eisenhower realised that the Suez affair had finished Eden. They did not correspond on matters of substance after early November, and

Eisenhower looked to the restoration of harmonious Anglo-American relations through Eden's successor. When Eden resigned in January 1957, Eisenhower wrote a tribute to him, stating that

> I cannot tell you how deeply I regret that the strains and stresses of these times finally wore you down physically until you felt it necessary to retire. To me it seems only yesterday that you and I and others were meeting with Winston almost daily – or nightly – to discuss the next logical move of our forces in the war. Now you have retired, I have had a heart attack as well as a major operation, and many others of our colleagues of that era are either gone or no longer active. The only reason for recalling those days is to assure you that my admiration and affection for you have never diminished; I am truly sorry that you had to quit the office of Her Majesty's First Minister.[32]

But Eisenhower's focus was on the new British prime minister, Harold Macmillan, who had been a close wartime associate of Eisenhower in North Africa and with whom Eisenhower formed a very warm personal and political relationship during their term of office together as US president and British prime minister, 1957–1961.[33]

Eisenhower never wavered in later years from his belief that the position which he had taken over Suez had been correct. Jonathan Aitken, in a biography of Richard Nixon, quotes a letter from Nixon to Julian Amery, a Conservative Member of Parliament, in 1987, in which Nixon wrote that 'Years later, after he had left office, I talked with Eisenhower about Suez. He told me that it was his major foreign policy mistake.'[34] Stephen Ambrose, however, in a review of Aitken's book, expressed scepticism that this had been Eisenhower's view. Ambrose wrote that 'Perhaps Eisenhower did say that to Nixon, but in my own interviews with Eisenhower in the mid-1960s, the former president said just the opposite. He was proud of what he had done with regard to Suez and insisted that he had been right to support Egypt.'[35]

Historians of Eisenhower's presidency have justifiably made reservations and qualifications to the somewhat over-enthusiastic and rather uncritical views of the revisionists on a wide range of policies, such as Taiwan, Cuba, Guatemala, Iran, the U-2 and other matters. On Suez, however, post-revisionist criticisms of Eisenhower are unconvincing. The most recent study of Eisenhower and Suez makes some relatively minor criticisms in the course of a broadly very supportive interpretation of Eisenhower's policies.[36] Through the prism of the Eden–

Eisenhower correspondence, even these minor criticisms seem carping. From the evidence of the correspondence, Eisenhower emerges as statesmanlike, perceptive and consistent in the exercise of very sound judgement throughout the crisis.

Notes

1 In 1951, the twenty-second amendment was added to the Constitution which imposed a limit of two terms as president. George Washington's retirement in 1797 after his second term established a two-term tradition, which was followed until Franklin Roosevelt ran for a third term in 1940 and for a fourth term in 1944. In 1951, the two-term tradition was given constitutional substance by means of the twenty-second amendment.

2 See for example, Arthur M. Schlesinger, Jr., *A Thousand Days: John F. Kennedy in the White House* (Boston: Houghton Mifflin, 1965). Schlesinger, a former Harvard University historian and a Kennedy aide, used Eisenhower as the counterpoise of a tired old leader lacking in ideas and vigour, in dramatic contrast to the dynamic young hero, John F. Kennedy.

3 Peter G. Boyle, 'Update: Eisenhower', *The Historian*, No. 43 (Autumn, 1994), p. 9.

4 Murray Kempton, 'The Underestimation of Dwight D. Eisenhower', *Esquire* (September, 1967), p. 108; Herbert Parmet, *Eisenhower and the American Crusades* (New York: Macmillan, 1972); Fred I. Greenstein, *The Hidden-Hand Presidency: Eisenhower as Leader* (New York: Basic Books, 1982); Stephen E. Ambrose, *Eisenhower* (2 vols; New York: Simon and Schuster, 1983–84).

5 Chester Pach and Elmo Richardson, *The Presidency of Dwight D. Eisenhower* (rev. edn, Lawrence: University Press of Kansas, 1991).

6 Warren F. Kimball (ed.), *Churchill and Roosevelt: the Complete Correspondence* (3 vols; Princeton: Princeton University Press, 1984).

7 Peter G. Boyle (ed.), *The Churchill-Eisenhower Correspondence, 1953–1955* (Chapel Hill: University of North Carolina Press, 1990).

8 The letters from Eisenhower to Eden are in the Prime Minister's Papers in the Public Record Office, Kew, Surrey, along with copies of letters from Eden to Eisenhower. The letters from Eden to Eisenhower are in the Eisenhower Library in Abilene, Kansas, along with copies of letters from Eisenhower to Eden. Peter Boyle is currently working on an edition of *The Eden–Eisenhower Correspondence, 1955–1957*, to be published by the University of North Carolina Press.

9 Eden to Eisenhower, July 27, 1956, PREM 11/1177, T337/56, PRO. Citations to the letters in this piece are to the copies in the Public Record Office.

10 Eisenhower to Eden, July 27, 1956, PREM 11/1177, PRO.

11 Eisenhower to Eden, July 31, 1956, PREM 11/1177, PRO.

12 Eden to Eisenhower, August 5, 1956, PREM 11/1177, T352/56/PRO.

13 Eisenhower to Eden, August 10, 1956, PREM 11/1177, T365/56, PRO.

14 Eden to Eisenhower, August 27, 1956, PREM 11/1177, T377/56, PRO.

15   Eisenhower to Eden, September 3, 1956, PREM 11/1177, T381/56, PRO.
16   Eden to Eisenhower, September 6, 1956, PREM 11/1177, T387/56, PRO.
17   Eisenhower to Eden, September 9, 1956, PREM 11/1177, T391/56, PRO.
18   Anthony Eden, *The Memoirs of Anthony Eden, Volume III: Full Circle* (London: Cassell), pp. 486–7.
19   Eden to Eisenhower, October 1, 1956, PREM 11/1177, T423/56, PRO.
20   Selwyn Lloyd, *Suez, 1956: a Personal Account* (London: Cape, 1978), p. 160.
21   W. Scott Lucas, *Divided We Stand: Britain, the U.S. and the Suez Crisis* (London: Hodder and Stoughton, 1991), pp. 227–64; Keith Kyle, *Suez* (London: Weidenfeld and Nicolson, 1991), pp. 291–391.
22   Eisenhower to Eden, October 30, 1956, PREM 11/1176, T486/56, PRO.
23   Eden to Eisenhower, October 30, 1956, PREM 11/1176, T483/56, PRO.
24   Eden to Eisenhower, October 30, 1956, PREM 11/1176, T485/56, PRO.
25   Eisenhower to Eden, October 31, 1956, PREM 11/1176, T488/56, PRO.
26   Eden to Eisenhower, November 5, 1956, PREM 11/1176, T520/56, PRO.
27   Lucas, *Divided We Stand*, pp. 265–97; Kyle, *Suez*, pp. 392–499.
28   Eisenhower to Eden, November 6, 1956, PREM 11/1176, T534/56, PRO.
29   Eden to Eisenhower, November 7, 1956, PREM 11/1176, T537/56, PRO.
30   Eisenhower to Eden, November 7, 1956, PREM 11/1176, T538/56, PRO.
31   Eisenhower to Eden, November 29, 1956, PREM 11/1176, T598/56, PRO.
32   Eisenhower to Eden, January 10, 1957, PREM 11/1176, PRO.
33   The tradition of exchanging regular correspondence between the American president and British prime minister was continued by Eisenhower and Macmillan, 1957–1961.
34   Richard Nixon to Julian Amery, January 21, 1987, Julian Amery Papers. Quoted, Jonathan Aitken, *Nixon: a Life* (London: Weidenfeld & Nicolson, 1993), p. 244.
35   Stephen E. Ambrose, Review of Jonathan Aitken, *Nixon: a Life, Foreign Affairs*, Vol. 73, No. 4 (July/August, 1994), p. 168.
36   Cole C. Kingseed, *Eisenhower and the Suez Crisis of 1956* (Baton Rouge: Louisiana State University Press, 1995).

10
Lyndon Johnson, Harold Wilson and the Vietnam War: a *Not* So Special Relationship?

Sylvia A. Ellis

Introduction

The Vietnam war dominated United States foreign policy during the Presidency of Lyndon B. Johnson, and yet the international dimensions of the conflict are only now being explored in any depth by historians. George Ball, US Under-Secretary of State, famously admitted that Vietnam 'made it very hard to get attention on anything else, that judgements tended to be colored by the Vietnamese situation . . . we were getting things totally distorted. . . . In fact, I once drew a map for Dean Rusk [Secretary of State] and said, "this is your map of the world". I had a tiny United States with an enormous Vietnam lying right off the coast.' As an example of this Ball mentioned that the Johnson administration 'pressed the British . . . hard to stay in line on Vietnam'.[1] This comment reveals just how important allied support and cooperation was to the Johnson administration. With only five other countries fighting alongside them – Australia, New Zealand, the Republic of Korea, Thailand and the Philippines – the diplomatic support of other key allies was crucial to America's propaganda war. No country's verbal support was more important than the United Kingdom's. Not only was Britain the US's closest ally, nominally at least, it was also a leading social democratic nation whose example was important, not least to the Commonwealth nations and in American liberal circles. However, the Wilson governments of 1964–70 found it exceedingly difficult to balance the demands of their transatlantic ally, who during a series of sterling crises was also their banker, with the outrage in their party and country at American action in South-East Asia. As a result, Harold Wilson's hopes for a close working alliance with the Americans, which he expressed during his first trip to Washington as Prime Minister, soon came under threat. Almost immediately tensions over Vietnam soured Anglo-American relations, and particularly the relationship between President Johnson and Prime Minister Wilson.

Most scholars of Anglo-American relations agree that the alliance between Britain and America weakened substantially during the mid- to late sixties, and have argued that this decline was epitomised, and perhaps even hastened by a frosty or at best cool personal relationship between Wilson and Johnson.[2] The deterioration in the quality of the transatlantic relationship can of course be attributed to a number of other factors, particularly that both countries were increasingly aware that Britain's role as a world power was rapidly diminishing: decolonisation was in full swing, the country was over-stretched militarily, and its economy was weakening. The power differential between Britain and America was therefore more acute. By May 1967 the US Embassy in Britain judged the 'special relationship' to be 'little more than sentimental terminology'.[3] That Johnson barely mentions Wilson and the British in his memoirs indicates that he did not see Anglo-American relations as a significant part of his years in office.[4] And while Wilson visited Washington seven times during Johnson's presidency, the visits were not reciprocated, Johnson never visited Great Britain during his five years in the White House.[5] The President's heart and mind were elsewhere: in South-East Asia. The Vietnam War clearly accentuated the decline in the strength of Anglo-American relations.

This chapter will therefore attempt to shed light on the complex relationship between two of the most colourful and puzzling characters in the political world of the 1960s and assess the extent to which Vietnam dominated and affected their public and private relationship. The common perception of the Johnson–Wilson relationship is one of master and servant, leader and follower. Left-wing political cartoonists in Britain expended much ink portraying the Prime Minister in a subservient role. Vicky in the *New Statesman* depicted Wilson as a willing boy scout wanting to carry Johnson's bags on Vietnam and the Dominican Republic.[6] And, in Gerald Scarfe's now notorious cartoon of April 1965, Wilson is shown licking Johnson's backside while the President remarks 'I've heard of a special relationship, but this is ridiculous.'[7] While portraying a gross oversimplification of their relationship, these satirists were right to highlight that the relationship between Wilson and Johnson was not one between equals. Despite this sort of attack Wilson tried desperately hard to portray his relationship with Johnson as one of mutual respect and allied interest. Few believed him.

The personal relationship: the myth of the positive

Despite the now common view that the relationship between Harold Wilson and Lyndon Johnson was strained, many of those who knew the two leaders contradict this perception. Many tell of good relations between the Prime Minister and the President. For instance, after Wilson's first meeting as Prime Minister with Lyndon Johnson, Tony Benn, MP and Postmaster General, noted in his diary that Wilson 'had got on excellently with President Johnson' and added that he thought they were 'both highly political animals and understand each other well'.[8] Edward Short, Labour Chief Whip, even went as far as to argue that

> The President and the Prime Minister were both down-to-earth politicians with much in common. The tough Texan and the homespun Yorkshireman hit it off famously and initiated an era of Anglo-American friendship which was closer than at any time since the war.[9]

Barbara Castle, Minister of Overseas Development and Transport Minister in the Wilson Government, also believes there was a close friendship between the two men, and is adamant Wilson believed he and LBJ were 'buddies'.[10] But the main perpetrator of the notion of a close, personal relationship was Wilson himself. He admired, respected and genuinely warmed to the American President, and moreover, appears to have believed in the public relations portrayal of a great friendship between the two of them. This is clearly borne out in his memoirs, where Wilson continually stresses the cordiality and intimacy of relations. And as late as 1986, Wilson was still describing Johnson as 'a very, very great man'.[11]

This British idea of a friendship appears to be based on some tangible evidence. For instance, the Americans treated the Prime Minister exceptionally well when he visited Washington. Wilson often boasted about the state receptions, lavish banquets, and the warmth of the welcoming speeches and toasts. Prompted by his aides, Johnson also tapped into Wilson's 'Mr Toad-like vainglory' by making Wilson feel that he was given special treatment, as in December 1965 when the Prime Minister and his wife, Mary, were invited to the annual ceremony of switching on Washington's Christmas lights.[12] Wilson proudly noted in his memoirs that this was 'the first invitation to a British Prime Minister since one to Mr. Churchill, twenty one years earlier.'[13] Johnson even engaged in over-the-top flattery. By July of 1966, LBJ appeared to be comparing Wilson to Churchill by talking of both men's courage and leadership qualities in a welcoming speech for the Prime Minister.[14] Considering Johnson had previously compared President Ngo Dinh Diem of South Vietnam to Churchill, perhaps Wilson should have been suspicious of such rhetoric. However, his reaction to this is telling. He recorded in his memoirs that during a week when the pressures of the sterling crisis had been immense, 'wildly exaggerated though it was, it was good to hear... when most epithets aimed in my direction had been as wide of the mark the other way'.[15] During a period when he was receiving increasing criticism at home, Wilson's recognition of the President's hyperbole did not prevent him from feeling that at least abroad he was appreciated and, perhaps, liked.

Meetings between Wilson and Johnson at the White House were frequently informal and they often met privately in the Oval Office. David Bruce, US Ambassador to Great Britain and an experienced diplomat, noted that such private meetings between heads of government were unusual and explained them in the following terms: 'I think seldom have two heads of state been such long-time master politicians in the domestic sense as these two. I think they found it extremely interesting to compare notes.'[16] Indeed, most discussions, formal and informal, usually began with the President and Prime Minister outlining their latest domestic political difficulties. Wilson would describe his handling of Parliament and in his first term in office, from October 1964 to April 1966, his paper-thin majority of between two and five. Johnson would lament the lack of Party loyalty within the American system and explain the conflicting pressures he faced on Vietnam from the hawks and doves in Congress.

On the surface, then, Wilson and his colleagues had every reason to believe that there was some degree of friendship between the British Prime Minister and the American President. Another reason Wilson may have believed in the closeness of his relationship with Johnson was that most of the cables and letters that passed between them were at least cordial and familiar in tone and content, and most of them were candid. Bruce commented that in correspondence 'there was no acrimony'; in fact it was 'really, extraordinarily polite correspondence, almost affectionate at times, even sentimental'.[17] The majority of the letters and cables that have been declassified verify this recollection. According to Bruce the Prime Minister and the President also addressed one another on a first-name basis.[18] Lady Bird Johnson noted in February 1968 at a dinner with one of her 'favorite Prime Ministers' at the White House that Wilson 'spoke of Lyndon as Lyndon, and he called me Lady Bird. The only other Chief of State that I remember using first names was Prime Minister Harold Holt from Australia.'[19] Holt's relationship with Johnson was, however, on a surer footing, not least because he was considered a 'true ally' and friend because he sent Australian troops to Vietnam. In Wilson's case, however, the use of first names could have been over-familiarity rather than an indication of intimacy. Wilson was known to speak on a Christian-name basis with his adversaries, including Ian Smith of Rhodesia, in his interpersonal approach to diplomacy. However, Lady Bird's comments suggest that in this case, the informality was not out of place.

The seemingly preferential treatment Wilson received in Washington clearly boosted his morale and convinced him of his closeness to Johnson. In a sense, Wilson had to believe his own propaganda regarding his relationship with the President in order that he could sell his government's line on Vietnam that the best way to influence the Americans was to remain loyal to LBJ. However, it appears that Wilson genuinely believed in the warmth of their relationship. This can be explained by Wilson's overestimation of his ability to establish good relationships with everyone and his well-known propensity for self-delusion, what Andrew Roth characterised as the 'Walter Mitty' factor.[20] Wilson continued to boast about the relationship even after the two statesmen left high office.

The personal relationship: the reality of the negative

Evidence of a poor or strained relationship between Wilson and Johnson is not only more numerous but is also more convincing. A number of Johnson's aides testify to the President's bad feelings towards Wilson. George Ball said that while 'LBJ had been impressed with Macmillan' he thought Wilson

> lacked Macmillan's consummate ability to deal on a friendly but slightly condescending basis... wore no patrician armor, was too ordinary, too much like other politicians with whom LBJ had to deal, and Johnson took an almost instant dislike to him.[21]

And as early as March 1965 David Bruce described in his diary the President's 'antipathy' for the Prime Minister.[22] Bruce's Deputy at

Grosvenor Square, Philip Kaiser, also noted that 'Wilson and Johnson were not temperamentally congenial.'[23] A senior Johnson aide also admits that 'they weren't friends', and that Johnson 'didn't feel comfortable' with Wilson because 'he felt Wilson didn't stay put'.[24] Many journalists and political colleagues recall Johnson's feelings about Wilson in less diplomatic language.

Along with the numerous accounts of Johnson's dismissive, and often scathing attitude towards the Prime Minister, it is clear that the President often tried to avoid or minimise his meetings with Wilson. For example, at the end of February 1965, Jack Valenti, LBJ's close aide at the White House, informed the President: 'Dean Rusk says there is no escape from seeing Prime Minister Wilson when he is here in April.'[25] And, shortly before Wilson's July 1966 visit to Washington, British diplomats were seriously concerned that Johnson might cancel the trip at the last minute, as he had postponed the visits of President Ayub Khan of Pakistan and Mr Shastri, Prime Minister of India the previous year.[26] Johnson also refused to take telephone calls from Wilson. Bruce continually restrained the Prime Minister from telephoning the President, instead insisting on preparing the ground first or alternatively encouraging the use of cables.

In spite of Wilson's protestations, on balance the weight of evidence suggests that his personal relationship with LBJ was limited, at best, and certainly one-sided. Yet at the time many in Britain were unaware of this reality. Certainly, it was possible to misread the situation; confusing signals were coming out of Washington at the time. Although Johnson apparently voiced his feelings about the Prime Minister quite readily in private, he never publicly conveyed his feelings in front of Wilson or his entourage. Indeed, David Bruce, while acknowledging talk of LBJ and Wilson not getting on, said:

> I never saw any instances of it because when they met each other – their talks, which were lengthy, were marked by the utmost courtesy. If either disliked the other, or if either were suspicious of the other, no onlooker like myself would have been made aware of it – I can only say that I never saw a sign of friction during their meetings.[27]

As the journalist Louis Heren noted, Johnson's 'old-fashioned Southern courtesy' may have been a factor here. Johnson could not 'bring himself to speak his mind in certain circumstances which may help to explain his apparent deviousness'.[28]

It is also clear that both Johnson's and Wilson's aides and advisers tried to shield the Prime Minister from the President's true feelings for him. For instance, in March 1964 when Wilson was still opposition leader, he appears to have misread his first meeting with LBJ. Wilson was convinced the trip to Washington had gone well yet the Johnson administration did not share this feeling. Richard Neustadt, a Harvard professor and special consultant to the President, noted during a trip to London in June and July of 1964, that if elected Wilson would have 'hopes for his own personal relationship which are quite different from the perceptions of reality held by many American officials' and hoped that a 'number of things' could be done 'to avoid shocking his sensibilities'.[29]

Neustadt was sent to London again after Wilson became Prime Minister to 'stress the importance of the "personal equation"' in the first formal talks with Wilson in December 1964. Derek Mitchell, the Prime Minister's Principal Private Secretary, met with Neustadt and recorded afterwards that Neustadt 'repeated the warning already given by him to the Prime Minister and others that the Prime Minister should not bank on everything going his way when he got face to face with the President'. He added that 'the President was not looking forward to the talks with anything approaching the same eagerness as the Prime Minister' because 'he had other problems on his mind, for example South-East Asia and a number of personnel matters. Thus preoccupied, he looked forward to the meeting 'as more of a chore than a major act of policy'.[30] All of this evidence indicates that even at this early stage misunderstandings were evident in the relationship between the Prime Minister and the President. Neustadt made this clear when he explained that

> It was known that the Prime Minister had received a strong impression from his personal meeting with the President which he had when he was Leader of the Opposition; and that he had been moved by the warmth of the message which was sent to him when he took up office. But the President himself had not the same recollection of the earlier meeting and the warm message of greeting was not more than the result of an instruction to officials to draft a warm message of greeting.[31]

Mitchell thought this assessment was a 'little one-sided' and later recalled that he advised Neustadt in the following way:

> it was a fact that the Prime Minister assumed he had a personal affinity with the President and if he were disabused of this in too

rude or unfeeling a way he might take it very hard. I said that I hoped that he would not look at this problem exclusively as one of conditioning the Prime Minister to the President. The opposite approach, difficult as it might be for Professor Neustadt and his colleagues in Washington, might pay handsome dividends.[32]

This advice may have been taken on board, especially when one considers the often lavish attention paid to Wilson on his many visits to Washington. Rusk argued in a memo to the President in March of 1965 that 'we have an excellent degree of understanding and cooperation in crucial foreign policy matters from the new Labor Government in Britain' and that 'anything we can do to maintain this state of affairs is in our best interests'.[33] Rusk recognised that if LBJ was willing to spend some time with the Prime Minister and use some of his undoubted charms on him then this would pay handsome dividends. Indeed, Tony Benn wryly commented after Wilson's visit to Washington in June 1967, at a time when British support for US policy in Vietnam was under intense domestic criticism, that the Prime Minister had been 'received with all the trumpets appropriate to a weak foreign head of state who has to be buttered up so that he can carry the can for American foreign policy'.[34] Throughout the Wilson–Johnson years, advisers on both sides of the Atlantic worked hard to ensure the personal relationship remained as warm as possible in order to ensure the mutuality of interests.

If we have by now undermined the myth of warm personal relations, is it possible to establish why the two men were not natural friends? One possible reason why Johnson did not warm to Wilson may lie in his attitude towards the British, although as with all discussions of LBJ the evidence is at times contradictory or conflicting. It could be argued that the President had a great deal of respect for the British. Along with expressing his preference for buying Hereford cattle, Johnson also spoke of his great admiration for the British, particularly their courage and determination during the Second World War and their abilities in diplomacy and negotiation. In February 1968, despite his great disappointment at the British government's announcement of its decision to withdraw troops from east of Suez, Johnson said in conversation with Henry Brandon:

> I'd be a slave today without the British and Churchill, if they had not done what they did in the first two years of World War II. They did it for America. I will not forget when Churchill came over here in 1941,

barefoot and his fly open, just before the clock struck twelve. I admire the character of the British, it is difficult to beat them in the clinches.[35]

Johnson's feelings for Churchill were undoubtedly genuine. His admiration for the British may have stemmed from his two visits to Great Britain: first, in the spring of 1945 as part of a delegation from the House Armed Services Committee visiting Europe following VE Day, and second, in November 1960 following a NATO Parliamentary Conference in Paris but it may also be that 'as with many Southerners' Johnson was 'proud of his English origins'.[36] David Bruce recalled in 1971 that:

> President Johnson had a strong feeling about England. I was rather surprised by it in the sense that coming from Texas . . . there remained in him a sort of atavism about England. He's very admiring of the British people – it's absolutely genuine – of their best qualities, of their vigor under hardship, of the skill in which they conducted their world affairs and administered their global role for a couple of hundred years or more. I would say he was strongly attuned to the British race, if you can call it that.[37]

But, although Johnson may have respected certain aspects of the British character, he was not instinctively attuned to the British way of life. Indeed, it could easily be argued that Johnson had a lack of empathy with the British which could be explained by his personal sense of geography. William McChesney Martin, while Chairman of the Federal Reserve Board, recalled to Henry Brandon what he thought were Johnson's true feelings towards England:

> First of all you have to know that he does not consider easterners . . . as real Americans. To him they look too much to Europe. Secondly, the line of Texas, Missouri, Minnesota to him is the real America. Those Texans who have gone to live in California are in his mind Texans who weren't able to make a go of it in Texas. In this picture, England figures about as large as North Dakota.[38]

Johnson recognised the unique nature of Anglo-American relations in terms of language, culture and tradition, but did not see them as being 'special' in any real sense due to Britain's decline as a great power and the rise in importance of other European nations, particularly West

Germany.[39] Moreover, Johnson did not want a close working alliance with Britain, or with any other European nation for that matter. Although Europe remained the first priority for US foreign policy and the commitment to NATO was as strong as ever, Johnson had no new initiatives on Europe. Indeed, George Ball admits that he took the lead on European policy and in general did not get much interference or guidance from Johnson in this.[40] Johnson clearly felt more at home with Latin American and Asian nations. His personal experience as a teacher of young, poor Mexican-Americans meant he felt he understood the problems of under-developed nations. His Presidential visits reflected this preference; overseas trips concentrated largely on the Western hemisphere and the Far East.

A second reason why the two leaders did not establish a close friendship, may be because the seeds of doubt about Harold Wilson were planted in Johnson's mind even before the 1964 General Election. Prior to Wilson's meeting with the President at the beginning of March 1964, LBJ was briefed on the opposition leader's personal and political characteristics. McGeorge Bundy, Special Assistant for National Security Affairs, thought LBJ would find Wilson 'interesting', 'seemingly sincere' but 'a cold man'.[41] The CIA felt he was a 'cold fish', 'possibly untrustworthy', but judged him to be a 'pragmatist' who was 'well aware of realities of power' and that his commitment to Anglo-US relations was not 'based solely on sentiment'.[42] Although this was a largely accurate picture of the Labour leader, some of the less flattering comments may have persuaded LBJ that Wilson was a difficult, devious man who was not to be trusted. And, unfortunately for Wilson, Lyndon Johnson's first presidential experience with a British Prime Minister had not gone well. Johnson had been furious after the visit of Prime Minister Douglas-Home in March 1964 when the Prime Minister had, by accident, led the press to believe that he had acted firmly in response to American criticism about British trade with Cuba, particularly the sale of Leyland buses. Johnson was furious at the imputation that he had allowed an allied leader, from an increasingly less important country, to speak to him in such a manner and, apparently, Johnson never spoke to Douglas-Home again. No such mistakes would be made with Wilson. In fact, over a year later Johnson still felt 'the wounds of what Home said about busses' even though, as McGeorge Bundy thought it necessary to point out, 'everyone else' had long since forgotten about that particular episode.[43] The President had no hesitation in telling Wilson during their first official meeting that he would 'never trust a British Prime Minister again, because all his experience showed their Washington visits to be concerned mainly with domestic electioneering'.[44] It is noticeable that throughout the Wilson–Johnson years, the Americans were particularly careful to avoid any unchecked statements or remarks by the British Prime Minister.

In addition to this, the President may have taken a moral stand against Wilson, despite his own marital infidelities. He certainly considered the question of security after being furnished with intelligence reports during the British General Election telling of Wilson's alleged affair with his secretary, Marcia Williams.[45] These reports appear to have originated in Britain and were picked up by the FBI's London mission. Charles Bates, the FBI legal attaché in London at the time, asserts that information surrounding Wilson's supposed liaison with his secretary was received by FBI Chief, J. Edgar Hoover, and duly passed on to President Johnson.[46] The same rumours were passed on to McGeorge Bundy via Richard Helms, the CIA's Deputy Director of Plans.[47] Shortly before Wilson's December visit, after a meeting with the President and his advisers, David Bruce also noted that such gossip was in circulation:

> The President made no allusion to what I had been confidently told was his prejudice against the Prime Minister, founded largely on gossip that the latter had conducted an irregular sexual connection with his secretary. This allegation had been muttered in certain circles during the campaign.... He received the assurance that the lady's husband would not bring a suit against Wilson, naming him as co-respondent, since the husband had been divorced, remarried, and was the father of a child of his second venture. Johnson is said to be puritanical in his views about such affairs, and heartily to disapprove of them.[48]

Certainly Johnson did not want Williams to accompany Wilson during his first trip to Washington in December 1964 and there can be no doubt that Johnson would have felt more confident in his dealings with the British Prime Minister in the knowledge that he had such information at his fingertips, especially given his axiom 'I never trust a man unless I have his pecker in my pocket.'[49]

Finally, it is worth asking what the two men had in common. It is safe to say that the only important personal characteristic shared by Wilson and Johnson was a total absorption in politics.[50] For that reason, if nothing else, they had a great deal of respect for each other as professional politicians. Both were great political campaigners who placed much emphasis on their perceived interpersonal skills. What else did they share? Perhaps, as commentators suggested at the time, both men felt they were not part of their country's ruling establishments.[51] They certainly had relatively humble origins: Johnson's comfortable, rural background in the Texas hill country and Wilson's lower-middle class upbringing in northern England meant both had no more than a middling social status. However, Johnson's high-school education was in marked contrast with Wilson's academic success as an Oxford don and although they may have come from modest backgrounds, they had not had similar life experiences and, apart from politics, had no shared interests.

Although both men had political principles, neither had clearly defined political philosophies, which contributed to misunderstandings over their potential for a close relationship. Tony Benn concluded that 'Johnson is an old style, folksy, warm-hearted New Dealer with much more in common with Wilson than Kennedy had or than he (Johnson) has with Home.'[52] But this was a misreading of Johnson and his politics, something Wilson was also guilty of according to Henry Brandon, the *Sunday Times* Washington correspondent:

> Like other Labour leaders, he was under the mistaken impression that there was little difference between a New Dealer and a British socialist. To him the Great Society was another way of talking about Labour's kind of socialism when in effect Johnson's approach to the welfare state did not prevent his being closer to business than to the labour unions.[53]

Wilson may therefore have assumed a closer political affinity than was in fact the case.

The political relationship

While there was no natural affinity between Wilson and Johnson, given their lengthy, four-year political relationship, it might be asked why a genuine friendship did not develop. The most obvious answer to this lies in the issues that dominated their working relationship.

Paul Gore-Booth, Permanent Under-Secretary in the Foreign Office, argued that 'With the Johnson Administration our relations were good.'[54] In many ways this was true. Despite problems over sterling, Vietnam, and Britain's decreasing world role, Washington and London were able to cooperate closely on remaining issues of mutual interest: NATO, the Middle East, Rhodesia and disarmament. The strong intelligence and nuclear links between the two countries also remained firmly intact. A healthy working relationship between Britain and America at the departmental levels was helped by the continuing strong ties between personnel within the American administration and the British government and foreign office. Sir Patrick Dean, British Ambassador to the United States, was admired by Johnson. Sir Michael Palliser, the Prime Minister's Assistant for Foreign Affairs, and Walt Rostow, the President's National Security Adviser, were old friends from Oxford who enjoyed working together at their respective stations. Harlan Cleveland, US Assistant Secretary of State for international organisations, had been one of Wilson's students at University College, Oxford, and most senior British cabinet members had met with officials in the Johnson administration prior to the 1964 election.

Still, in the mid-to late 1960s, Anglo-American relations were dominated by three particularly taxing problems. The worst of these in terms of the Wilson–Johnson relationship was Vietnam. Although sterling's difficulties overshadowed Anglo-American relations until devaluation in 1967, and the British decision to withdraw its troops from east of Suez was of greater significance to the special relationship in the long run, Vietnam caused the deepest and most open disagreements between London and Washington during the 1960s. One of the major reasons for this was the great personal, as well as political, significance Vietnam had for both Harold Wilson and Lyndon Johnson. It is with Vietnam that one can recognise that personality may have played a part in diplomacy.

The war dominated LBJ's time in office. Clearly it destroyed Johnson's plan for his own legacy to the nation – the Great Society. This huge programme of social and welfare legislation was stymied due to the diversion of funds to the war in South-East Asia. Between 1965 and 1969 the Johnson administration spent less than \$15 billion on Great Society programmes compared to a massive \$120 billion on the war in Vietnam.[55] The war swamped Johnson's daily agenda. He was kept closely informed on day-to-day events in Vietnam, on domestic and international reaction to them, and even got involved in choosing bombing targets.[56] As US casualties mounted and the war became bogged down in a stalemate, the President's physical and emotional health were clearly affected. By 1967 he regularly looked white-faced and tired; he was ageing prematurely. On 31 March 1968, the day Johnson announced he would not seek re-election as President, Lady Bird noted in her diary that 'his face was sagging and there was such pain in his eyes as I had not seen since his mother died.'[57]

The Wilson government was therefore faced with a complex president who, after his July 1965 decision to send large numbers of US ground troops to South Vietnam was increasingly obsessed by events in South-East Asia and the consequences of those events back home. If the Wilson government was not involved in this important matter, then Anglo-American relations inevitably would be strained during the Johnson administration. Moreover, given LBJ's views on loyalty and his growing paranoia that anyone who did not support him on Vietnam was against him in all things, the Anglo-American alliance faced the possibility of being jeopardised if the United Kingdom was not cooperative.

Throughout the Kennedy and Johnson years, the United States was alert to the propaganda benefits of making its involvement in South-East Asia part of an allied crusade to prevent communist domination of the area. The Americans welcomed, and in some cases demanded, troop deployments or other assistance in Vietnam from other countries. The addition of extra trained manpower would have helped ease the demand for American 'boys'. However, as many military strategists argued, the logistical and linguistic problems inherent in multi-national armed forces meant that the main benefits were psychological and political. In the 'zero-sum' atmosphere of the cold war, the Americans would have liked to have as many world powers as possible lining up on their side in Vietnam. The US understood that its ability to win the war, especially the propaganda war, would be enhanced if Vietnam could be turned into a wider international affair. Having Britain on its side was of particular importance because of its role in the Western Alliance and the UN Security Council. Britain was also a leading social democracy whose example counted. Any condemnation or ambivalence on the part of the US's professed closest ally would be seized upon by North Vietnam as proof of the weakness of America's cause. William Bundy, Assistant Secretary of State for Far East Affairs, later argued that a British commitment 'would have made a considerable psychological difference ... particularly in liberal circles, which was where the main criticism of the war came from'.[58] LBJ recalled telling Wilson in their July 1966 Washington meeting that, 'a platoon of bagpipers would be sufficient, it was the British flag that was needed'.[59] Or as Dean Rusk put it to the journalist Louis Heren: 'All we needed was a regiment. The Black Watch would have done.'[60]

The British steadfastly refused to become directly involved in the conflict, turning down repeated American requests for a British troop deployment in Vietnam. There were three main reasons for this refusal to contribute armed forces. Firstly as co-Chairman of the 1954 Geneva conference the British might well have a role to play in finding peace. Secondly, they were already over-stretched militarily in the Far East through their commitment of 50 000 troops to the Malaysian struggle against Indonesia. And thirdly, the war in Vietnam was increasingly unpopular at home and therefore presented the British government with domestic political problems. By 1966 the Parliamentary Labour Party (PLP) was deeply divided on the Government's policy of support for US action in Vietnam.

Britain's position had remained virtually unchanged since the 1954 Geneva Conference, when Britain and the Soviet Union became co-Chairs and subsequently took on the informal role of mediators on South-East Asian conflicts. Many in London were doubtful that the US could achieve any sort of military victory in Vietnam and were worried about the ever-increasing risk of Chinese intervention. However, the sanctity of the Anglo-American relationship demanded that Britain's true feelings on the conflict could not be made public, or even fully stated privately. Instead, the British gave the Americans diplomatic support and limited practical and technical assistance. This included the British Advisory Mission in South Vietnam (BRIAM), ostensibly four former Malayan police officers, headed by Sir Robert Thompson, sent to provide Saigon with expert assistance in administrative and police matters.[61] In reality, its role was to advise on counter-insurgency techniques the British had mastered during the Malayan emergency in the 1950s and help establish the strategic hamlets programme.[62] In return for British verbal support of American policy in South-East Asia, which was bound to be controversial under a Labour government, Wilson was kept abreast of latest developments in Vietnam and his attempts to start peace talks were sanctioned. US support for sterling may also have been an implicit *quid pro quo*, as Clive Ponting and others have suggested.[63]

Despite assurances from David Bruce and McGeorge Bundy, among others, that Wilson was doing as much as he could on Vietnam, the President, along with Dean Rusk and Walt Rostow, was never entirely convinced of this. LBJ also believed that Britain's role as co-Chairman of the Geneva Conference was being used by Wilson as a convenient 'fig-leaf' behind which to hide.[64] The first real breach on this issue, and perhaps the earliest clear example of strain in the personal and political relationship, came on the night of 10 February 1965 when Wilson incurred Johnson's wrath by telephoning the President to express concern over the first bombing raids of North Vietnam and to suggest that he come to Washington to discuss the matter. Johnson sharply pointed out this was not Korea and Wilson was not Clement Attlee:

> I won't tell you how to run Malaysia and you don't tell us how to run Vietnam .... If you want to help us some in Vietnam send us some men and send us some folks to deal with these guerillas. And announce to the press that you are going to help us. Now if you don't feel like doing that, go on with your Malaysian problem. . . .[65]

Apparently, this incident did much to damage Johnson's view of Wilson. Transcripts of the conversation show that Johnson resented British interference on this issue. He saw the Prime Minister as merely posturing for domestic consumption and felt the British might be entitled to more of a say in the war's progress if they deployed troops in Vietnam.[66] On this occasion, early in the life of the Labour government, Wilson had failed to judge the limits of his relationship with Johnson.

In late March 1965 there was another mini-crisis in Anglo-American relations over the American use of CS gas. Wilson faced a major backbench revolt on this issue. The British Foreign Secretary, Michael Stewart, on a visit to Washington at the time, expressed 'in the strongest terms' British disapproval of this action. He argued that the use of gas and napalm bombs inflicted undue suffering and was of limited military value, and warned the Americans they might lose their moral position as a consequence. He also expressed the Prime Minister's extreme annoyance at the lack of prior warning. The Americans characterised the British reaction as a 'stupid fuss'.[67] Johnson's reluctance to see Wilson or Stewart later that year was explained by Bruce with reference to Vietnam: 'He regards attempts on the part of the British to insinuate themselves into Vietnamese affairs as irrelevant and unimportant. He believes Wilson, for his own domestic political purposes, wishes to capitalise on a supposed close relationship with Johnson that is non-existent.'[68] For a brief period between December 1965 and April 1966 the relationship did look quite rosy in terms of cooperation and was almost friendly. Wilson's December 1965 visit to Washington proved successful and according to Bruce, Wilson had every right to be pleased with the visit, for 'President Johnson has been favourably impressed by him, and their relationship will be more intimate than heretofore.' Bruce also noted in March 1966 that the British Embassy received 'almost daily copies of messages passing between the Prime Minister and the President. Their tone is cordial to the point of being on both sides effusive. The President is clearly grateful for the support given him by the PM on Vietnam.'[69]

However, events in Vietnam again dictated that this picture couldn't last. A more serious diplomatic rift came on 29 June 1966 when Wilson finally placed limits on British support for American action in Vietnam. Aware of the outrage that American bombing of oil installations in Hanoi and Haiphong would provoke in Britain, the Prime Minister dissociated Britain from this action. Although Wilson warned the President in advance that this could be his only response, LBJ was still furious. Philip Kaiser, Bruce's chief of mission, explained: 'When we bombed Hanoi, Wilson felt compelled to criticise us, though he did so rather mildly. Johnson reacted with typical vehemence, sharply castigating the prime minister. As a consequence, relations between the two men, never too warm, deteriorated temporarily.'[70] William Bundy, Assistant Secretary of State for Far Eastern Affairs, agreed on the effect of Wilson's statement: 'the President just didn't trust Wilson, particularly since the...disassociation. He thought he was trying to make time politically....there's no doubt in the President's mind this established Wilson, as far as I know unchangingly, as a man not to go to the well with.'[71]

Another occasion that revealed stresses in the relationship was the Wilson–Kosygin peace initiative of February 1967 when Wilson's claims of intimacy and influence with LBJ were rather embarrassingly shattered. By this time the Labour government was under immense pressure from within his own party and from anti-war groups to act on Vietnam. Wilson had long sought to assuage criticism of British support for the Americans by acting as an 'honest broker' or peace mediator. This led to a series of peace moves, or 'gimmicks' as his detractors called them, with the most notable ones being the Patrick Gordon-Walker fact-finding tour of South-East Asia in April/May 1965, the Commonwealth Peace Mission of June 1965, the Harold Davies mission of July 1965 and George Brown's peace plan of November 1966. By not criticising the Americans, Wilson argued he could gain more influence with Johnson. When the seven-day visit to Britain of Russian Premier Alexei Kosygin in February 1967 coincided with a Tet bombing pause, Wilson took the opportunity to play the role of statesman and got permission from the Americans to ask the Russians to send out peace feelers to the North Vietnamese. Washington promised the British they would not begin bombing again until after Kosygin left Britain.

One can only speculate on the extent of Russian influence in Hanoi, but both Britain and the United States felt the Soviets appeared willing to encourage the North Vietnamese to the peace table. Britain was, however, clearly acting in the name of, and with the consent of, Washington. Prior to the scheduled meeting with Kosygin, Wilson and his Foreign Secretary, George Brown, had asked the Americans if there was anything that they could offer in way of opening talks. Washington, by now tired of third-party attempts at finding peace and still preferring a military solution to the conflict, routinely gave their approval to offer the Phase A–Phase B formula. This proposed that the US would stop bombing on the condition that on their doing so, Hanoi would stop North Vietnamese army infiltration of the South, followed by a joint de-escalation of hostilities.

At their first meeting, Wilson proposed a Geneva-type conference to arbitrate over Vietnam but both the Americans and Kosygin felt that this was a premature suggestion. Obviously, in seeking to re-establish British co-chairmanship of another Geneva conference, Wilson appeared to the Americans to be seeking to maintain an important role for his government and his country. Although this was to some extent true, Wilson does appear to have had genuine humanitarian concerns over the continuing casualties of the Vietnam war.

Kosygin did, however, respond to Phase A–Phase B, asking for a written version of it, which he could present to the North Vietnamese. The British, believing they had had a draft approved by the Americans, handed the text to Kosygin. However, that evening the Americans sent a redrafted text to be given to the Russians to replace the earlier one. The new terms were much harder than the old ones. They said that the US would order a cessation of bombing of North Vietnam as soon as they were assured that infiltration from North Vietnam to South Vietnam had stopped. The phrase *had stopped* was obviously more hard-line than *would stop* following the cessation of bombing.

This action placed the British in a most embarrassing situation with Kosygin. Wilson was extremely angry at Washington's change in policy at the last moment. He later said in his memoirs that:

> We were staggered.... No one could understand what had happened. I said that there could be only three explanations. One, which I was reluctant to believe, was that the White House had taken me – and hence Mr. Kosygin – for a ride. Two ... that the Washington hawks had staged a successful take-over. Three ... that the authorities were suffering from a degree of confusion about a possible and unfortunate juxtaposition of certain parts of their anatomy, one of which was their elbow.[72]

Or as the Foreign Office put it: 'there was a state of unutterable, anatomical confusion in the higher part of the Administration'.[73] Johnson, in his memoirs, insisted that Wilson had not received specific approval from Washington to deliver the first draft.[74] But in a meeting with Wilson during the Prime Minister's visit to Washington in June of 1967, Johnson 'did not try to deny' Wilson's belief that 'there had been a change of policy under pressure by their hawks'.[75] Either way, the British looked foolish over the incident.

Despite the loss of credibility on the part of the British, Wilson and Kosygin continued their talks. On the last day of Kosygin's visit, Sunday 12 February, a last-ditch attempt to encourage peace talks was formulated at Chequers. Wilson proposed that the bombing truce be extended so that Hanoi could have time to respond to the terms outlined in the revised document. In rather chaotic and frantic circumstances, the American representative, Chester Cooper, waited for Washington's response in an upstairs bedroom at Chequers, while Wilson did his best to forestall Kosygin's departure with talk on such subjects as geology and technology. Cooper pleaded with Washington to come to a decision fast as Kosygin was about to leave and, to prove this, hung the telephone out of the bedroom window so they could hear the Premier's cars and accompanying motorcycles revving up to leave. But only after Kosygin had returned to his London hotel did an answer come. Wilson and Brown dashed across London to inform Kosygin that bombing would not resume if, before 10 a.m. on Monday (only nine hours away), Washington could have Hanoi's assurance that infiltration had stopped.[76]

This time-span was totally unreasonable, even after the British persuaded Washington to extend the deadline by a further six hours. This was still insufficient time in which to pass the message from Moscow to Hanoi, and for people to assemble and debate the offer. Despite this, Kosygin informed the British he would pass the message to Hanoi at once. Not surprisingly, no reply had come from Hanoi by the time of the deadline and bombing recommenced.

The Americans had also failed to brief the British fully on simultaneous peace efforts, including a letter from Johnson to Ho Chi Minh. Wilson was extremely embarrassed by Johnson's obvious lack of faith in his ability to represent American interests adequately and clearly felt humiliated and personally slighted by Washington's hardening of their position. He also felt a chance for peace had been lost and said so publicly, calling it a 'missed opportunity', which further fuelled the situation. William Bundy argued that the failure of this peace initiative had 'great significance as a source of lasting distrust and feeling of misunderstanding on both sides, between the President and Wilson. If they were not too well off before, they were infinitely worse after this'[77] Certainly by early March 1967 press speculation about Johnson's annoyance with Wilson's peace moves was rife. The *Observer* reported that 'Mr. Wilson's standing' in Washington had 'declined sharply over the past weeks. This is a result of what is regarded as his grossly exaggerated account of how near to success he came in his efforts with Mr. Kosygin to achieve peace in Vietnam.' According to the correspondent, President Johnson 'accused Mr Wilson of having ludicrously magnified his role to reap a domestic political dividend'.[78] For the remainder of 1967 the US put some effort into trying to conciliate Wilson, primarily due to a fear of further British 'dissociations'. Walt Rostow visited England shortly after the Kosygin fiasco and patiently listened to British grievances. Although Johnson did not see Anglo-American relations as particularly 'special', he still recognised the symbolic value of British diplomatic support on Vietnam and did not relish a crisis in Anglo-American relations during already troubled times in America's foreign affairs.

Conclusion

Given the nature and difficulty of understanding any relationship between human beings – never mind between politicians of such complexity as Wilson and Johnson – it is difficult to comment on the relationship between the two statesmen with any certainty. The evidence at times appears contradictory but in many ways it merely reflects the fact that the relationship between the President and the Prime Minister was not static, but instead had distinct peaks and troughs. There were periods, usually after one of Wilson's visits to Washington, when the relationship saw marked improvement, but the possibility of a close, working relationship developing into a cordial, personal one ended in July 1966 with Wilson's dissociation from the bombing of Hanoi and Haiphong. Johnson felt betrayed by this action and their mutual suspicions of one another increased greatly. The President was convinced that the Prime Minister acted purely out of domestic concerns and firmly believed that Britain had reneged on its South East Asia Treaty Organisation commitments; Wilson was beginning to question LBJ's conduct of the Vietnam war. This incident soured relations and the chances of a meaningful friendship developing were greatly reduced. The débâcle surrounding the Wilson–Kosygin peace initiative the following year effectively ended any intimacy between the President and the Prime Minister. Philip Kaiser observed that the relationship between President Johnson and Prime Minister Wilson 'had its ups and downs' and that, at best, they 'developed a shaky rapport'.[79] This appears to be the most accurate assessment of an ambiguous partnership. The relationship did change over time with the highs and lows in the relationship paralleling disputes over Vietnam.

There was no personal chemistry or ideological common ground between Wilson and Johnson. Those who served in both the Kennedy and the Johnson administrations acknowledge that the special relationship lost its emotional charge during the Johnson years.[80] If compared with the earlier relationships between the heads of the US and the UK, say with Roosevelt–Churchill, Eisenhower–Macmillan and Kennedy–Macmillan, and with the later relationships between Reagan and Thatcher and between Clinton and Blair, the Wilson–Johnson relationship was indeed cool. Given Johnson's obsession with Vietnam, it could be argued that any British prime minister who took such decisions as keeping out of Vietnam and devolving Britain's defence role would have had difficulty establishing a close personal relationship with any American president. Moreover, Johnson's own problems of paranoia and self-esteem – his fixation over leaks and his demands for complete loyalty from colleagues and allies – would equally have caused any prime minister problems. And, with Wilson's domestic difficulties over sterling and Vietnam, it is hard to see how he could have done more to ensure a close personal relationship. He could have stayed out of peace negotiations and could have said less on the whole issue of Vietnam but in so doing would have risked an internal split in the Labour Party and may have threatened the very life of his government. And, while never explicitly linked, Wilson was aware that his diplomatic support on Vietnam helped in negotiations over sterling.

Yet it is also worth asking whether feelings of loyalty to LBJ may have blinded Wilson over Vietnam, especially in the years after devaluation. Did Wilson's belief in his close personal relationship with LBJ and the President's demands for absolute loyalty add 'an emotional constraint about coming out against LBJ' as Barbara Castle suggests?[81] Or did Wilson fear Johnson's forceful personality? Would the President have used American power and influence against Britain if Wilson dissociated completely on Vietnam? Given the President's obvious obsession with the war, and his unpredictability, this possibility could not be ruled out. Wilson and the Foreign Office would have been aware that the President had never contacted Douglas-Home after the 'buses to Cuba' incident. Moreover, Wilson believed strongly in the Anglo-American alliance, and given the many areas of practical cooperation between Britain and America, to risk such a breach would have been unthinkable to the Prime Minister and his advisers.

Ultimately, the relationship between Harold Wilson and Lyndon Johnson was not a happy one. Not only was there much dishonesty in it – with Johnson pretending to like a Prime Minister he clearly had contempt for on many occasions – but, unfortunately for Wilson, historical timing was not on his side. Anglo-American relations were bound to go through a period of serious readjustment in the 1960s due to Britain's ever-weakening economic position, but to face that realignment at a time when the US was faced with the quagmire that was Vietnam meant that diplomacy was inevitably more complicated. That it was Lyndon Johnson who was President at this time meant Anglo-American relations faced not only readjustment and complications but also volatility.

Notes

1　George Ball, Oral History Transcript, LBJ Library, Interview II, Tape 1, p. 17.
2　Alan P. Dobson, *Anglo-American Relations in the Twentieth Century* (London: Routledge, 1995); David Dimbleby & David Reynolds, *An Ocean Apart: the Relationship between Britain and America in the Twentieth Century* (London: Guild Publishing, 1988); Ritchie Ovendale, *Anglo-American Relations in the Twentieth Century* (Macmillan, 1998).
3　Cable from Bruce to Rusk, 8 May 1967, NSF, Country File, UK, Box 211, File: UK, Vol. XI, Memos, 4/67–6/67, Doc. 92a, Lyndon Baines Johnson Presidential Library, Austin, Texas [henceforth LBJL].
4　Lyndon Baines Johnson, *The Vantage Point: Perspectives of the Presidency, 1963–69* (New York: Holt, Rinehart and Winston, 1971). Only the Wilson–Koysgin peace initiative is covered in any detail.
5　Once as Leader of Her Majesty's Opposition, six times as Prime Minister.
6　Vicky, *New Statesman*, 7 May 1965.
7　Gerald Scarfe, *Private Eye*, No. 88, Friday, 30 April 1965, p. 1.
8　Tony Benn, *Out of the Wilderness, 1963–67* (London: Arrow, 1991), 4 March 1964, p. 97.
9　Edward Short, *Whip to Wilson* (London: Macdonald & Co., 1989), p. 97.
10　Author's interview with Baroness Castle of Blackburn, 28 April 1993.
11　Lord Wilson of Rievaulx, International Forum, Lyndon B. Johnson and the World, Fifth Annual Presidential Conference: Lyndon Baines Johnson: a Texan in Washington, 11 April 1986, Hofstra University, Hempstead, New York.

LIBRARY, UNIVERSITY COLLEGE CHESTER

12 Philip Ziegler, *Wilson: the Authorised Life* (London: Weidenfeld & Nicolson, 1993), p. 188.
13 Harold Wilson, The *Labour Government 1964–70* (Harmondsworth: Penguin, 1974), p. 188.
14 Ibid., p. 265.
15 Ibid., p. 342.
16 Transcript, David Bruce Oral History Interview, Tape I, 9/12/71 by Thomas H. Baker, p. 11, LBJL.
17 Ibid, p. 14/15.
18 Transcript, David Bruce Oral History Interview, Tape II, 9/12/71 by Thomas H. Baker, p. 15, LBJL.
19 Lady Bird Johnson, *A White House Diary* (London: Weidenfeld & Nicolson, 1970), p. 630.
20 Andrew Roth, *Sir Harold Wilson: Yorkshire Walter Mitty* (London: Macdonald and Jane's, 1977).
21 George Ball, *The Past Has Another Pattern: Memoirs* (New York: W.W. Norton & Company, 1982), p. 336.
22 David Bruce Diaries, 22 March 1965, Virginia Historical Society, Richmond, Virginia.
23 Philip Mayer Kaiser, *Journeying Far and Wide: a Political and Diplomatic Memoir* (New York: Macmillan, 1992), p. 226.
24 Interview with author.
25 Jack Valenti to the President, 26 February 1965, GEN CO, Box 76, Folder CO305 UK, 1/1/65–7/1/65, LBJL.
26 *The Times*, 17 April 1965, p. 8.
27 Transcript, David Bruce Oral History Interview, Tape II, 9/12/71 by Thomas H. Baker, p. 15, LBJ Library.
28 Louis Heren, 'Anglo-U.S. Friendship Comes Under Strain', *The Times*, 23 February 1968.
29 Memorandum on the British Labour Party and the MLF, prepared by Richard E. Neustadt, 6 July 1964, *New Left Review*, No. 51, 1968, p. 21.
30 Public Record Office, Kew [henceforward: PRO]: PREM 13/193, Note of a Conversation with Professor Neustadt and D. Mitchell, Prime Minister's Visit to Washington, Top Secret, 29 November 1964.
31 Ibid.
32 Ibid.
33 Dean Rusk, Memo for the President, 22 March 1965, NSF, Country, UK, Wilson Visit, 4/15/65, LBJL.
34 Benn, 1 June 1967, p. 501.
35 Henry Brandon, *Special Relationship: a Foreign Correspondent's Memoirs from Roosevelt to Reagan* (London: Macmillan, 1988), p. 231.
36 Louis Heren, 'Anglo-U.S. Friendship Comes Under Strain', *The Times*, 23 February 1968.
37 Transcript, David Bruce Oral History Interview, Tape II, 9/12/71 by Thomas H. Baker, p. 11, LBJL.
38 Brandon, p. 204.
39 Frank Costigliola, 'LBJ, Germany, and the "End of the Cold War"' in Warren I. Cohen & Nancy Bernkopf Tucker (eds), *Lyndon Johnson Confronts the World: American Foreign Policy 1963–1968* (Cambridge University Press, 1994), p. 174.

40 Transcript, George W. Ball Oral History Interview, Tape II, p. 17, July 9, 1971, LBJL.
41 Memo, McGeorge Bundy to the President, 1 March 1964, File: UK, Meetings with Wilson, 3/2/64, UK Country File, NSF, LBJL.
42 CIA Biographic Statement on Harold Wilson, NSF, Country File, UK, Box 213, File: UK, Wilson Visit Briefing Book, 12/64, Doc. 9m LBJL.
43 Memo, McGeorge Bundy to the President, 3 June 1965, NSF, Country File, UK, Vol. V, Memos 6/65, Box 208, Doc. 11a, LBJL.
44 Wilson, p. 46.
45 David Bruce Diaries, December 5 1964; Stephen Dorill and Robin Ramsay, *Smear! Wilson and the Secret State* (London: Grafton, 1991), pp. 44–5.
46 David Leigh, *Wilson Plot: How the Spycatchers and Their American Allies Tried to Overthrow the British Government* (New York: Pantheon Books, 1988), p. 69.
47 Stephen Dorril & Robin Ramsay, *Smear! Wilson and the Secret State* (London: Grafton, 1992), p. 56.
48 David Bruce Diaries, 5 December 1964.
49 Denis Healey, *The Time of My Life* (London: Penguin, 1989), p. 319.
50 Stewart Alsop, 'The Interesting Mr. Wilson', *The Economist*, December 1964.
51 Ibid.
52 Benn, p. 106, 27 April, 1964.
53 Henry Brandon, *Special Relationship: a Foreign Correspondent's Memoirs from Roosevelt to Reagan* (London: Macmillan, 1988), p. 209.
54 Paul Gore Booth, *With Great Truth and Respect* (London: Constable, 1974), p. 332.
55 Vivienne Sanders, *The USA and Vietnam, 1945–75* (London: Hodder & Stoughton, 1998), p. 108.
56 Ted Gittinger (ed.), *The Johnson Years: a Vietnam Roundtable* (Austin: University of Texas, 1993), p. 78.
57 Lady Bird Johnson, p. 642.
58 David Dimbleby, BBC1 Interview with William Bundy in David Dimbleby and David Reynolds, *An Ocean Apart: the Relationship between Britain and America in the Twentieth Century* (London: Guild, 1988), p. 252.
59 Wilson, p. 264.
60 Louis Heren, *No Hail, No Farewell* (London: Harper & Row, 1970), p. 231.
61 *Hansard*: House of Commons Debate, Fifth Series, Vol. 646, Col. 13, 23 October 1961; PRO: PREM 11/4759, Confidential Aide Memoire, 'British Aid to Vietnam', 13 July 1964.
62 Report on 'Developments in Viet-Nam Between General Taylor's Visits – October 1961–October 1962', JFK Library, NSF, Vietnam, Box 197, 10/1/62–6/30/63, Document 21.
63 Clive Ponting, *Breach of Promise: Labour in Power 1964–1970* (London: Penguin, 1989).
64 Prime Minister to President, June 14, 1966, NSF, Files of Walt Rostow, Box 12, Wilson Visit, LBJL; Background Paper, Visit of Prime Minister Wilson, July 27, 1966, NSF, UK, Wilson Visit, LBJL.
65 PRO: PREM 13/692, Record of a Telephone Conversation between the Prime Minister and President Johnson on Thursday, February 11 at 3.15 am; Wilson, p. 80.

66   PRO: PREM 13/692, Record of a Telephone Conversation between the Prime Minister and President Johnson on Thursday, February 11 at 3.15 am.

67   Memorandum for the President from McGeorge Bundy, 22 March 1965, *Foreign Relations of the United States (FRUS)*, 1964–68, Vol. II (Washington, DC: US Government Printing Office, 1996), p. 469.

68   David Bruce diaries, 22 March 1965.

69   David Bruce Diaries, 3 March 1966.

70   Kaiser, p. 209.

71   Transcript, William Bundy Oral History Interview, Tape IV, 2/6/69 by Paige E. Mulhollan, p. 25 & 36, LBJL.

72   Wilson, *Labour Government*, p. 458.

73   PRO: PREM 13/1919, Record of a Conversation between the Prime Minister and the President of the United States of America at the White House on the morning of Friday, 2 June, 1967, Confidential Annex to the Visit of the Prime Minister to Canada and the United States, 1–3 June, 1967.

74   Lyndon B. Johnson, p. 254.

75   PRO: PREM 13/1919, Record of a Conversation between the Prime Minister and the President of the United States of America at the White House on the morning of Friday, 2 June, 1967, Confidential Annex to the Visit of the Prime Minister to Canada and the United States, 1–3 June, 1967.

76   Chester L. Cooper, *The Lost Crusade: the Full Story of US Involvement in Vietnam from Roosevelt to Nixon* (London: MacGibbon & Kee, 1970), p. 365–7.

77   Transcript, William Bundy Oral History Interview, Tape 4, 2/6/69 by Paige E. Mulhollan, p. 27, LBJL.

78   *The Observer*, 5 March 1967.

79   Kaiser, pp. 209 & 230.

80   Transcript, McGeorge Bundy Oral History Interview, by David Nunnerly, John F. Kennedy Presidential Library, Boston, p. 7.

81   Author's interview with Baroness Castle, 28 April 1993.

Index